LIVING WITH GHOSTS: *A Reader*

Writings on Coloniality, Decoloniality, Hauntology, and Contemporary Art

PACE

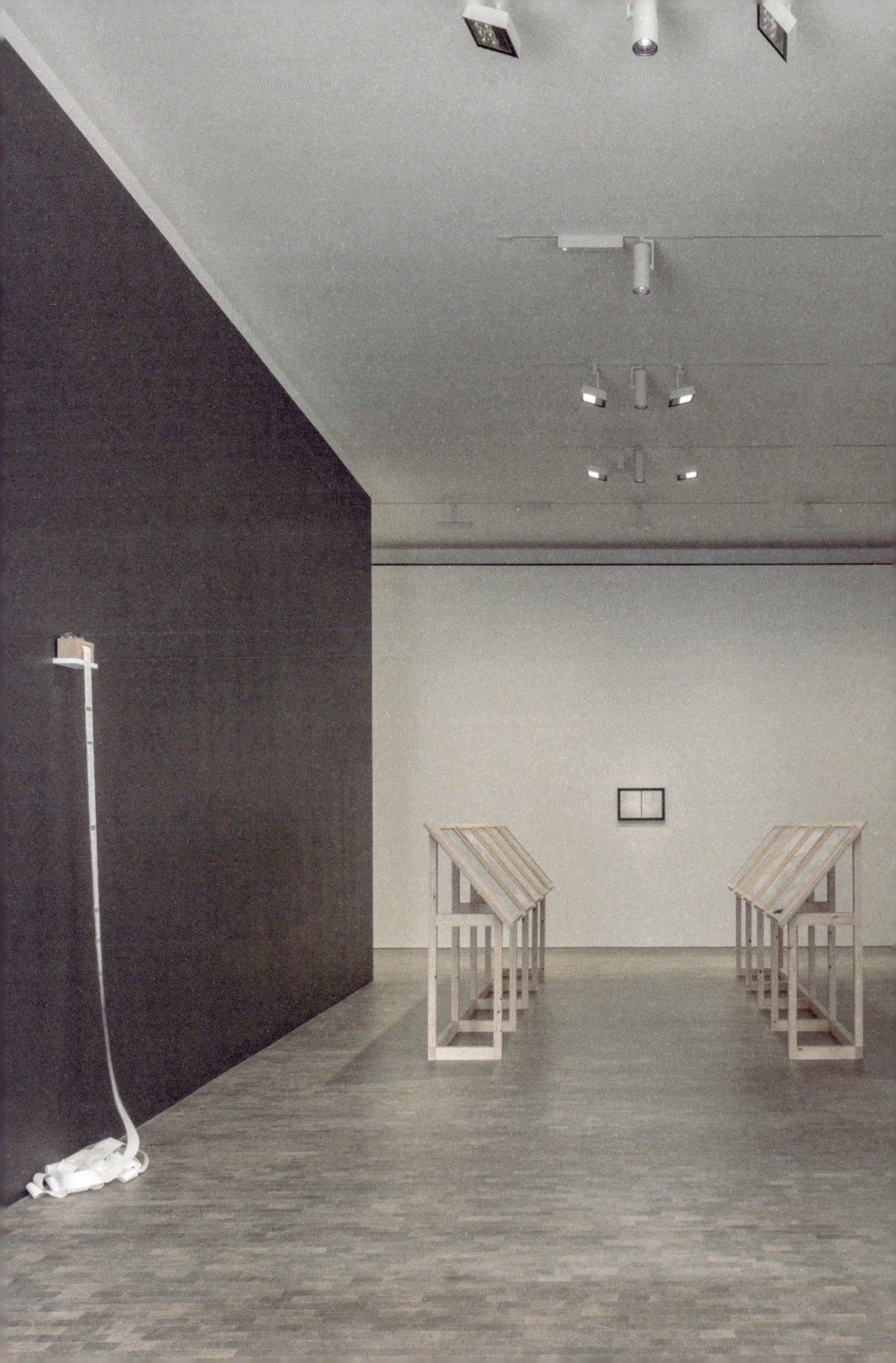

CONTENTS

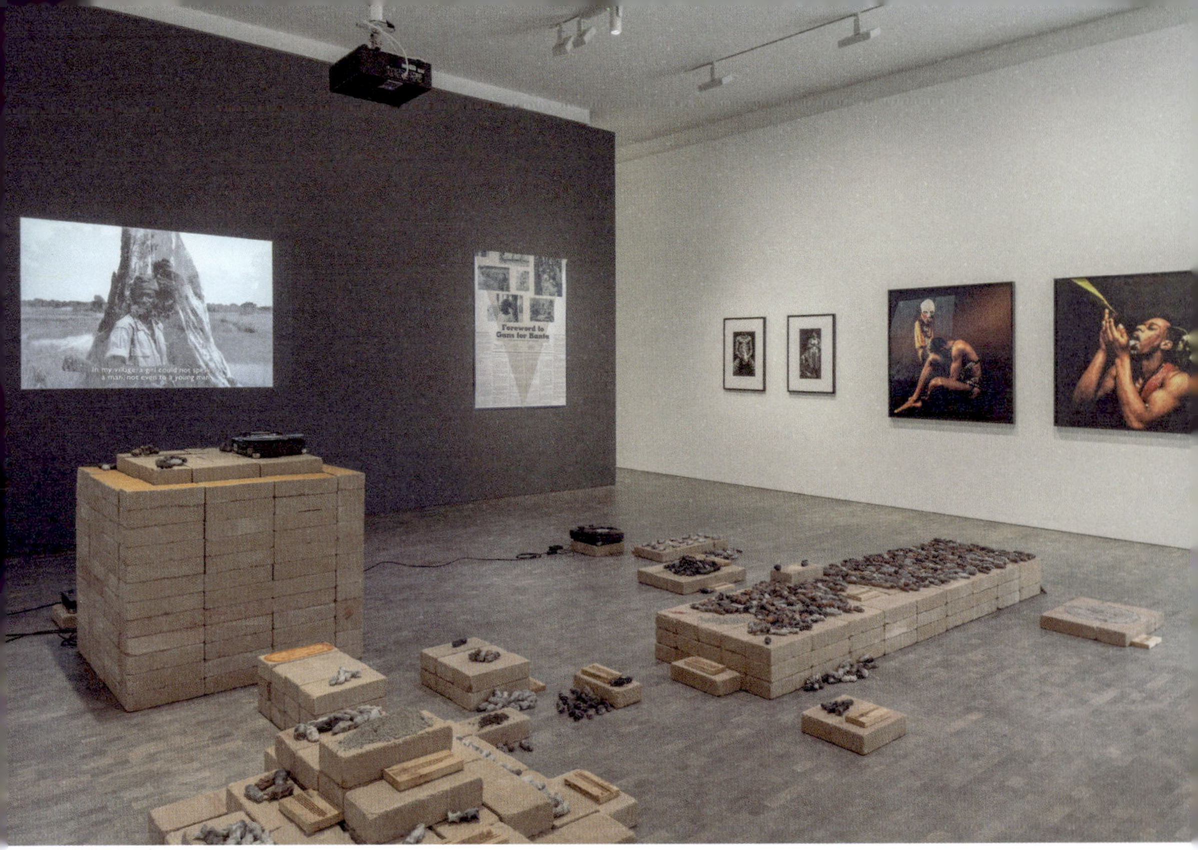

Page 2 and above:
Living With Ghosts, Installation View, Pace Gallery, London

INTRODUCTION

This reader stems from the accumulation of four years of research, beginning as a critical theoretical project, which then morphed into an exhibition, and now sits somewhere between (and yet is in excess of) the two. Whether realised in its written or gallery-bound formats, *Living with Ghosts* explores the ways the unresolved traumas of Africa's colonial past and its incomplete project of decolonisation continue to haunt the global present. Critical to this overarching project is its interrogation of the primal, yet strangely excised, position of Africa and its diasporas in the matrix of modernity, with particular consideration given to the spatial, temporal, psychological, and spiritual a/effects of such historical and ongoing processes of spectralisation on both postcolonial Africa and the wider world. Largely informed by the groundbreaking work of thinkers working in postcolonial and decolonial intellectual traditions, from Achille Mbembe and Sylvia Wynter to Walter D. Mignolo and Sabelo J. Ndlovu-Gatsheni, *Living with Ghosts* takes seriously the claim that the world-historical ruptures kickstarted by modernity in the 15th century cannot be thought apart from the consonant violences of slavery, colonialism, imperialism, and the transhistorically adaptive logics of Euro-centred power these violences birthed, known as "coloniality."[1] And equally, that coloniality cannot be thought apart from a subjugated, though resilient, field of otherwise possibility that has *always* refused and resisted coloniality's impositions, known as "decoloniality."[2]

What this reader aims to foreground is precisely how this modernity-coloniality-decoloniality paradigm, when refracted through the historical experiences and contemporary realities of the African postcolony – the central staging ground of modernity's *unending* drama – engenders a thoroughly disjunctive space-time that in turn reveals a spectral constellation of multiple, interpenetrating, absent-present spatialities and temporalities. This is to say that in purposely centring the geographically dispersed, geologically expropriated, and epistemologically phantomised entity that is Africa, one arrives at the non-presentness of an (accumulated) present and the non-hereness of an (entangled) here, in other words, a stubborn, uncanny, extra-ontological condition of ghostly (non-)being that Jacques Derrida aptly terms a "hauntology."[3]

Living with Ghosts critically attends to these ghosts, spirits, and phantoms that abound in the modern calamities of Africa's historical becoming from the 15th century to the present day, what some have referred to as modernity's colonial *longue durée*. As Derrida argues, ghosts, or what he calls *specters*, are both dead and alive, visible and invisible, material and immaterial, past and present, future and past. By virtue of their disorienting, "non-sensuous sensuous" manifestations, specters refuse and exceed the fixities and certainties imposed by post-Enlightenment orders of knowledge and thus inhabit an unassimilable realm of unknowability that transgresses the historically determined boundaries of Western ontology and epistemology. Most importantly, Derrida proposes that without this acknowledgement of

1 • Such logics, also known as the "colonial matrices of power," work on varying levels of abstraction, from the conceptual planes of ontology, epistemology, and aesthetics – the presumed legitimacy and neutrality of Eurocentric conceptions of space, time, beauty, spirituality, and the human – to the more concrete registers of political economy – the hegemony of capitalistic modes of production, the nation-state model, and Western-style "democracy." See Walter D. Mignolo and Catherine E. Walsh, *On Decoloniality: Concepts, Analytics, and Praxis*, 2018, and Sylvia Wynter, "Unsettling The Coloniality of Being/Power/Truth/Freedom: Towards The Human, After Man, Its Overrepresentation - An Argument," *The New Centennial Review*, Vol. 3, No. 3, Fall 2003, 257-337.
2 • Ibid.
3 • Jacques Derrida, *Specters of Marx: The State of the Debt, the Work of Mourning and the New International*, trans. Peggy Kamuf (New York and London: Routledge), 1994, 10.

the specter's radical foreignness, without a negation of our habituated desires to disavow, bury, or exorcise the haunting visions the specter conveys, we cannot arrive at the possibility of global justice.

It then follows that spectral encounters bear a transformative capacity to produce hitherto unforeseen ethical and political possibilities. This is because to be haunted by the specter is to be urgently reminded of repressed individual and collective traumas, and of one's *relation* to that trauma; it is to be impregnated with a desire to excavate dormant freedom dreams that lay buried in the wreckages of history; it is to be made uncannily aware of the disorienting entanglement of past, present, and future, and of the mutual entwinement of *here* and *there*. In other words, via the irreducibly affective encounter that is a haunting, specters *move* us to act; by instantiating an alternative politics of memory, they prevent us from falling into the blinded comforts of historical amnesia while also urging us to attend to the unfulfilled emancipatory tasks left behind by those who came before us.

Yet, modifying and extending Derrida's arguments, along with many other thinkers of the "spectral turn," – an amorphous body of thought that emerged in the 1990s with its primary locus of enunciation in Europe and the United States[•4] – this reader (re)centers African history, politics, and critical thought. An epistemological reorientation of this sort is long overdue and entirely necessary for it does not merely "supplement" hauntology discourses with an Africanist or Third Worldist flavour but exposes the inherent conceptual gaps and oversights, the racialised and colonial occlusions and exclusions, that is, *the ghosts*, that haunt these Euro-centred critical theoretical discourses. Via the trenchant critiques offered throughout this reader, one ought to come to the realisation that the aforementioned demand for "global" justice impelled by the specter is by definition meaningless or less it expresses an explicit alignment with what most concerns us here, the demand for *decolonial* justice.

NOTES ON CURATORIAL METHODOLOGY

As the contents of this reader elegantly demonstrate, the conceptual explorations set out in this introduction evidence a decolonial orientation to history, aesthetics, and the production of knowledge, and so cannot rely on conventional models of curatorial practice which, conditioned by post-Enlightenment logics of disciplinarity and its epistemological corollaries, problematically attempt to separate aesthetics from politics, the sensuous from the discursive, the artwork from the lecture, and the visual artist from the writer or speaker.

This second iteration of *Living with Ghosts* at Pace Gallery, London, as with the first iteration at the Wallach Art Gallery, New York, refuses such categorical delimitations by expanding "the exhibition" beyond the confines of the gallery space.[•5] The curatorial framework instead views text-based materials (such as this reader) and presentational or performative lectures as *equally constitutive* segments of the exhibition that exist *alongside* the selected artworks. In blurring the distinctions and/or creating more horizontal relationships between artwork and text/lecture, artist and writer/lecturer, lecture and performance, this

4 • See María Del Pilar Blanco and Esther Peeren (eds.), *The Spectralities Reader: Ghosts and Haunting in Contemporary Cultural Theory,* (London and New York: Bloomsbury), 2013.
5 • The first iteration of *Living with Ghosts* took place at the Wallach Art Gallery, New York, March 26 - April 10, 2022. Comprising three overlapping acts, including an intimate gallery display, an art-film screening programme, and a live virtual lecture series, the exhibition gathered several artists and thinkers, including John Akomfrah, Kader Attia, Zarina Bhimji, Filipa César, T.J. Demos, Rotimi Fani-Kayode, Onyeka Igwe, Bouchra Khalili, Serubiri Moses, Abraham Oghobase, and Emma Wolukau-Wanambwa.

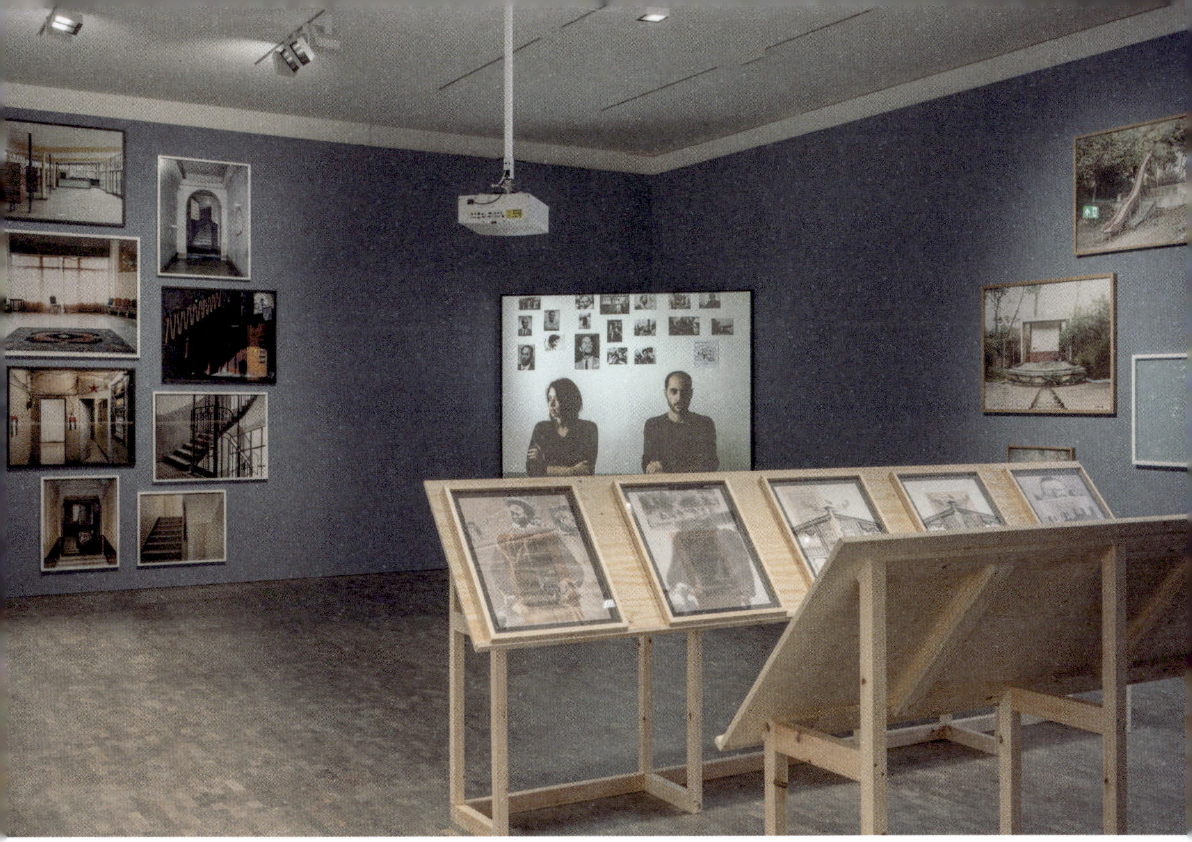

project (of which the reader is one segment) views exhibitions, not merely as abstracted sites for aesthetic "appreciation" but as politically situated venues ripe for the production, transmission, and reception of socially transformative knowledges. Evidenced from its convening of a thinking multitude, *Living with Ghosts* emphasises the grander, ongoing project of decoloniality and the pragmatic necessity of horizontal, interdisciplinary collaboration between writers, curators, artists, poets, academics, activists, designers, scientists, policy-makers, and so on, in bringing about a more just, decolonial future.

Hence, this reader is not "about" the artworks on display in the galleries – even though many of the artworks are illustrated in the following pages – but is intended to function as an independent pedagogical resource for scholars and an interested public curious about the publication's explorations through the conceptual junctures of African post/de-coloniality and hauntology. This reader constitutes one among two other overlapping "acts" within the fragmented spatio-temporal unfolding of *Living with Ghosts* – these other acts include the gallery-bound display of artworks and the lecture series. Because the reader will outlast the other timebound acts, it is to be considered as the residual *afterlife* of *Living with Ghosts*. Further, just as the specter notably evades a metaphysics of the singular, this exhibition, and the reader especially, attempts a textual *performance* of the specter's disjunctive modalities of (dis)appearance through a collaging of excerpts, texts, and conversations by contributors who are dead and alive, who hail from various regions of the world, and who express differing though complimentary theoretical and political commitments and sensibilities.

Living With Ghosts, Installation View, Pace Gallery, London

The reader begins with a conceptual diptych: textual excerpts from both Achille Mbembe and Jacques Derrida. Both philosophers' meditations on time, space, history, memory, and justice, have deeply influenced the tone and direction of *Living with Ghosts.* Between Mbembe's pioneering theorisations on the African postcolony as inhabiting a unique "time of entanglement," a non-linear temporality in which "different forms of absence become mixed together" to Derrida's strikingly resonant proposition that intergenerational justice – especially if we are to consider those that have been, are, and will continue to be subjugated by the colonial matrices of power – necessarily hinges on a disjunctive relation to time, on the "non-contemporaneity with itself of the living present," we arrive at a seemingly self-evident collision between the paradigms of the postcolonial and the hauntological.

From this thematic juncture, we move on to a series of visual and textual sources that forthrightly address the ghosts of mid-20th century African decolonisation movements. Included here is the epilogue from C.L.R. James' much lauded work, *A History of Pan-African Revolt*, 1969, where James provides a detailed historical account of the ongoing struggles for liberation in various parts of the African continent and in its American and Caribbean diasporas, between 1939 and 1969. Taking note of the dashed hopes of this revolutionary epoch, crystallised by the swift collapse of several newly independent African states into military dictatorships, James, like many others gathered in this reader, argues that "The states which the African nationalist leaders inherited were not in any sense African" and further that "the newly independent African state was little more than the old imperialist state only now administered and controlled by black nationalists."

Sabelo J. Ndlovu-Gatsheni launches a similar critique in his essay, arguing, with analytic precision, that newly independent African states only managed to achieve a juridical form of freedom, which ought to be distinguished from the more radical, liberatory implications of decolonisation. Decolonisation, as Ndlovu-Gatsheni and various other decolonial thinkers understand it, connotes a thorough delinking from the epistemological architectonics of colonial modernity, which includes the nation-state model as well as capitalistic modes of production. The shortcomings of these mid-century anti-colonial movements, that is, their failure to deliver on the insurrectionist promise of a new world order, leads Ndlovu-Gatsheni to adopt rather hauntological language. He describes decolonisation as an incomplete project, as a "terrain of illusions of liberation and myths of freedom." Paired with James' historical writings, which situate Africans' struggles for liberation in an extended time frame that predates the mid-20th century, beginning with the Haitian Revolution in the 18th century (not to mention the numerous slave revolts that occurred on the continent and in the Americas two centuries further back), it becomes clear that the ghostly terrain of loss, disillusionment, delayed arrival, and arrested possibility that Ndlovu-Gatsheni describes is *immanent* to the condition of modernity and is what inflects the African postcolonial condition with an irreducibly hauntological character.

My essay on John Akomfrah and Black Audio Film Collective as well as my conversation with Bouchra Khalili centres on the indisputably vital role of aesthetics in articulating and mediating the ghostly historical space-time of the postcolonial realm. Both Akomfrah's and Khalili's art practices often trace, with poetic and formalist verve, the seemingly bygone revolutionary histories outlined above, of African anti-colonial nationalist movements and Third World internationalist networks that lasted from the 1950s to the 1970s. Here, I theorise how both artists' works produce a poetics of the spectral, what Derrida terms a "spectropoetics." These texts make a case for the unique capacity of lens-based media, specifically moving images, to conjure specters and therefore haunt viewers. In both pieces, I pay considerable attention to the formal methods deployed by these artists' works, taking note of the political, historical, and philosophical implications of their formal innovations, whether that be in the use of montage, colour filtration, sound scores, archival fragments, or written/vocalised texts. What must be clarified here (and this also applies to the selection of artworks in the gallery-bound act) is that Akomfrah and Khalili's artworks do not illustrate or merely reflect upon the conceptual structures elucidated by this reader but in fact materialise, modify, and complicate these very structures. It also goes without saying that I would not have come to many of the theoretical junctures elaborated earlier had it not been for the affective power of some of these aesthetically intelligent artworks, which, once more, work *alongside* and not *for* the adjacent critical texts.

Oscillating between the autobiographical and the historical, Emmanuel Iduma's anecdotal passages continue with a reflection on spectral aesthetics by way of responding, in an unmistakably literary register, to some of the images used in Abraham Oghobase's *Constructed Realities*, 2022. Oghobase's photo-conceptual work overlays translucent colonial archival images depicting British colonial officials and colonised Nigerian subjects with one-page text excerpts from *The Dual Mandate in British Tropical West Africa*, penned in 1922 by Lord Frederick Lugard, Nigeria's first governor-general. Lugard's colonial rhetoric starkly reveals the anxiety-ridden ideologies and discourses that were required for the establishment of British-administered colonial states in Africa in the late 19th and early 20th centuries. Covering numerous branches of the colonial state apparatus, from hut taxation to education to, rather ironically, "the evils and extenuations of slavery," viewers of these archival texts are left haunted by the bureaucratic aesthetics of colonial governance, by the colonial state's exploitative and expropriative practices of labour and natural resource extraction, by its unaccountable and illegitimate modes of necropolitical rule, and by its dubious creation of racial and civilizational difference – all logics that, as James and Ndlovu-Gatsheni lucidly demonstrate, were inherited by the supposedly "postcolonial" African state at the dawn of independence, and which in turn perpetuate the African postcolony's neo-colonial servitude in a 21st century context of rapacious global financial capitalism.

Walter D. Mignolo's essay on the work of Sylvia Wynter (and in turn, Wynter's theorising on the "Jamesian poiesis," after the work of C.L.R. James) forcefully grapples with the aforementioned colonial logics. Both Mignolo and Wynter are primarily concerned with the nearly imperceptible structures of power – what Mignolo calls the "colonial matrices of power" and what Wynter calls the "coloniality of being" – which not only determine the hierarchical ordering of global economies and nation-states in favour of Euro-American interests, but on a deeper symbolic and psychological level, dictate what even counts as "knowledge" and who gets to be human. Following Wynter, who meticulously argues that the most damaging legacy of colonial modernity has been the invention of "Man," – a white, straight, male, property-owning onto-epistemological category that "overrepresents" itself as if it were the only way to be human – it appears that we can only arrive at a decolonial future through, as Frantz Fanon similarly posed, the creation of a new human, one whose ontological sustenance and self-coherence does not depend on the ontological abjection of racialised/colonised Others and the more-than-human world.•[6]

If indeed, coloniality, at its basis, comprises a transhistorical matrix of intersecting hierarchies and heterarchies of power that operate on the abstract, quasi-immaterial plane of ontology and epistemology, but which, in turn, produce uncannily concrete material a/effects in the world, then we can conceive of coloniality as a ghost, as a spectral entity that belongs to the "past" but continually lingers in and haunts the present. In the excerpted sections from a recent interview with Avery F. Gordon, she theorises ghosts and hauntings along similar lines, taking heed of hauntology's more psychic registers. In the interview, Gordon describes haunting as "a way we're notified that what's been suppressed or concealed is very much alive and present, interfering with us and with the systems of repression that produce concealment and blockage." Thinking back to Derrida, who relates the spectral encounter with the potential realisation of justice, Gordon similarly proposes that confronting ghosts impels an active sense of "something to be done." Interestingly, Gordon's framing of hauntings, as catalytic yet melancholic events, complicates conventional psychoanalytic understandings of trauma by making us view trauma not as a pathological state of paralysis or compulsive repetition but as an originary hauntological site that spurs perpetual action and therefore engenders a potential (decolonial) futurity.

Returning to Mignolo and Wynter, they both argue that in order to think beyond the neo-colonial present and bring a transformed decolonial world into being, one must, on the one hand, engage in a rigorous deconstructive process that aims to identify and disaggregate coloniality's logics, and on the other hand, partake in a reconstructive project that critically re-centres and re-animates alternative modes of knowing and being that have been discredited, erased, and subjugated by colonial modernity's homogenising scientific rationalism. As Adjoa Armah's contribution makes evident, these alternative onto-epistemologies, many of which include African indigenous systems of thought, exist *in the present* as resilient non/counter-modern zones, which we ought to take seriously. Regarding "hauntology," which as pointed out earlier is largely derived from Euro-American intellectual genealogies (which are littered with all kinds of colonial phantasms), Armah offers a decolonial understanding of the concept via her meditations on the charged photographic negatives she collects on the coasts of Ghana. Armah expands on the "-graphy" of photography, using the suffix as a "descriptive science" that allows her to contend with historiography and cartography simultaneously.

6 • Frantz Fanon, *The Wretched Of The Earth*, trans. Richard Philcox, (New York: Grove Press), 1963, 239.

By methodologically mobilising West African animistic thought, which views physical reality as a material realm wherein immaterial forces can and do interfere, Armah's writing on these ghostly photographic negatives frames such indigenous systems of thought as *always already* hauntological. Thinking back to Derrida, one then wonders if the specter, which confounds Western ontology and epistemology, is precisely the trace, the seething non-present presence of various indigenous thought systems, whose internal logics *exceed* colonial reason, and whose exorcism from the sphere of modernity secure yet *haunt* the very definition of "the modern."

As Mbembe reminds us, "African social formations are not necessarily converging toward a single point, trend, or cycle. They harbor the possibility of a variety of trajectories neither convergent nor divergent but interlocked, paradoxical." Joshua Segun-Lean would agree, thinking through the aftermaths of various mass uprisings on the continent over the last half-decade, from the #ENDSARS protests in Nigeria and the #FixTheCountry protests in Ghana to the Sudanese Revolution and the #RhodesMustFall movement in South Africa, all of which have challenged the legitimacy of the African postcolonial nation-state and its reliance upon tyrannical modes of militarised governance, mass-poverty-inducing neoliberal economic policies, patriarchal and queerphobic oppression, and environmentally destructive processes of corporate enrichment, among many other colonial instruments of domination. Segun-Lean thinks with and through the fugitive choreography of these betrayed citizens as they gather around and reclaim urban public space. We are made palpably aware that the entropic charge that drives and guides these movements evidences an anarchic surplus, an "aggressive vitality," that exceeds the "living present" via an aggregation of multiple pasts, stretching back years, decades, centuries. And simultaneously, that these fierce refusals of the securitised state's "call to order" bring the possibility of a different world into view – an alternative future – if only for a brief duration.

Inflecting Armah's reflections through Segun-Lean's, I am led to consider whether that animating spectral call that is both future and past, that both implicates those who are no longer and those who are not yet born, that depends on the fundamental inseparability of life and death, belongs to an *otherwise*, "circular" conception of time and the cosmos, one that modernity's discontents know all too well – of "living dead" ancestors in the spirit realm who guide us, who interfere on our behalf, who have borne witness to what has happened and what might happen, and who we remain in *continuous* conversation with.[•7] When we forget to "feed" these ancestral spirits, they become hungry and wreak all manners of havoc in the physical world, giving rise to an all-too-familiar haunted, disjunctive present.[•8] Therefore, if these indigenous knowledges teach us anything at all, it is that we must boldly detach ourselves from coloniality's rituals of memorial disavowal, which attempt to bury, silence, or exorcise the ghosts that speak from our old and new colonial wounds. Instead, by actively feeding and communing with these ghosts, in other words, by *living with them*, we develop an expanded and layered historical consciousness of the catastrophic global present while also nurturing our desire for, and anticipation of, a more just future.

7 • Notions of "circular" time and the "living dead" are borrowed from Kas Saghafi via his theorising on Derrida's writings on survivance and phantasms. Saghafi briefly distinguishes the "circular" from the "cyclical" – whereas the latter connotes a revolving, non-linear *succession* of life and death, the former does away with the presupposition of the separability of life and death, rather asserting their spatial and temporal co-presence. This is not unlike various African indigenous cosmological schemes in which the physical world of the living is ontologically sutured to the spirit world of the dead. See Kas Saghafi, "Dying Alive," *Mosaic*, Vol. 43, No. 3, September 2015, 25.

8 • See Malidoma Patrice Somé, *Of Water and The Spirit: Ritual, Magic, and Initiation in the Life of an African Shaman*, (London: Penguin Compass), 1994, 9-10.

Achille Mbembe: Excerpt from *On the Postcolony*

University of California Press, 2001

What distinguishes our age from previous ages, the breach over which there is apparently no going back, the absolute split of our times that breaks up the spirit and splits it into many, is again contingent, dispersed, and powerless existence: existence that is contingent, dispersed, and powerless but reveals itself in the guise of arbitrariness and the absolute power to give death any time, anywhere, by any means, and for any reason. More precisely, it is the current face of arbitrariness over the *longue durée*, yet not just any arbitrariness, but arbitrariness in its comedy and stark horror, a real shadow that, while totally devoid of beauty, does not lack clarity; not just any arbitrariness, but arbitrariness as human and contingent violence with the distinctive feature of committing acts of destruction that, in their starkness, scale, and "knockout" effects, have the peculiar characteristic of concealing human suffering, burying it in an infinite circle centered, so to speak, everywhere. This is, then, the arbitrariness that accomplishes its own work and validates itself through its own sovereignty, and thereby permits power to be exercised as a right to kill and invests Africa with deaths at once at the heart of every age and above time.

But the question of the violence of tyranny was already posed to Africans by their remote and their recent past, a past slow to end. This obsession is found in African awareness in the nineteenth century. The slave trade had ramifications that remain unknown to us; to a large extent, the trade was the event through which Africa was born to modernity. Colonialism also, in both its forms and its substance, posited the issue of contingent human violence. Indeed, the slave trade and colonialism echoed one another with the lingering doubt of the very possibility of self-government, and with the risk, which has never disappeared, of the continent and Africans being again consigned for a long time to a degrading condition. In many ways, the form of domination imposed during both the slave trade and colonialism in Africa could be called phallic. During the colonial era and its aftermath, phallic domination has been all the more strategic in power relationships, not only because it is based on a mobilization of the subjective foundations of masculinity and femininity but also because it has direct, close connections with the general economy of sexuality. In fact, the phallus has been the focus of ways of constructing masculinity and power. Male domination derives in large measure from the power and the spectacle of the phallus—not so much from the threat to life during war as from the individual male's ability to demonstrate his virility at the expense of a woman and to obtain its validation from the subjugated woman herself.

Thus, it was through the slave trade and colonialism that Africans came face to face with the *opaque and murky domain of power*, a domain inhabited by obscure drives and that everywhere and always makes animality and bestiality its essential components, plunging human beings into a never-ending *process of brutalization*. It is these lines of separation—and of continuities—that African philosophy has failed to take up. Underlying the problem of arbitrariness and tyranny, as we have sketched it, of course lies the problem of freedom from servitude and the *possibility of an autonomous African subject*.

It is to focus on these issues that I have deliberately abstained from theorizing that would involve examining how, in sub-Saharan Africa, the critical power of reason could be retained or by what means could be ensured its triumph against all sorts of superstitions, customs, and habits.

To ask whether Africa is separated from the West by an unbridgeable gulf seems pointless. In an attempt to force Africa to face up to itself in the world, I have tried to state, in the most productive possible way, some general questions suggested by concepts drawn from social theory—notably those notions used generally for thinking about time, the bonds of subjection, the ways domination is validated, the collapse of historic "possibles" or their extensions, the symbolic constitution of the world, constraint and terror as limits of what is human, and relations to transcendence and finitude. Where these concepts were manifestly incapable of describing the particular figures of reason in African history and the practices of our time, I have invented different modes of discourse, *a different writing*.

By focusing the discussion on what I have called the "postcolony," the aim was not to denounce power as such, but rather to rehabilitate the two notions of *age* and *durée*. By age is meant not a simple category of time but a number of relationships and a configuration of events—often visible and perceptible, sometimes diffuse, "hydra-headed," but to which contemporaries could testify since very aware of them. As an age, the postcolony encloses multiple *durées* made up of discontinuities, reversals, inertias, and swings that overlay one another, interpenetrate one another, and envelope one another:•[1] an *entanglement*. I also wanted to pose the whole question of *displacement*. To do so with even a minimum of relevance, it was necessary to reject theories that—by proclaiming not only "the death of God" and "man" but also of "morality" and the "subject" at the risk of bringing about the disappearance of any axiological reference point and any object other than "oneself"—reduce individuals to mere flows of drives and networks of "desires," to libidinal machines. The central concern was to rethink the theme of the African subject emerging, focusing on him/herself, withdrawing, in the act and context of *displacement* and *entanglement*.

Displacement is not simply intended to signify dislocation, transit, or "the impossibility of any centrality other than one that is provisional, ad hoc, and permanently being redefined."•[2] While willing to take up a philosophical perspective when needed, I started from the idea that there is a close relationship between subjectivity and temporality—that, in some way, one can envisage subjectivity itself as temporality. The intuition behind this idea was that, for each time and each age, there exists something distinctive and particular—or, to use the term, a "spirit" (*Zeitgeist*). These distinctive and particular things are constituted by a set of material practices, signs, figures, superstitions, images, and fictions that, because they are available to individuals' imagination and intelligence and actually experienced, form what might be called "languages of life."

This "life world" is not only the field where individuals' existence unfolds in practice; it is where they exercise existence—that is, live their lives out and confront the very forms of their death. On this basis, I then asked what is the set of particular signs that confers on the current African age its character of urgency, its distinctive mark, its eccentricities, its vocabularies, and its magic, and make it both a source of terror, astonishment, and hilarity at once? What gives this set of things significations that all can share? In what languages are these significations expressed? How can these languages be deciphered?

1 • See M. Foucault, "Revenir à l'histoire," *Dits et écrits* (Paris: Gallimard, 1994), 278–80.
2 • As suggested by P. Michel in "De la notion de la 'transition': Remarques épistémologiques," *Cahiers internationaux de sociologie* 96 (1994): 214.

This line of thought led me to ask, for example, about the *fact* and the sign of the potentate, the relations between the government of people and the multiplication of things, the various forms of indigence, and the problem of excess and laughter, or of finitude and madness, as stated in the languages and practices of the supernatural and the divine.[3]

From the outset, there were two difficulties. First, every age, including the postcolony, is in reality a combination of several temporalities.[4] In the case of the postcolony, to postulate the existence of a "before" and an "after" of colonization could not exhaust the problem of the relationship between temporality and subjectivity, nor was it sufficient to raise questions about the passage from one stage (before) to the other (after), and the question of *transit* that such passage raises, or again to recognize that every age has contradictory significations to different actors. It was still necessary to know how, for each time, this multiplicity of times was to be re-inscribed not only in the *longue durée*, but also in indigenous *durées*. And then it was necessary to think about the status of that peculiar time that is *emerging time*.

To think relevantly about *this time that is appearing*, this *passing time*, meant abandoning conventional views, for these only perceive time as a current that carries individuals and societies from a background to a foreground, with the future emerging necessarily from the past and following that past, itself irreversible. But of central interest was that peculiar time that might be called the *time of existence and experience*, the *time of entanglement*. There was no way to give a plausible account of such time without asserting, at the outset, three postulates. First, this time of African existence is neither a linear time nor a simple sequence in which each moment effaces, annuls, and replaces those that preceded it, to the point where a single age exists within society. This time is not a series but an *interlocking* of presents, pasts, and futures that retain their depths of other presents, pasts, and futures, each age bearing, altering, and maintaining the previous ones.

Second, this time is made up of disturbances, of a bundle of unforeseen events, of more or less regular fluctuations and oscillations, not necessarily resulting in chaos and anarchy (although that sometimes is the case); moreover, instabilities, unforeseen events, and oscillations do not always lead to erratic and unpredictable behaviors on the actors' part (although that happens, too).

Finally, close attention to its real pattern of ebbs and flows shows that this time is not irreversible. All sharp breaks, sudden and abrupt outbursts of volatility, it cannot be forced into any simplistic model and calls into question the hypothesis of stability and *rupture* underpinning social theory, notably where the sole concern is to account for either Western modernity or the failures of non-European worlds to perfectly replicate it.

3 • These are some reasons our problematic has little in common with current discussions in the United States on "postcoloniality" or "subaltern" consciousness. On these latter see A. Quayson, *Postcolonialism: Theory, Practice, or Process?* (Cambridge: Polity Press, 2000); G. C. Spivak, *A Critique of Postcolonial Reason* (Cambridge: Harvard University Press, 1999); E. Shohat, "Notes on the "Postcolonial," *Social Text* 31–32 (1992): 84–113; G. Prakash, "Postcolonial Criticism and Indian Historiography," *Social Text* 31–32 (1992); G. Prakash, "Subaltern Studies as Postcolonial Criticism," *American Historical Review* 99, 5 (1994): 1475–90; G. Prakash, *After Colonialism: Imperial Histories and Postcolonial Displacements* (Princeton: Princeton University Press, 1995); D. Chakrabarty, "Postcoloniality and the Artifice of History: Who Speaks for 'Indian' Pasts?" *Representations* 37 (1992).

4 • For some discussions of time in general, see F. Braudel, "Histoire et sciences sociales, la longue durée," Annales ESC, 4 (1958); K. Pomian, *L'ordre du temps* (Paris: Gallimard, 1984); P. Osborne, *The Politics of Time: Modernity and Avant-Garde* (London: Verso, 1995).

African social formations are not necessarily converging toward a single point, trend, or cycle. They harbor the possibility of a variety of trajectories neither convergent nor divergent but interlocked, paradoxical. More philosophically, it may be supposed that the present *as experience of a time* is precisely that moment when different forms of absence become mixed together: absence of those presences that are no longer so and that one remembers (the past), and absence of those others that are yet to come and are anticipated (the future). This is what this book endeavors to interpret. I felt that what distinguishes the contemporary African experience is that this emerging time is appearing in a context—today—in which the future horizon is apparently closed, while the horizon of the past has apparently receded.•[5]

Moreover, to focus on *time of entanglement* was to repudiate not only linear models but the ignorance that they maintain and the extremism to which they have repeatedly given rise. Research on Africa has hardly stood out for its attempts to integrate nonlinear phenomena into its analyses. Similarly, it has not always been able to account for complexity. On the one hand, it has assimilated all non-linearity to chaos, forgetting that chaos is only one possible corollary of unstable dynamic systems. In addition, it has underestimated the fact that one characteristic of African societies over the *longue durée* has been that they follow a great variety of temporal trajectories and a wide range of swings only reducible to an analysis in terms of convergent or divergent evolution at the cost of an extraordinary impoverishment of reality. Further, research on Africa has literally impoverished our understanding of notions such as rationality, value, wealth, and interest—in short, what it means to be a subject in contexts of instability and crisis.•[6]

5 • Read J. Ferguson, *Expectations of Modernity: Myths and Meanings of Urban Life on the Zambian Copper Belt* (Berkeley and Los Angeles: University of California Press, 1999).
6 • A. Mbembe and J. Roitman, "Figures of the Subject in Times of Crisis," *Public Culture* 7, 2 (1993).

Jacques Derrida: Excerpt from *Specters of Marx: The State of the Debt, the Work of Mourning and the New International.*

Routledge, 1994

Someone, you or me, comes forward and says: *I would like to learn to live finally.*

Finally but why?

To learn to live: a strange watchword. Who would learn? From whom? To teach to live, but to whom? Will we ever know? Will we ever know how to live and first of all what "to learn to live" means? And why "finally"?

By itself, out of context—but a context, always, remains open, thus fallible and insufficient—this watchword forms an almost unintelligible syntagm. Just how far can its idiom be translated moreover?

A magisterial locution, all the same—or for that very reason. For from the lips of a master this watch word would always say something about violence. It vibrates like an arrow in the course of an irreversible and asymmetrical address, the one that goes most often from father to son, master to disciple, or master to slave ("I'm going to teach you to live"). Such an address hestitates, therefore: between address as *experience* (is not learning to live experience itself?), address as *education*, and address as *taming* or *training* [dressage].

But to learn to live, to learn it *from oneself and by oneself*, all alone, to teach *oneself* to live ("I would like to learn to live finally"), is that not impossible for a living being? Is it not what logic itself forbids? To live, by definition, is not something one learns. Not from oneself, it is not learned from life, taught by life. Only from the other and by death. In any case from the other at the edge of life. At the internal border or the external border, it is a heterodidactics between life and death.

And yet nothing is more necessary than this wisdom. It is ethics itself: to learn to live—alone, from oneself, by oneself. Life does not know how to live otherwise. And does one ever do anything else but learn to live, alone, from oneself, by oneself? This is, therefore, a strange commitment, both impossible and necessary, for a living being supposed to be alive: "I would like to learn to live." It has no sense and cannot he *just* unless it comes to terms with death. Mine as (well as) that of the other. Between life and death, then, this is indeed the place of a sententious injunction that always feigns to speak like the just.

What follows advances like an essay in the night—into the unknown of that which must remain to come—a simple attempt, therefore, to analyze with some consistency such an exordium: "I would like to learn to live. Finally." Finally what.

If it—learning to live—remains to be done, it can happen only between life and death. Neither in life nor in death *alone*. What happens between two, and between all the "two's" one likes, such as between life and death, can only maintain *itself* with some ghost, can only *talk with or about* some ghost [s'entretenir *de quelque fantôme*]. So it would be necessary to learn spirits. Even and especially if this, the spectral, *is not*. Even and especially if this, which is neither substance, nor essence, nor existence, *is never present as such*. The time of the "learning to live," a time without tutelary present, would amount to this, to which the exordium is leading us: to learn to live *with* ghosts, in the upkeep, the conversation, the company, or the companionship, in the commerce without commerce of ghosts. To live otherwise, and better. No, not better, but more justly. But *with them*. No *being-with* the other, no *socius* without this *with* that makes *being-with* in general more enigmatic than ever for us. And this being-with specters would also be, not only but also, a *politics* of memory, of inheritance, and of generations.

If I am getting ready to speak at length about ghosts, inheritance, and generations, generations of ghosts, which is to say about certain *others* who are not present, nor presently living, either to us, in us, or outside us, it is in the name of *justice*. Of justice where it is not yet, not yet *there*, where it is no longer, let us understand where it is no longer *present,* and where it will never be, no more than the law, reducible to laws or rights. It is necessary to speak *of the* ghost, indeed *to the* ghost and *with* it, from the moment that no ethics, no politics, whether revolutionary or not, seems possible and thinkable and *just* that does not recognize in its principle the respect for those others who are no longer or for those others who are not yet *there*, presently living, whether they are already dead or not yet born. No justice—let us not say no law and once again we are not speaking here of laws—seems possible or thinkable without the principle of some *responsibility*, beyond all living present, within that which disjoins the living present, before the ghosts of those who are not yet born or who are already dead, be they victims of wars, political or other kinds of violence, nationalist, racist, colonialist, sexist, or other kinds of exterminations, victims of the oppressions of capitalist imperialism or any of the forms of totalitarianism. Without this *non-contemporaneity with itself of the living present*, without that which secretly unhinges it, without this responsibility and this respect for justice concerning those who *are not there*, of those who are no longer or who are not yet *present and living*, what sense would there be to ask the question "where?" "where tomorrow?" "whither?"

This question arrives, if it *arrives,* it questions with regard to what will come in the future-to-come. Turned toward the future, going toward it, it also comes from it, it proceeds from [*provient* de] the future. It must therefore exceed any presence as presence to itself. At least it has to make this presence possible only on the basis of the movement of some disjointing, disjunction, or disproportion: in the inadequation to self. Now, if this question, from the moment it comes to us, can clearly come only from the future (whither? where will we go tomorrow? where, for example, is Marxism going? where are we going with it?), what stands *in front of* it must also precede it like its origin: *before* it. Even if the future is its provenance, it must be, like any provenance, absolutely and irreversibly past. "Experience" of the past as to come, the one and the other absolutely absolute, beyond all modification of any present whatever. If it is possible and if one must take it seriously, the possibility of the question, which is perhaps no longer a question and which we are calling here *justice*, must carry beyond *present* life, life as *my* life or *our* life. *In general.* For it will be the same thing for the "my life" or "our life" tomorrow," that is, for the life of others, as it was yesterday for other others: *beyond therefore the living present in general.*

To be just: beyond the living present in general—and beyond its simple negative reversal. A spectral moment, a moment that no longer belongs to time, if one understands by this word the linking of modalized presents (past present, actual present: "now," future present). We are questioning in this instant, we are asking ourselves about this instant that is not docile to time, at least to what we call time. Furtive and untimely, the apparition of the specter does not belong to that time, it does not give time, not that one: "Enter the ghost, exit the ghost, re-enter the ghost" (*Hamlet*).

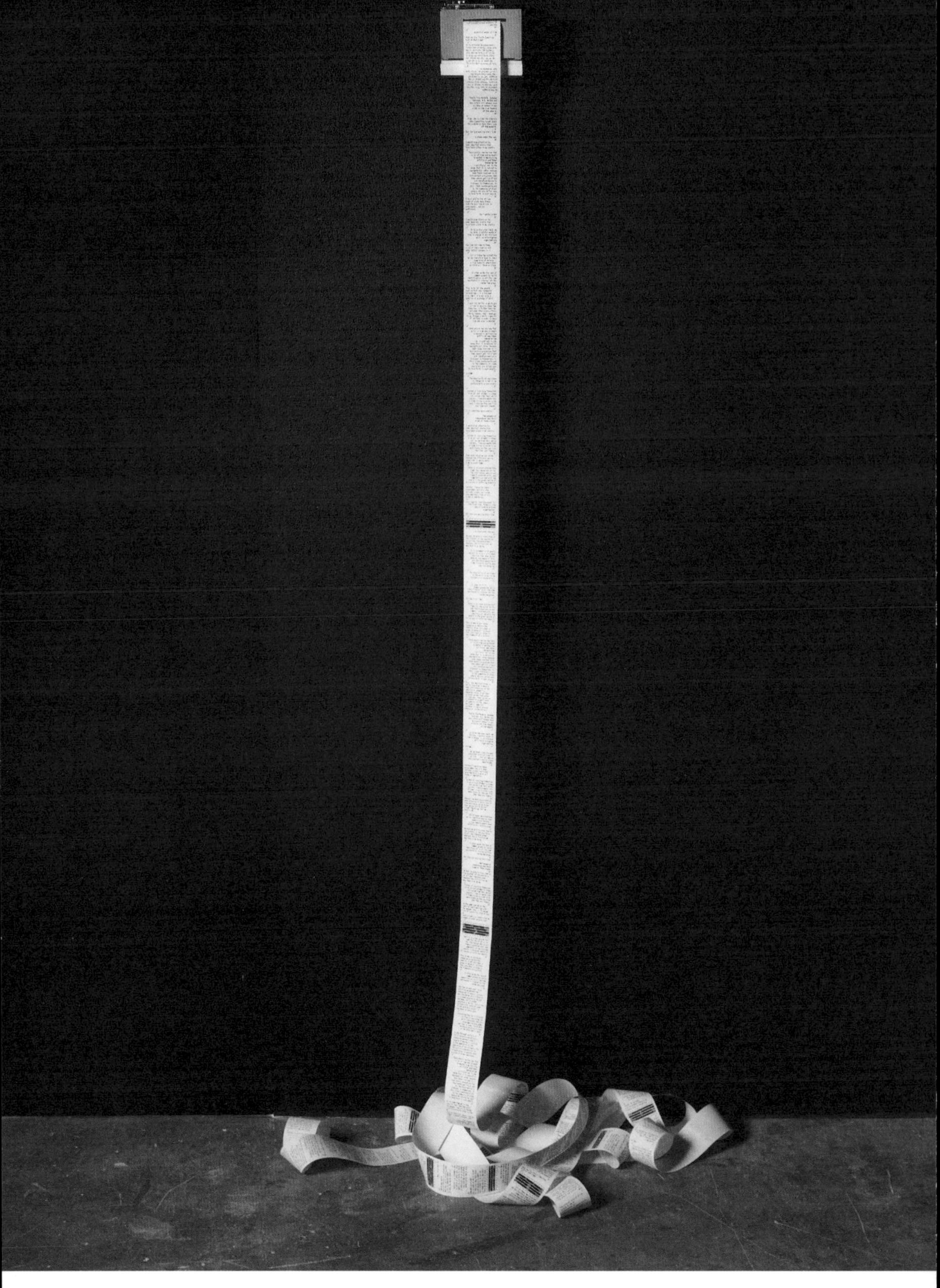

Nolan Oswald Dennis. *biko.cabral (time/place)*, 2020. Receipt Printer, microcontroller. Variable dimensions.

even those involved in it
have certain prejudices that
they cannot get rid of and
are therefore basically
dishonest to themselves, to
their black counterparts and
to the community of black
people who are called upon
to have faith in such people.
.b^

I have said to the African
heads of state many times,
that the aid from Africa is
very useful, but not
sufficient.
.c^

its rightful place
.b^

I would draw attention to
some important events that
have taken place in my country
.c^

It is on the other hand, we
believe, a painful waste of
time to engage in any dialogue
with racially-bigoted
organisations
.b^

the time had come to take
stock of the situation and
make radical changes in it
.c^

Out of these two situations
we can therefore hope to reach
some kind of balance -
a true humanity where power
politics will have no place.
.b^

.c^

In other words the lack of
common ground for solid
identification is all the time
manifested in internal strifes
inside the group.
.b^

This is to let the people
realize that they conquered
colonialism - it's finished
his time - it's not only a
question of a change of skin
.c^

It must not be that a white guy
is free to move to Cape Town
tomorrow, to Durban tomorrow,
and some other place without
being indexed, and I have got
to go through a whole rigmarole
of red tape in order to move
from one area to another.
.b^

.c^

These people realise now that
a lot of time and strength
is wasted in maintaining
artificial and token
nonracialism
- artificial not in the
sense that it is natural to
segregate but rather because
even those involved in it
have certain prejudices that
they cannot get rid of and
are therefore basically
dishonest to themselves, to
their black counterparts and
to the community of black
people who are called upon
to have faith in such people.
.b^

in time.
.c^

The peculiarity of our place
in the world is not to be
confused with anyone else's
.b^

.c^

Instead of involving themselves
in an all-out attempt to stamp
out racism from their white
society, liberals waste lots

C.L.R. JAMES
Epilogue: The History of Pan-African Revolt: A Summary, 1939–1969

PM Press, 1969

I have to review the thirty years from 1938 when this book was published to 1969. This involves the social, using the word in the broadest sense, and the political activity, defeats and successes of hundreds of millions of people in Africa; tens of millions in the United States; and a few million in the West Indies who make up in intensity and potentiality for the insignificance of their numbers. Apart from the mere mass of the material, few periods in history exceed, in fact approach, the range of achievement, change, dramatic events and striking personalities of this particular period in history. Under these circumstances it is necessary even, at the cost of a few hundred words, where words are so precious, to make clear what can be done and what cannot be done, in fact to set the tone and the mood in which this review must be approached.

Anatole France (now, alas, low in critical estimation) made many not only witty but wise observations: A famous ruler, after many successes not excluding failures, called together the wise men of his kingdom and told them he wanted them to study and report to him the facts and the understanding of History. The learned old men accepted the responsibility, gathered their assistants and their materials and retired for twenty years. They then returned with twenty volumes in which they had summarized the facts and the significance of History. By this time the monarch was an old man and he complained: "How do you expect me at my age to cope with all that, to read far less to study twenty large volumes? Go away, summarize the twenty volumes so that I will be able to read them." The historians went away and after twenty years one very old man with a long beard returned with a single volume. "Sire," he said, "my fellow scholars are all dead. I have summarized it all and here it is in one volume." The monarch lay on what he knew to be his death bed, and he bitterly complained. "You mean to say that I will never know the facts and the significance of History? How can I read even that large single volume which you bring to me?" The old historian put the book aside and told him: "Sire, I can summarize the history of man for you so that you can understand it before you die: They were born, they suffered, they died."

I wish my readers to understand the history of Pan- African Revolt during the last thirty years. They fought, they suffered—they are still fighting. Once we understand that, we can tackle our problems with the necessary mental equilibrium.

First Africa: I shall take only two of the nearly fifty African States, which have won their independence or increased their powers. The first is what we know today as Ghana, the second is Kenya. It helps that I have known personally the national leaders of both countries.

I. AFRICA

Gold Coast to Ghana

There lived in Accra a sub-chief called Nii Kwabena Bonne III. He was also a businessman. He made a short campaign through the country enlisting the support of the Chiefs. He then, on January 11, 1948, called a boycott on the purchase of European imported goods. The boycott was as complete as such an undertaking could be. It became general in the Colony and Ashanti and lasted until the February 24.

During the boycott events of immense symbolical significance took place. Native administrations, up to this point, like the Chiefs, tools of the Government, now used their legal position to impose fines upon those who did not cooperate in the boycott of European goods. Groups of young men went around the towns maintaining the boycott by force when necessary.

It was only on February 11 that the Government intervened. There was a series of meetings between the Chamber of Commerce and Nii Bonne III, with the Colonial Secretary in the Chair. It was agreed that prices should be lowered for a trial period of three months. Nii Bonne III then called off the boycott.

Meanwhile, the Ex-Servicemen's Union planned to present a petition to the Governor setting forth their grievances on Monday, the February 24, 1948, but they postponed it until Saturday the 28th. On that day the Ex-Servicemen's Union began their march. In the course of it they changed the prescribed route and announced their determination to march on Christiansborg Castle, the residence of the Governor. They found a squad of police in their way and in the course of the dispute which followed, the Superintendent of Police, a white man, fired at the ringleaders, killed two of them and wounded four or five. The news spread into the industrial district of Accra where the people or the first time in a month were buying European goods. They were already dissatisfied because they believed that the goods were not being sold to them at the prices stated in the published agreement, which had preceded the calling off of the boycott. The news of the shooting precipitated an outburst of rage. The people attacked the European shops and looted them. The police were unable to restore order for two days, Saturday the 28th and Sunday the 29th. There was destruction of property by fire and in the two days fifteen persons were killed and 115 injured in Accra alone: There were other disturbances in various parts of the Colony. The most important were at Koforidua where the outbreak began after the arrival of a lorry with men from Accra. They broke out in Kumasi and district on Monday, March 1st, an hour after the arrival of the train from Accra.

Nkrumah says that he and his organization, the United Gold Coast Convention, had nothing whatever to do with the disturbances, and, as we shall see, there is every reason to believe him.

These are the bare facts of the case. When, however, we look a little more closely in the light of after-events, an often analyzed logical movement discloses itself. These were no ordinary riots of a hungry populace over high prices. The first stage of every revolution is marked by a great mass movement of the populace, usually led by representatives of the old order. M. Georges Lefebvre of that great school of historians, the French historians of the French Revolution, has established that the bourgeois revolution in France in 1789 was preceded by mass rioting during what he calls the "crisis of the monarchy" which took place in 1788, one year before the popular eruption which captured the Bastille on July 14, 1789.•[1] In this case we are in the middle of the twentieth century.

The first outburst takes the form of an economic boycott that lasted a month, but it is led by a Chief and supported by the Chiefs. The people of Accra follow exactly the course that the masses of the people have followed in every great revolution. The only organization at hand was the organization of ex-servicemen, and when they began their march they were at once reinforced by large numbers of spectators and sympathizers. Whatever had been the original intention of the ex-servicemen, these sympathizers encouraged them to take the road to the Governor's Castle. Anti-racial cries were frequently uttered.

Among the remarks were such as "This is the last European Governor who will occupy the Castle." (They were not far wrong; he was the last but one.) The crowd directed a heavy fusillade of stones against the police. When the police tried to stop them, they shouted insults at the European officers and invited the Africans in the ranks to abandon their duty. It seems that they were successful. For when the Superintendent finally gave the order to fire, the Africans did not shoot and he himself had to seize a rifle from the nearest man to fire the shots which caused the casualties. Superintendent Imray had with him at the time only ten men. The idea that a crowd of 2,000, many of them men who had seen battle, was cowed by the shooting is ridiculous. They could have swept the ten men away in ten seconds, and as there was only two officers and twenty men at Christiansborg, the Castle could easily have become another Bastille. In these situations you have to work by inferences, similar conjunctures in previous historical situations and an absence of prejudice against crowds and against Africans. The crowd retreated because it realized that to sweep away the petty resistance which faced it would be to initiate a battle for which it knew it was not prepared. Therefore, as crowds will do under such circumstances, it preferred to retreat.

I am here using the report of the investigations made later by a Colonial Office Commission, and it must be remembered first that at moments like these what the crowd is really thinking and the motives of its actions are profoundly difficult to recapture after the actions have taken place; and in any case a Government Commission is not exactly the body which would know whom to question, how to elicit the answers that matter, and even to understand what evidence it does manage to collect. The Commission calls the crowd a "lawless mob." That was precisely what it was not. It was acting instinctively according to certain fundamental laws of revolution and we shall see that it obeys these laws to the very end.

We should note these incipient actions carefully because, unless there is a great unsettlement of the settled policy of His Majesty's Government and the other European powers, that is precisely what is going to take place over vast areas of colonial Africa. What has really taken place can be summed up as follows:

1. The people on a national scale have mobilized and organized themselves during the boycott and felt their power, and they have

1 • A few words here were omitted from earlier editions. See Publisher's Foreword.

been able to do so rapidly because this first step is taken under their traditional leaders, their Chiefs.

2. The call to the African police not to obey their European officers and not to shoot was not an accident. It takes place at the beginning of all revolutions. Neither was it spontaneous. Already, during the boycott, at the trial of a local chief on a charge arising out of the enforcement of the boycott, posters had appeared in Accra calling upon the police to strike and to refuse to obey the orders of the European officers.

3. The march on Christiansborg Castle and the shouts that the Governor would be the last European governor show that out of the confidence built up in the month-long boycott, the people had proclaimed the ultimate slogan of the revolution, the end of imperial rule.

They knew what they wanted. If they turned aside from the direct march to the Castle and hesitated before sweeping aside the police, it was because they understood the consequences of such actions. They had been waiting for somebody to lead them and they welcomed Nkrumah as a person to do so. Lawless mob indeed. Within eighteen months Nkrumah was going to call a Ghana Constituent Assembly in Accra, which would be attended by 90,000 people. Within two years these people would carry out a policy of Positive Action in which the life of the whole country would be brought to a standstill with the utmost discipline and order. Within three years they would give Nkrumah a vote of 22,780 out of a possible 23,122.

Nkrumah was taken out of jail to be made Leader of Government Business. Then after years of in-fighting he finally achieved the independence of the Gold Coast in 1957.

The Myth of Mau Mau

Not African beliefs and tribal practices but land and white settlers on the land were to be decisive in shaping the character of the black revolt in Kenya. The railway made possible the export of cash crops by Europeans settled on the fertile temperate land of the Kenya Highlands. A policy of encouraging white settlement, a new policy in Africa, soon received the official blessing of the Foreign Office. Subsequently, under Colonial Office supervision, European settlement rapidly became the most powerful influence in the social, economic, and political development of the new country.

It was in the first decade of the twentieth century that this new Kenya took shape. One of the largest early applications for land (500 square miles) was made in April 1902 by the East Africa Syndicate, a company with a strong South African interest. With only a dozen settlers established at the beginning of 1903, in August the Commissioner, Sir Charles Eliot, sent his Collector of Customs, A. Marsden, to South Africa to encourage settlers to migrate to the country. By the end of 1905 over a million acres of land had been leased or sold by the Protectorate authorities. In 1906 a large party of Boer "Irreconcilables" trekked overland from the Transvaal to the Kenya highlands; others poured in by boat from Britain and South Africa.

Thus began something new in an African colony: the struggle to make it a "white man's country."

Nowhere in Africa was there such a struggle as began before 1914 and lasted decade after decade until it culminated in the independence of Kenya nearly fifty years later. Between 1903 and 1906 important areas of Kikuyu land were alienated. Some 8,000 shillings was paid in compensation to 8,000 Kikuyu, but more than 3,000 received nothing at all. Commissioner Eliot was to write that "no one can doubt that the rich and exceptionally fertile district of Kikuyu is destined to be one of the chief centers of European cultivation, and the process of settlement is facilitated by the fact that there are gaps where there is no native population."

By 1914, the exclusive "White Highlands" was already a reality, and the Europeans were demanding the conventional right of British colonists to elect their own representatives to the Protectorate's Legislative Council.

The struggle was continuous. Ultimately (by the early 1950s) the Africans, mainly but not entirely Kikuyu, took to arms, and from encampments and hiding places in the forests raided settled establishments and slew white farmers and those Africans who supported the British regime. Dedan Kimathi and Waruhiu Itote ("General China") were generally acknowledged as the senior leaders of the nationalist armies. Food, funds, arms, medical supplies could be secured only by immense risks and labors. In some parts the Home Guard was strong, in others weak. In some areas the chief was sympathetic, in others he was a dedicated "loyalist." There were some wonderful leaders whose names ought to be recorded—Kimathi himself, Stanley Mathenge, China, and Tanganyika in Nyeri, Matenjagwo, Kago, and Mbaria Kaniu in Fort Hall, and Kimbo, the cattle-raider, operating between Nanyuki and Maivasha. The difficult terrain prevented easy lateral communication within the forest itself, and the campaign soon developed into a series of local battles of attrition, ridge by ridge.

Though defeated in the Reserves, and with some surrendering to the British Security Forces, nonetheless many men and women in the forest continued their resistance. Their aim, apart from surviving and carrying on the struggle for land and freedom, was to attract international attention to their cause. No outside help was forthcoming, and the Emergency did not give rise to a major political investigating commission from Britain.

From 1953 to 1955, Kimathi sought to provide an overall perspective of the resistance in the forest. At one point, while in the forest, Kimathi was reported to have said: "I do not lead rebels but I lead Africans who want their self-government and land. My people want to live in a better world than they met with when they were born. I lead them because God never created a true and real brotherhood between white and black so that we may be regarded as people and as human beings who can do each and every thing."

Yet the plain fact is that the nationalist army in the forests was defeated by the huge forces sent by the British Government to maintain the colonial regime. Some 50,000 Kikuyu and other revolutionaries were detained in special camps to undergo special training to cure them of the mental disease which the British authorities discovered as the cause of their refusal to submit. Jomo Kenyatta was given a long prison sentence and, having served it, was confined far away from the center of Kenya politics.

Despite this reconstitution of physical and military authority the British found that they could no longer govern the people of Kenya. Constitutional manipulation and constitutional maneuver were worked out, agreed upon by the British Parliament and its experts, only to meet rejection and failure. In the end Kenya had to be granted political independence. The stories spread about "Mau Mau" have been exposed for the anti-African myths that they are. There is nothing inherently African about "Mau Mau." Their social organization and corresponding beliefs being broken up and persecuted by the British, what was (by the British) labeled as Mau Mau was an *ad hoc* body of beliefs, oaths, disciplines newly created for the specific purpose of gathering and strengthening the struggle against British imperialism, its military, political and economic domination and, in particular, the Christianity it sought to inject and impose.

Independence and After

In the Gold Coast and in Kenya we have the two extremes of the African struggles for independence. Nothing in modern history was more starting than the rapidity with which other African states achieved political independence. In Algeria the French imperialists had an experience similar to the Kenya experience. The French military had established what they considered military power over the necessarily not-well-organized Algerian nationalist forces. They believed that they had established control over the political resistance. They engineered General de Gaulle into power in France in order finally to teach Algerians that they were French. But the General understood a revolutionary upheaval better than they did. He realized that whatever the strength of guns and of prisons, the colonial mentality of accepting domination was broken and could never be restored. To the fury of the French imperialists and army he worked out an independence agreement with the Algerian nationalists, saving what he could for French finance and capital. Such was the disappointment and anger of the French generals in particular that they tried to assassinate him. So blatant was their attempt that some of them had to be tried and even jailed. Such was the naked proof of the rapacity of that small section of the population of an advanced civilization, which profited by imperialism. Similarly, thousands of Frenchmen who had lived well by exploiting the Algerian people left Algeria and returned to France.

The murder of Lumumba and the tireless efforts of the late Tshombe dramatized the attempt by Belgian imperialism to maintain its exploitation of the vast mineral wealth of the Congo, while giving some token recognition to the irresistible movement for national independence.

The dozen years that have unfolded since the winning of independence by the Gold Coast in 1957 are some of the most farranging and politically intense that history has known. African state after African state has gained political independence with a tumultuous rush that was not envisaged even by the most sanguine of the early advocates of independence. The names of leaders obscure the political reality. What is to be noted is that Kenyatta, Nkrumah, Banda, to take the best-known names, were all imprisoned by the British Government and *had to be released to head the independent states*. The British Government, as did the French and Belgian, found that despite their soldiers, their guns and planes, they could not rule. The colonial mentality having been broken, the only way to restore some sort of order or, to reject a word now corrupted and offensive, the only way to have a viable society was to transfer the man in jail to be the head of state. In no other way could the African people once more accommodate themselves to any social structure.

They accepted the African leader and his African colleagues. But that is precisely why in African state after African state, with almost the rapidity with which independence was gained, military dictatorship after military dictatorship has succeeded to power, the most depressing of all being the overthrow of what had appeared to be the most progressive and successful of the new African governments—the government of Mali. What are the reasons for this rapid decay and decline of African nationalism? The best known and the reason most often advanced by Africans and advocates of African independence is the continued exploitation by the industrial and finance-capital of Europe and the United States. Even people no more than casually informed are aware of the continual lowering of the prices of the commodities, most often single-crop or unit-minerals, produced by the African countries, and the raising of the prices of the manufactured goods needed by the newly independent African countries in their necessarily frantic efforts to modernize themselves. Banks, and old industries with new African names working through local agents (such as the East Indian community in Kenya), continue to control the life of the newly independent African communities. "Aid," so small in quantity and so large in publicity, would gladly be dispensed with, if economic independence were automatically to result from political independence.

However, without minimizing the continuing economic subordination of the newly independent African states, there are objective reasons for the apparent decline, in fact abrupt disintegration and resort to crude military dictatorship in African state after African state.

The states which the African nationalist leaders inherited were not in any sense African. With the disintegration of the political power of the imperialist states in Africa, and the rise of militancy of the African masses, a certain political pattern took shape. Nationalist political leaders built a following, they or their opponents gained support among the African civil servants who had administered the imperialist state, and the newly independent African state was little more than the old imperialist state only now administered and controlled by black nationalists. That these men, western-educated and western-oriented, had or would have little that was nationalist or African to contribute to the establishment of a truly new and truly African order was seen most clearly by the late Frantz Fanon, and he established his still constantly increasing reputation by his untrammeled advocacy of revolt against these black nationalist regimes. Uncompromising revolt he saw as the only means of ridding Africa of the economic and psychological domination by Western civilization which, independence or no independence, seemed certain to keep Africa and Africans hewers of wood and drawers of water to Western civilization. Sekou Toure of Guinea seemed to be the only African leader who aimed at building a society which would use European techniques to strengthen and develop the African heritage. But not only was Guinea a very small and very underdeveloped state, but the Moscow assistants whom he hoped would help him, plotted to overthrow his regime and Guinea did not make the progress which would set an example for Africa. That example, however, was to come from Tanzania, under the leadership of Dr. Nyerere. The impact that the policies of Tanzania has made upon Africa and can in time make upon the rest of the world, underdeveloped or advanced, has already established the African state of Tanzania as one of the foremost political phenomena of the twentieth century. Tanzania is the highest peak reached so far by revolting blacks and it is imperative to make clear, not least of all to blacks everywhere, the new stage of political thought which has been reached. But first to establish some idea of what is happening in other areas of Negro political reality and response since 1938.

II. SOUTH AFRICA

Since the end of World War II nowhere has any regime in the world (or for that matter any modern historical regime) made it more clear what is its primary and permanent concern. This preoccupation is the repression and containment of the increasing revolutionary rejection of its exploitation and oppression by the millions of blacks on whose backs it lives and thrives. Such is the record which the South African regime of whites daily registers in contemporary history aided by the benevolent neutrality of Europe and America, and the border states that it seeks to build and strengthen against political destruction by a self-conscious independent African continent.

All that will be attempted here is to give what is usually neglected, the pressure—the objective social pressure—which the South African blacks, the most highly developed in Africa, exercise on the very vitals of the South African regime.

A Prime Minister of South Africa, Mr. B.J. Vorster, made it absolutely clear that the regime had no intention of giving political rights to urban Africans. Speaking in Parliament on April 24, 1968, he said:

> They remain there because they cannot provide employment for themselves. But the fact that you employ those people, does not place you under any obligation to grant them political rights in your parliament. Surely the fact that you work for a man does not give you the right to run his affairs? . . . It is true that there are blacks working for us. They will continue to work for us for generations, in spite of the ideal we have to separate them completely. . . .

The fact of the matter is this; we need them, because they work for us, but, after all, we pay them for their work. . . . But the fact that they work for us can never entitle them to claim political rights. Not now, nor in the future . . . under no circumstances can we grant them those political rights in our own territory, neither now nor never.

> That indicates the fear that white South Africa has of the blacks. Any examination of South Africa's labor laws and policies will show the pretense and the reality of the status of Africans in the urban areas. More than 4,000,000 Africans live in the urban areas. In spite of desperate measures to limit the flow of Africans into the towns, the urban African population doubled between 1945

and 1960, when 3,471,233 were counted in the census. For twelve of those remarkable fifteen years, the Nationalist government was busily engaged in applying its policy of keeping the races apart.

For better appreciation of the situation, one should study the racial composition of the thirteen principal urban areas, listed in the accompanying table. These centers of industrial and commercial activity have been designated "white" areas although their white population is far less than their non-white.

The greatest concentration of industry is on the Witwatersrand, where there are twice as many non-whites as whites and Africans alone outnumber whites by over half-a-million.

Population of Principal Urban Areas 1960 (Approximate)

	African	Whites	Coloreds	Asians
Johannesburg	650,912	413,153	59,467	28,993
Cape Town	75,200	305,155	417,881	8,975
Durban	221,535	196,398	27,082	236,477

The purpose of the Urban Areas Act is to control the influx of Africans into the urban areas; to set apart areas for their accommodation; to direct their labor; and to impose strict regulations for their control and movement. In short, it aims at providing whites with black labor without allowing blacks to acquire residential, social and other rights in the areas where they are employed. Try as they will, the South African whites cannot isolate or circumscribe the black population. The simple truth is that without the participation of the black population the South African economy would fall apart.

Here are some figures, published by the Anti-Apartheid Movement in February 1969.

Population (mid-1967)

	Numbers	Percentage
Africans	12 3/4 million	68
Whites	3 1/2 million	19
Coloreds	1 3/4 million	10
Indians	1/2 million	3

88 percent of Coloured people live in the Cape. 83 percent of the Indian people in the Natal. They are debarred from living on the Orange Free State.

Distribution of population by race in each of the four largest cities (percent)

	Whites	Africans	Coloreds	Indians
Johannesburg	36	56	5	3
Cape Town	38	9	52	1
Durban	29	32	4	35
Pretoria	49	47	2	2

There have been created three so-called African states, Transkei, Ciskei and Tswanaland, labeled Bantustans so as to create some sense of race and nation separate from white South Africa. That cannot alter nor mitigate the remorseless pressures of the blacks of South Africa against the whites. The imprisonings, the tortures and the shootings now have been met by guerrilla warfare substantially authenticated. One thing is certain. The existing regime in South Africa can continue to exist only by the increasing persecution and brutal repression of the existing blacks. History in general, and the particulars of this history, indicate a violent end to this regime sooner or later, and sooner rather than later.

III. THE UNITED STATES

1952 was the first year in seventy-one years that there were no lynchings. But that does not mean that the bodies of black men who had offended whites were no longer found floating in shallow waters, or that at times black men disappeared, their relations and friends uncertain whether they had gone North or had been liquidated by white racists. The National Association for the Advancement of Colored People, a predominantly middleclass organization, chiefly of blacks but including sympathetic whites, concentrated on the abolition of legal discrimination against Negroes and earned notable successes. Legal struggles and mass action reacted on each other. The famous bus boycott in Montgomery, Alabama, began on December 5, 1955, and this action, of a range and solidity unprecedented, unloosed a flood which became a torrent. On June 5, 1956, a Federal court ruled that racial segregation on Montgomery city buses violated the Constitution. Later that year, the Supreme Court upheld a lower court decision which banned segregation on Montgomery buses. Federal injunctions prohibiting this segregation were served on city, state and bus company officials on December 20. At mass meetings, Montgomery blacks called off the year-long bus boycott, and buses were integrated on December 21.

Congress passed the Civil Rights Act of 1957, the first federal civil rights legislation since 1875. That very year. President Eisenhower, with obvious reluctance to take such a step, ordered federal troops to Little Rock, Arkansas, to prevent interference with school integration at Central High School. That was on September 24. These episodes might have seemed to be merely unusual types of struggles which in the past had been halfheartedly projected or even attempted. Rapidly they showed themselves to be precipitants of the greatest social crisis the United States had known since the Civil War.

It was black students who initiated this struggle. On February 1, 1960 four students from a North Carolina college started a sit-in movement at Greensboro, North Carolina, in a five and dime store. By February 10 the movement had spread to fifteen Southern cities in five states. In March, one thousand Alabama State students marched on the State Capitol and held a protest meeting. In April the Student Nonviolent Coordinating Committee was organized on the Shaw University campus. In May, President Eisenhower signed the Civil Rights Act of 1960, but that was insignificant in comparison with the tremendous movement that now began among blacks: the masses of the population in city after city; the groups of "Freedom Riders"—black young men and women who faced the bombs, bullets, whips and prisons of the South, official and unofficial; the black students on the campuses; black youths in the schools. Let it not be forgotten that both the New Left and the revolutionary defiance of campus authority by white students began to take shape as a direct result of the black students turning from protests by asking for reforms to protests by revolutionary action.

It would be a mistake here to attempt to give details about either events or personalities. Even to name some is to omit and thereby discriminate against others. It may be said, however, that names such as LeRoi Jones, Stokely Carmichael, Eldridge Cleaver, Rap Brown, Malcolm X, Martin Luther King, the Black Panthers, are household names not only among young people in the United States but among white populations all over the world. Summer after summer has seen tremendous struggles by the black masses, led by unknown, obscure, local leaders. Perhaps the most significant was that which followed the assassination of Dr. Martin Luther King, the world-famous black leader. The American government placed a cordon of troops around the White House and government buildings and areas in Washington. They then abandoned the city, the capital of the United States, to the embittered and insurgent blacks, who constitute a majority of the Washington population. The question to be asked: what else could the government have done?

One can only record the question most often and most seriously asked: can any government mobilize the white population, or a great majority of it, in defense of white racism against militant blacks? The only legitimate answer lies in the continuing militancy or retreat of the black population. This population is at least 30 million in number, strategically situated in the heart of many of the most important cities in the United States. If the black population continues to resist racism, the militants and youth actively and the middle classes sympathetic or neutral, then the physical defeat of the black struggle against racism will involve the destruction of the United States as it has held together since 1776.

IV. THE CARIBBEAN

The Caribbean is a small area where British and French have ruled for centuries and where at the present one or two British territories have been granted what is known as independence. There are a few points that are to be made about these extraordinarily significant but on the world scale minute territories.

First of all, it is only recently that a British scholar, Sir Richard Pares, in a work called Merchants and Planters, has made it clear that as far back as the middle of the eighteenth century the slaves actually ran the plantations—those plantations that were the source of so much wealth, which contributed so substantially to the advancement of the advanced countries. Merchants and Planters is a study of the Caribbean and was published for the Economic History Society at the Cambridge University Press. Pares notes that:

> in all the inventories which are to be found among the West Indian archives it is very usual for the mill, the cauldron, the still and the buildings to count for more than one-sixth of the total capital; in most plantations one-tenth would be nearer the mark. By far the greatest capital items were the value of the slaves and the acreage planted in canes by their previous labor.

So that the greatest capital value (about 1760) of the sugar plantations, was the labor of the slaves and the acres they had planted. All sorts of economists do all sorts of studies about the West Indies but they don't know that the real value of those precious economic units was the slaves and the land they had developed by their labors. This escapes nearly all, except this English scholar.

Pares goes on to say: "Yet, when we look closely, we find that the industrial capital required was much larger than a sixth of the total value. With the mill, the boiling house and the still went an army of specialists—almost all of them slaves, but none the less specialists for that."

There was an army of slaves, but they were specialists. This tremendous economy that made so much wealth, particularly for British society—it was the slaves who ran those plantations. Pares drives home the point: "They were not only numerous but, because of their skill, they had a high value. If we add their cost to that of the instruments and machinery which they used, we find that the industrial capital of the plantations without which it could not be a plantation at all, was probably not much less than half its total capital."

Pares obviously feels it imperative to reiterate what he no doubt has failed to find in previous studies. "But when we examine specifications of the Negroes, we find so many boilers, masons, carters, boatswains of the mill, etc., that we cannot feel much confidence in our categories, especially when we find individuals described as 'excellent boiler and field Negro'"

So that about 1766 Negroes ran the plantations. A man is described as an excellent boiler and field Negro, but this prevents us from putting such persons on either side of the line. He not only worked in the fields but also did the necessary technical work. Further complication arises from the fact that specialist jobs were awarded to the sickly and the ruptured. The sickly or the ruptured were given the technical jobs to do—we have to look afresh at the rapid spread of technical skill.

That gives an entirely different picture of the kind of civilization that was in existence in the West Indies well before the French Revolution of 1789. In the United States in general skilled labor was the preserve of whites. There were no white laborers in the Caribbean. There is other evidence elsewhere and it seems legitimate to say that the slaves ran the society. If they had been removed the society would have collapsed. That in fact is perfectly clear in certain writings about Trinidad and Tobago.

This is the process whereby the inhabitants of these Caribbean islands have made an astonishing mastery of the techniques of Western civilization. Race prejudice, however, continues to be subtly, and not so subtly, a dominant feature of the social structure of the islands. What has happened is that the population, without any native background (the Amerindians were all wiped out), have been compelled to master the languages and the techniques of Western civilization which they have done with astonishing skill. The struggle for African and black independence is studded with distinguished individuals of Caribbean origin: Rene Maran, winner of the Prix Goncourt in 1921 for his exposure in his novel *Batouala* of French degradation of the African peoples in Africa, where be worked as a civil servant; Marcus Garvey, George Padmore, Frantz Fanon, Aime Cesaire, Stokely Carmichael . . . But this mastery of certain aspects of Western civilization has been able to exercise itself fully only in Western Europe and the United States for the imperialists continue, as they have done from the beginning, to dominate the economic and finances of the territories. The only difference today is that black men administer the imperialist interests. The situation is highly explosive. Whereas the economy continues to be a colonialist economy of the seventeenth century, completely dominated by foreign powers, the population is a modern population, a population of the twentieth century, learned in the languages and techniques of Western civilization and highly developed because of the smallness of the islands and the close relations between what is technically known as urban and rural. A federation was attempted in the British islands, the British being anxious to rid themselves of the responsibility of these islands, the Caribbean being now an American sea. But the federation fell apart. The reason is very simple: A federation meant that the economic line of direction should no longer be from each island to London, previously the financial and economic capital of each territory. The new lines of direction should have been from island to island. But this involved the break-up of the old colonial system. The West Indian politicians preferred the break-up of the federation.

What is the situation in the islands, what is inherent there and what may break out at any minute, is proved by the revolt that has in 1969 broken out in the island of Curafao, dominated by Dutch oil interests.

The revolt was a revolt of workers and unemployed youth and they burned down business houses of a value variously estimated between 15 and 40 millions (Dutch money). On the surface the revolt was a spontaneous process against Westcar, a sub-contractor of Shell Oil, who lowered salaries and laid off workers. But the ensuing strike spread to Shell, representing more than 90 percent of the national income. The workers marched on Parliament and when the marchers clashed with a column of armed police the eruption broke out.

Meanwhile, 300 political prisoners are in the penitentiary. According to local law, they can be kept there if need be for two years while their cases are being investigated.

Nominally "peace" would have been achieved by the arrival of 600 Dutch marines, but not in 1969. An uneasy peace was really secured by the resignation of the Democratic Government which had been in power for fourteen years. Facing a Revolution, it has agreed to hold elections. It is freely stated by leaders of the Working Class Front that if the Democratic Government is re-elected, the events of May will be repeated with even greater devastation.

Herbert Specer, President of the Federation of Petroleum Workers, states what is the obvious truth: "In the last analysis the significance of the May revolt is that people want change, and if they don't get it anything could happen." Small as they are, their historical origin and development have been such that these Caribbean islands can make highly significant contributions to the economics and politics of a world in torment. That is exactly what Castro's Cuba has done.

V. "ALWAYS OUT OF AFRICA"

For many hundreds of years, in fact almost (though not quite) from the beginning of the contact between Western civilization and Africa, it has been the almost universal practice to treat African achievement, discoveries and creations as if Western civilization was the norm and the African people spent their years in imitating, trying to reach or, worse still, if necessary going through the primitive early stages of the Western world. We therefore will, before we place it historically, state as straightforwardly as possible the historical achievements that are taking place today in an African state.

First the Tanzanian Government has nationalized the chief centers of economic life in the territory. That though important and necessary is not sufficient to create a new society. Less and less is nationalization becoming a landmark of a new society—today right-wing military dictators (Peru) and the Catholic hierarchy (with the blessing of the Pope) are ready to nationalize and even confiscate. The Government of Tanzania has gone further. In the Arusha Declaration of 29 January 1967 it aims at treating a new type of government official:

PART FIVE: THE ARUSHA RESOLUTION
Therefore, the National Executive Committee, meeting in the Community center at Arusha from 26.1.67 to 29.1.67, resolves:

> A. *The Leadership*
> Every TANU and Government leader must be either a Peasant or a Worker, and should in no way be associated with the practices of Capitalism or Feudalism.
>
> No TANU or Government leader should hold shares in any company.
>
> No TANU or Government leader should hold Directorship in any privately-owned enterprises.
>
> No TANU or Government leader should receive two or more salaries.
>
> No TANU or Government leader should own houses which he rents to others.

For the purposes of this Resolution the term "leader" should comprise the following: Members of the TANU National Executive Committee; Ministers, Members of Parliament, Senior Officials of organizations affiliated to TANU, Senior Officials of Para-Statal organizations, all those appointed or elected under any clause of the TANU Constitution, Councilors, and Civil Servants in high and middle cadres. (In this context "leader" means a man, or a man and his wife; a woman, or a woman and her husband).

> Such a resolution would probably exclude 90 percent of those who govern and administer in other parts of the world, developed or underdeveloped. The Government aims at creating a new type of society, based not on Western theories but on the concrete circumstances of African life and its historic past.
>
> Perhaps the most revolutionary change of all, it will reconstruct the very system of education in order to fit the children and the youth,

> in particular the youth in secondary education, for the new society which the Government of Tanzania seeks to build. The simplicity with which Dr. Nyerere states what his government proposes to do disguises the fact that not in Plato or Aristotle, Rousseau or Karl Marx will you find such radical, such revolutionary departures from the established educational order.

Alongside this change in the approach to the curriculum there must be a parallel and integrated change in the way our schools are run, so as to make them and their inhabitants a real part of our society and our economy. Schools must, in fact, become communities— and communities which practice the precept of self-reliance. The teachers, workers, and pupils together must be the members of a social unit in the same way as parents, relatives, and children are the family social unit. There must be the same kind of relationship between pupils and teachers within the school community as there is between children and parents in the village. And the former community must realize, just as the latter do, that their life and well-being depend upon the production of wealth— by farming or other activities.

This means that all schools, but especially secondary schools and other forms of higher education, must contribute to their own upkeep; they must be economic communities as well as social and educational communities. Each school should have, as an integral part of it, a farm or workshop which provides the food eaten by the community, and makes some contribution to the total national income.

> This is not a suggestion that a school farm or workshop should be attached to every school for training purposes. It is a suggestion that every school should also be a farm; that the school community should consist of people who are both teachers and farmers, and pupils and farmers. Obviously, if there is a school farm, the pupils working on it should be learning the techniques and tasks of farming. But the farm would be an integral part of the school and the welfare of the pupils would depend on its output, just as the welfare of a farmer depends on the output of his land. Thus, when this scheme is in operation, the revenue side of school accounts would not just read as at present: "Grant from Government . . . ; Grant from voluntary agency or other charity . . ." They would read: "Income from sale of cotton (or whatever other cash crop was appropriate for the area) . . . ; Value of the food grown and consumed . . . ; Value of labor done by pupils on new building, repairs, equipment, etc. . . . ; Government subvention . . . ; Grant from . . ."

Perhaps nothing shows more clearly the radical, the revolutionary, the complete break with Western habits and Western thought than the new attitude to the Tanzanian farmer. Some of them have followed the advice given to the African farmer officially and unofficially by Westerners: wishing him and his country well, they have encouraged him to individual effort, essentially capitalistic. Following this advice farmers in certain districts of Tanzania (mainly the slopes of the Kavirondo Mountain) have followed this Western type of agriculture with success. Note now the economic, in fact the political attitude of the Tanzanian

Government to this type of farmer. Reviewing Tanzania "After the Arusha Declaration" Dr. Nyerere outlines the cooperative socialist community Tanzania aims at. He continues:

> This is the objective. It is stated clearly, and at greater length, in the policy paper. We must understand it so that we know what we are working towards. But it is not something we shall achieve overnight. We have a long way to go.
>
> For what has been happening over recent years is quite different. We have not been enlarging and modernizing our traditional family unit as much as abandoning it in favor of small-scale capitalist farming. Many of our most dynamic and energetic farmers, especially those with the most initiative and willingness to learn new techniques, have been branching out on their own as individuals. They have not been enlarging their farms by joining with others in a spirit of equality, but by employing labor. So we are getting the beginnings of the development of an agricultural laboring class on the one hand, and a wealthier employing class on the other. Fortunately, this development has not gone very far; we can arrest the trend without difficulty. But we must not make this change by persecuting the progressive farmers; after all, we have been encouraging them in the direction they have been going! Instead we must seek their cooperation, and integrate them into the new socialist agriculture by showing them that their best interests will be served by this development. For energy and initiative such as these farmers have displayed will be very important to our progress. We need these people.

This is something new in the history of political thought. The cooperative villages aimed at are called Ujamaa and Dr. Nyerere has called the whole new attempt to create a new society Socialism. In our view he is entitled to do so, and a proper respect for what the Tanzanian Government is doing demands that it be related to traditional and contemporary concepts of socialism.

First of all, no one today believes that what exists in Russia and Eastern Europe is, in any sense of the word, socialist; that is to say, a society having achieved and aiming at even more comprehensive stages of liberty, equality and fraternity, social relations higher than those achieved by the most advanced parliamentary democracy. That is socialism, or it is worse even than capitalist decay being then a deliberate and conscious fraud. Worse still, most unfortunately, certain of the new African states, anxious to rid themselves of the capitalist stigma, have invented a new category labeled African socialism. Worthy of repetition is the exposition of this African socialism by one newly independent state.

> *Adaptability*
>
> 15. African Socialism must be flexible because the problems it will confront and the incomes and desires of the people will change over time, often quickly and substantially. A rigid, doctrinaire system will have little chance for survival. The system must:

(i) make progress towards ultimate objectives; and

(ii) solve more immediate problems with efficiency.

16. No matter how pressing immediate problems may be, progress toward ultimate objectives will be the major consideration. In particular, political equality, social justice and human dignity will not be sacrificed to achieve more material ends more quickly. Nor will these objectives be comprised today in the faint hope that by so doing they can be reinstated more fully in some unknown and far distant future.

Whenever was there a state, beginning with the state of Adam and Eve, that did not, could not, proclaim that it had in mind ultimate objectives while paying attention to immediate needs? That is not socialism. It is nonsense. It is not African. It is bureaucratic balderdash, to which we are now well accustomed in advanced as well as in underdeveloped fakers—a bold attempt by newcomers to dress the old reality in new clothes.

Far more important than this fakery is the recognition by President Kaunda of Zambia that the attempt merely to ape European ways, which has brought such wide fields of disaster to Africa, must not only be rejected but that there are new African paths to be explored. In his significantly named "Humanism in Zambia" President Kaunda says:

This is a key point, for if the distribution of wealth is not done properly, it might lead to the creation of classes in society and the much-valued humanist approach that is traditional and inherent in our African society would have suffered a final blow. If this happened the world as a whole, and African in particular, would be all the poorer for it. For you would then have the "haves" and the "have-nots." Politically you would be creating room for opposing parties based on "the oppressed" and "the oppressor" concept which again would not be in keeping with the society described above; a society in which the Chief as an elected or appointed leader of the people held national property like land in trust for the people, and he was fully aware that he was responsible to them. He knew, too, that his continuing to be their head depended on his people's will.

President Kaunda wants to show how important it is for Africans to break cleanly with the ideas of European well-wishers, that African progress depends on educating first a small number of Africans and then an increasing number who will gradually (without undue haste) educate more and more African natives to capitalist energies and the moderate mastery of parliamentary democracy. His rejection of this concept is total.

Now we must ask again what effects will persistently increasing levels of specialization have on our much valued traditional society in our country. This field of specialization drives people to resort to new groups in society. In other words, people with common interests group together, partly because of the community of their interests and partly as the means of promoting and protecting the welfare of their group. For example, a carpenter will find his own interests are not the same as those of the commercial farmer. The teacher finds that his interests differ from those of the mine worker. And so the whole list of different interests can be outlined. This point is, all this gives birth to a new disintegrative tendency. This, as can be seen, cuts right across the traditional society which has been described above as a mutual aid society which was an accepting and inclusive community.

Despite the low-level of economic development in African states, this new African conception of the future of Africa lays claim not only to a future, but also to deep roots in the past. President Kaunda insists on this:

> The traditional community was a mutual aid society. It was organized to satisfy the basic human needs of all its members and, therefore, individualism was discouraged. Most resources, such as land, might be communally owned and administered by chiefs and village headmen for the benefit of everyone. If, for example, a villager required a new hut, all the men would turn to forests and fetch poles to erect the frame and bring grass for thatching. The women might be re sponsible for making the mud-plaster for the walls and two or three of them would undoubtedly brew some beer so that all the workers would be refreshed after a hot but satisfying day's work. In the same spirit, the able-bodied would accept responsibility for tending and harvesting the gardens of the sick and infirm.

This new recognition so characteristic first of Tanzania and now of Zambia does not turn its back on the modernization necessary in the modern world. Once more let the African President speak: from what has been said above, it is clear that we cannot ourselves expect to achieve once again the Man-centered society without very careful planning. And in this direction nothing is more important than institutions of learning.

Here the model is or will have to be that so clearly delineated by Dr. Nyerere. That is the essence of the matter. And the newly independent African states are in such crises that success in Tanzania and real strides forward in hard-pressed Zambia can initiate a new road for Africa—the mobilization of the African people to build an African society in an African way.

It would be a great mistake not to make clear how reality corresponds with—and indeed carries further—the highest stages so far reached by Western political thought. Lenin had no illusions about the Russian Revolution. He knew that socialism in the Marxist sense was impossible in the Russia he knew, and in 1923 was leaving behind. In the last days he increasingly drew attention to two important aspects and needs of the Russia which he insisted on calling Socialist Russia, despite the fact that the great majority of the Russian population consisted of illiterate peasants. The Soviet State, he insisted in those last days, was not new. Behind the Marxist terminology and proletarian window dressing was the same old Czarist state, not even a bourgeois state but a "bureaucratic-serf state." His proposals to alter these we need not go into. It is sufficient to know that Dr. Nyerere has seen through the reactionary, bureaucratic colonialist state which he inherited, and has gone further than anyone in the determination to break it up and make a new type of state.

Lenin also knew, none better, that the Soviet official had to leave high-flown theorizing and personally go to work among the backward Russian peasants. In perhaps the most moving of his many statements of what the people needed from the Marxist officials of the Government, he says:

> Less argument about words! We still have too much of this sort of thing. More variety in practical experience and more study of this experience! Under certain conditions the exemplary organization of local work, even on a small scale, is of far greater national importance than many branches of the central state work. And these are precisely the conditions we are in at the present moment in regard to peasant farming in general, and in regard to the exchange of the surplus products of agriculture for the manufactures of industry in particular. Exemplary organization in this respect, even in a single volost, is of far greater national importance than the "exemplary" improvement of the central apparatus of any People's Commissariat; for three and a half years to such an extent that it has managed to acquire a certain amount of harmful inertness; we cannot improve it quickly to any extent, we do not know how to do it. Assistance in the more radical improvement of it, a new flow of fresh forces, assistance in the successful struggle against bureaucracy, in the struggle to overcome this harmful inertness, must come from the localities, from the lower ranks, with the exemplary organization of a small "whole," precisely a "whole," i.e. not one farm, not one branch of economy, not one enterprise, but the *sum total* of economic exchange, even if only in a small locality.
>
> Those of us who are doomed to remain on work at the center will continue the task of improving the apparatus and purging it of bureaucracy, even if in modest and immediately achievable dimensions. But the greatest assistance in this task is coming, and will come, from the localities.

Note in particular one of his last sentences: "We who are doomed." Lenin wanted to go and work among the peasants. The great Marxist would have understood the profoundly socialist and human conception which has moved Dr. Nyerere to break to pieces the old system of education and substitute a genuinely socialist and humanist procedure for the youth of Tanzania. In a conversation with Dr. Nyerere, the present writer (having previously read his writings) drew his attention to this particular passage from Lenin and what Lenin was striving to teach as far back as 1923. The African leader said that he did not know it—he had arrived at his conclusion by himself and with his people. It is sufficient to say that socialist thought has seen nothing like this since the death of Lenin in 1924, and its depth, range and the repercussions which flow from it, go far beyond the Africa which gave it birth. It can fertilize and reawaken the mortuary that is socialist theory and practice in the advanced countries. "Marxism is a Humanism" is the exact reverse of the truth. The African builders of a humanist society show that today all humanism finds itself in close harmony with the original conceptions and aims of Marxism.

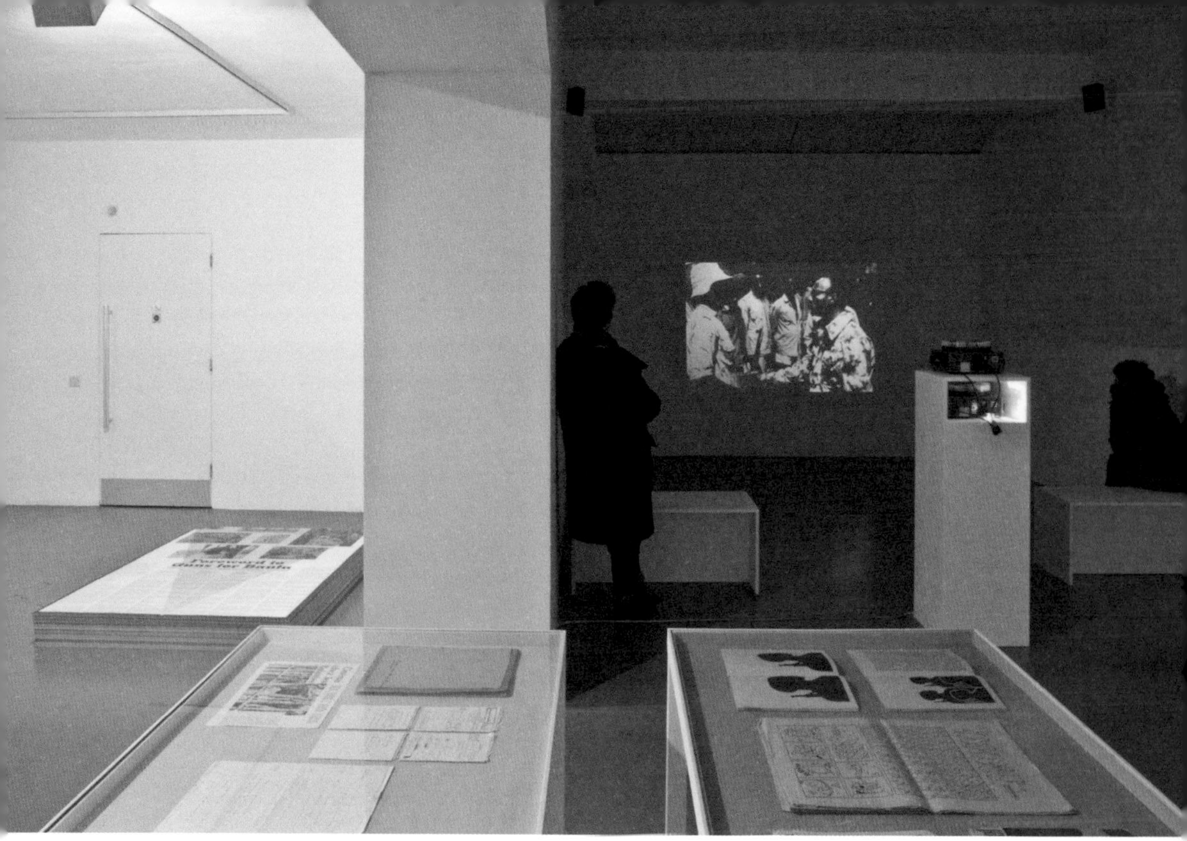

Mathieu Kleyebe Abonnenc, *Foreword to Guns for Banta*, Gasworks, London, 2011. Installation view.

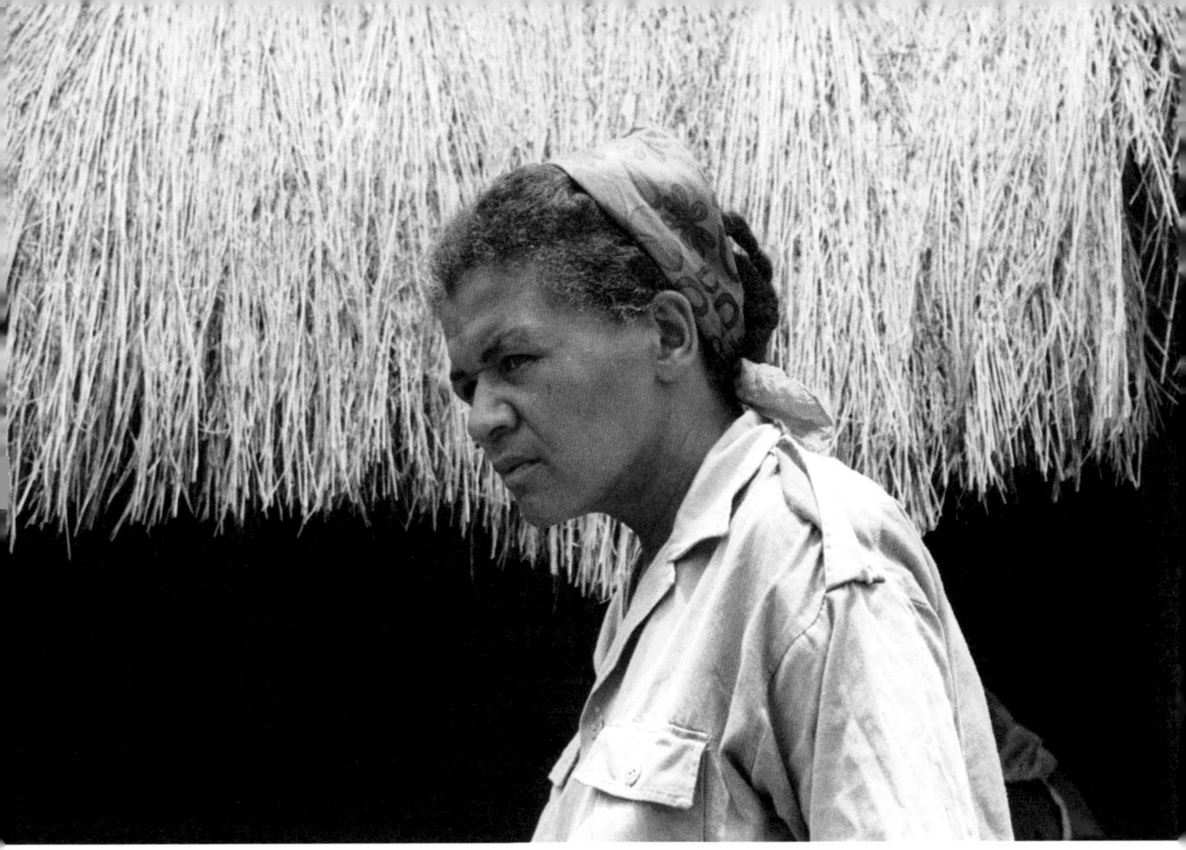

Set photographs of the shooting of the film *Guns for Banta* by Sarah Maldoror, 1979.

SABELO J. NDLOVU-GATSHENI

Myths of Decolonization and Illusions of Freedom

CODESRIA, 2013

In a Habermasian type of scenario, liberation would be subservient to emancipation; and, decolonization, likewise, would still be covered over and managed by the emancipating rhetoric of modernity, either liberal or Marxist. In other words, if 'emancipation' is the image used by honest liberals and honest Marxists from the internal and historical perspectives of Europe or the US, then looking at the world history from outside of those locations [...] means coming to terms with the fact that there is a still further need for 'liberation/de-coloniality' from the people and institutions raising the flag of 'emancipation.' Thus, in this precise sense, emancipation cannot be the guiding light for liberation/de-coloniality but the other way round: liberation/de-coloniality includes and re-maps the 'rational concept of emancipation.' In this complexity, we need a relentless critical exercise of awareness of the moments when the guiding principle at work is liberation/decoloniality and when, on the other hand, the irrational myth directs social actors in their projects for political, economic and spiritual (epistemic, philosophical, religious) decolonization.
– Walter D. Mignolo

The momentous people's uprisings rocking the North African region since January 2011, culminating in the collapse of the oppressive regimes of Zine el Abidine Ben Ali of Tunisia and Hosni Mubarak of Egypt in quick succession as well as the collapse of Colonel Muammar Gaddafi's forty-two years of iron rule in Libya, and his death in the process, have put to rest notions of an 'end of history and the last man' that was popularized by Francis Fukuyama at the end of the Cold War. The popular uprisings by the masses indicated beyond doubt the continuing ability of the ordinary people to make history. Massiah (2011:2) identified one of the key lessons from the uprisings that rocked the Maghreb region as the opening to the possibility of a new phase of decolonization and depicted this new phase as relating to the 'passage from the independence of states to self-determination of the people'. These uprisings which no social scientist or journalist was able to predict and forecast compel us to revisit the African past and rethink the limits of the decolonization process that culminated in the achievement of juridical freedom by African colonies from the late 1950s onwards.

The process of decolonization which Zeleza (2003: vi) calls the 'proudest moment' of African nationalism, is believed to have marked the triumphalism of black liberatory nationalism over white exploitative and oppressive colonialism. Being liberated and/or emancipated were subsumed under the rubric of decolonization to mean a single state of being. The day each of the African colonies achieved political independence is celebrated annually as 'independence day' throughout the African continent save perhaps for Ethiopia that was never colonized. But even Ethiopia celebrates its triumphalism over Italian invasion at the famous battle of Adowa in 1896. There is no doubt that decolonization occupies a nerve centre of pride in African historiography and nationalist humanism. Those who actively participated and led the struggles for decolonization became heroes of the African nationalist revolution and founders of the postcolonial African states.

This chapter re-evaluates the decolonization process in order to understand its grammar and eventually unpack it as a process that was never completed and, therefore, continues to obscure and hide the disempowering colonial matrix of power that prevented the re-birth of Africa as a confident and brave postcolonial world. Decolonization is better understood as a terrain of illusions of liberation and myths of freedom. This intervention is in no way meant to down play the sacrifices some Africans made in the name of decolonization. It is common knowledge that Nelson Mandela spent twenty-seven years in prison while many others like Eduardo Mondlane of Mozambique, Amílcar Cabral of Guinea-Bissau, Chris Hani and Solomon Mahlangu of South Africa, Jason Ziyaphapha Moyo and Herbert Chitepo of Zimbabwe all lost their lives. The analysis is meant to expose the ideational traps constructed by colonial modernity that diluted the liberatory ethos of decolonization and channelled it towards emancipation that did not question the alienating logic of modernity itself but called for reforms within the same system.

Moreover, the chapter articulates three core arguments. The first is that, for one to gain a deeper meaning of decolonization and its limits one needs to unpack its grammar. By its 'grammar' I mean its genealogy, ethical and ideological aspects as well as its political assumptions and implications. In unpacking the core essence of decolonization I engage with two utopic registers of liberation and emancipation that are subsumed under decolonization discourses. I disentangle liberation from emancipation as I reveal the myths and illusions of freedom bequeathed Africa by decolonization. The second is that decolonization largely manifested itself in the form of juridical freedom albeit of a complicated nature that was mistakenly conflated with popular freedom for the ex-colonized peoples. This argument is explicated by analysing the problematic character of the African postcolonial state that emerged from colonial rule rather than from African society and operated through coercion rather than consent to impose its will on the African people.

The final argument is that existing studies of decolonization have been blinded by nationalist celebratory politics to the extent of ignoring the ordinary citizens' new struggles aimed at liberating themselves from the domination, exploitation and repression of the postcolonial state. Therefore the chapter provides details of strategies the ordinary citizens use to liberate themselves from the postcolonial, neocolonized African state and which continues even today by taking the form of popular uprisings in North Africa with potential ripple effect on sub-Saharan Africa.

DISENTANGLING 'EMANCIPATION' FROM 'LIBERATION' IN THE DECOLONIZATION DISCOURSE

Some critics would probably think simplistically that disentangling 'emancipation' from liberation is an exercise in futility. Those who might think so are totally mistaken because without clearly disentangling both terms, failure it would be difficult to realize that the active forces of the colonial matrix unleashed by colonial modernity always fought to dilute liberation struggles into emancipatory struggles that ended up celebrating the achievement of democracy instead of freedom. The post-1994 South African situation speaks volumes about how the liberation movement was disciplined into an emancipatory force that finally celebrated the achievement of liberal democracy instead of decolonization and freedom. This means the day was won by liberals rather than nationalists. The other example is that of slaves who were emancipated rather than liberated to the extent that they continued to languish at the bottom of the racial-hierarchy of societies like the United States of America and engage in further civil rights struggles to change their oppression and domination.

So there is, indeed, a real danger in African studies accepting that the utopic registers of emancipation and liberation can be used interchangeably to mean freedom. Emancipation and liberation are related utopic registers but they do not mean the same thing and their genealogies are different. In his studies of philosophies of liberation, Dussel (1995, 2000) makes it clear that emancipation belongs to the discourse of the European Enlightenment and is today a common term used in liberal and Marxist discourses. Dussel's argument is reinforced by that of Walter D. Mignolo who argues that:

> The concept of emancipation belongs to the universe of discourse framed by the philosophical and historical concepts of modernity, which becomes apparent if we look at the particular intersection of Theo-and Ego-politics that later, in the eighteenth century, gave rise to the idea of emancipation—the Reformation. In terms of philosophical modernity, the Reformation was a crucial break-through for the emergence of critical self-reflexivity and it is easy to see how—and why—the concept of emancipation emerged from the 'transition' to 'freedom of subjectivity' and 'critical self-reflexivity' from lack thereof that began with the Reformation. The individual freedom sought to some degree within the Church by Luther became more and more autonomous through secularization until its detachment in Descartes dictum, 'I think, therefore I am,' in Kant's transcendental subject and in Hegel's freedom of subjectivity and critical self-reflexivity (Mignolo 2007: 467).

Emancipation was used in the eighteenth century to refer to three historical events, namely the Glorious Revolution of 1668 in England, the independence of the colonists in America from the British colonial empire (American Revolution of 1776) and the French Revolution of 1789 (Mignolo 2007: 455). In these three events emancipation was with reference to the bourgeois revolutions that did not fight against the edifice of modernity but for reformism and class ascendancy within the same capitalist system.

Emancipation is always informed by the reformist spirit rather than total change. It is more of a strategy used by oppressive systems to deal with opposition by opening up new concessions while gaining a new lease of life. As Mignolo (2007: 445) argues, emancipation 'proposes and presupposes changes within the system that doesn't question the logic of coloniality'. The most dangerous assumption in this thinking is that freedom for the non-Western world had 'to be planned, dictated, and executed from Europe or the US itself only' (Mignolo 2007: 457). This thinking led to such ideas of decolonization as mere transfer of power from white colonialists to black nationalists.

It is also ideas of emancipation that underpin present-day Western powers' use of military power and violence as part of their crusade to introduce liberal democracy and human rights on non-Western parts of the world. The example of the invasion of Iraq is an indication of this mentality. Such military adventures, which were justified on the basis of emancipation were seen reality as a continuation of the spread of Western modernity by force to engulf the non-Western world, especially the Islamic world that is seen as resisting some aspects of cultural imperialism, including embracing Christianity. Even Marxism was informed by the spirit of emancipation; hence it did not question the logic of Western modernity and its colonial mission but simply emphasized the emancipation of the working class instead of the bourgeoisie. Today, part of the dominant Western discourse is about emancipation of the multitudes (Hardt and Negri 2000).

Understood from this perspective, emancipation is different from liberation notwithstanding that they are two sides of the same coin of modernity/coloniality. The genealogy of liberation is in resisting the imposition of Western modernity and revolting against the darker and negative aspects of Western modernity such as the slave trade, imperialism, colonialism, apartheid and neocolonialism. In Africa, the genealogy of liberation discourse is traceable to slave revolts and primary resistance, and in the Diaspora to the 1781 Tupac Amaru Uprising in Peru and the 1804 Haitian Revolution. The resisters who participated in these struggles did not fight for internal reform within Western modernity and its logic of imperialism and colonialism. The revolutions in Peru and Haiti challenged and questioned the whole edifice of Western modernity and its concomitant logic of slavery, imperialism and colonialism. The clarion call was for independence not reform of the system as emancipatory demands tended to do. Liberation is the expression of aspirations of the oppressed non-Western people who desired to de-link with the oppressive colonial empires. Its grammar had a double meaning: political economic independence and epistemological freedom.

Ideally, African liberation was expected to destroy the colonial state and culminate in the creation a new dispensation of freedom, equality and justice. Mignolo (2007: 454), in his differentiation of emancipation from liberation, posed some crucial questions: Who needs emancipation? Who needs liberation? Who benefits from emancipation? Who benefits from liberation? Who are the agents and the intended targets of emancipating or liberatory projects? What subjectivities are activated in these projects? Does the distinction even matter when emancipation has a universal ring that seems to cover the interests of all oppressed people in the world? It is clear from this chapter that emancipation is a watered-down variant of liberation in the sense that it does not take into account the hierarchies of oppression and exploitation introduced by Western modernity across the world mediated by race. Emancipation was a strategy of the white bourgeoisie that questioned only the excesses of the logic of imperialism and colonialism such as the slave trade and apartheid, for instance.

Those who wanted liberation were the colonized people who desired a rebirth as free citizens and new, liberated beings. But the decolonization project in Africa was permeated by both imperatives of emancipation and liberation coexisting uneasily and tendentiously. The agenda of decolonization was hijacked by the 'native bourgeoisie' and channelled towards emancipation. The 'native bourgeoisie', despite its black colour, was a creation of colonial modernity and had imbibed colonial languages and embraced Western cultures; as such it aspired to occupy the positions monopolized by the white colonial bourgeoisie. Its agenda was limited to replacing the colonial white bourgeoisie (Fanon 1961: 87).

The emancipatory strand in the decolonization project was easily embraced by the 'native bourgeoisie' that was not really opposed to colonial modernity but wanted to be accommodated within the system. On this point Peter Ekeh argued that:

> In many ways, the drama of colonization is the history of the clash between European colonisers and African bourgeois class. Although native to Africa, the African bourgeois class depends on colonialism for its legitimacy. It accepts the principles implicit in colonialism but rejects the foreign personnel that rule Africa. It claims to be competent enough to rule, but has no traditional legitimacy. In order to replace the colonisers and rule its own people, it has invented a number of interest- begotten theories to justify that rule (Ekeh 1975: 96).

Reverend Ndabaningi Sithole, a leading Zimbabwean nationalist and historian of nationalism, celebrated how colonial modernity eradicated tribalism in Africa and proclaimed that the African political trajectory was moving from tribalism to nationalism and to modernity (Sithole 1968: 98). What Sithole and his bourgeois class were fighting for was not very different from what the British bourgeoisie wanted during the Glorious Revolution of 1668. The difference was only that colonial modernity had added the race element to the African situation as a variable in bourgeois power struggles.

The black native bourgeoisie that spearheaded the decolonization project stirred it in the direction of emancipation rather than liberation. As long as decolonization was conceived in emancipatory terms, its failure to fulfil Fanon's expectations of total, complete and instantaneous substitution of the colonial species and colonial subject with another liberated and confident African species and the birth of 'new men, new language and new humanity' were inevitable. Fanon emphasized that, 'The production of the new men is solely a result of their act of obtaining their freedom' (Fanon 1961: 1968a). Decolonization did not result in complete reversal of the order of society whereby, 'The last shall be first and the first shall be last' and the 'native goes from "animal" to "human"' (Fanon 1968a: 102).

At another level, Grosfoguel (2007: 219) argued that de-colonization must not be articulated in terms of conquering power over the juridical political boundaries of a state akin to the old national liberation and socialist strategies of taking power. Such approaches ignored global coloniality which operates without a direct colonial administration. This means that decolonization that was simply aimed at the elimination of colonial administrations amounted to a myth, a 'postcolonial world', because from direct colonialism African states fell directly into neocolonialism.

In the 1960s and 1970s, revolutionary African cadres like Amílcar Cabral (1969: 75) became worried about the 'ideological deficiency' of the decolonization movements. Cabral urged the existing African liberation movements to pay particular attention to the form of society they wanted to construct at the end of colonial rule. He clearly understood that the attainment of political independence was not the same thing as national liberation. He was concerned about the failure of African nationalist leaders to distinguish between genuine national liberation and neocolonialism (Cabral 1969: 89).

Cabral was not alone in this endeavour to rescue the liberatory ethos of decolonization that was being confused with emancipation. Kwame Nkrumah was also very vocal about the dangers of neocolonialism being taken for African freedom. He was very concerned about the vulnerability of postcolonial African societies to the 'extended tentacles of the Wall Street octopus' (Nkrumah 1965). Nkrumah visualized postcolonial Africa as trapped within the snares of 'neocolonialism' which he called the 'last stage of imperialism' (Nkrumah 1965). He was indeed very correct. Slavoj Žižek even derided the logic of decolonization in these words:

> One is tempted to say that the will to gain political independence from the colonizer in the guise of a new independent nation-state is the ultimate proof that the colonized ethnic group is thoroughly integrated into the ideological universe of the colonizer (Žižek 2000: 255).

This critical analysis of the myths of decolonization and its illusions of freedom takes us to the higher order question of what constitutes decolonial resistance and liberation for the African people. In simple terms, African resistance to colonial modernity had to exceed the terms and constraints imposed on Africa by Western modernity. Such resistance was expected to create decolonization as a double operation that involved the liberation of both the colonizer and the colonized. The end product was to be 'de-coloniality' which Mignolo defined thus:

> De-coloniality, then, means working towards a vision of human life that is not dependent upon or structured by the forced imposition of one ideal society over those that differ, which is what modernity/coloniality does and, hence, where decolonization of the mind should begin. The struggle is for changing the terms in addition to the content of the conversation (Mignolo 2007: 459).

At the time of writing this book, the majority of those who led the nationalist inspired decolonization process had already displayed signs of capitulation to the dominant world constructed by Western and colonial modernities. Replacement of white colonial administrators at the state level was celebrated as independence and as freedom in countries like Zimbabwe and South Africa. In Zimbabwe they celebrate 'independence day' every April and in South Africa they have celebrated 'freedom day' since 1995. In both countries, the African political elite proclaimed the policy of reconciliation, which Ibbo Mandaza correctly characterized as:

> The mourn of the weak, even when pronounced from positions of apparent moral superiority over oppressors and exploiters of yesterday. The reconciliation exercise, therefore, serves largely a political function, facilitating the necessary compromise between the rulers of yesterday and the inheritors of state power, within the context of incomplete decolonization (Mandaza 1999: 79).

Mandaza also emphasized that what is generally celebrated as the postcolonial state 'has no life of its own, it has no essence; it is a state modeled on the (European) bourgeois state but without a national bourgeoisie that would otherwise provide it an anchor and even a semblance of independence' (Mandaza 1998: 3). All this analysis underscores the fact that a postcolonial world was never born; rather what decolonization facilitated was a postcolonial neocolonized world.

At the abstract level one can still begin to identify some of myths of decolonization. For instance, the idea of politically sovereign and economically independent postcolonial states ignored the crucial reality of entrapment of these states within the snares of the global colonial matrix of power that denies African leaders policy space to chart any autonomous economic or political trajectory. To argue that colonial situations ceased to exist after the demise of colonial administrations some fifty years ago also constitutes a myth of a decolonized postcolonial African world. Grosfoguel (2004: 320-321) added credence to this argument:

> For the last 50 years, states that had been colonies, following the dominant Eurocentric liberal discourses [...] constructed ideologies of 'national identity,' 'national development,' and 'national sovereignty' that produced an illusion of 'independence,' 'development,' and 'progress.' Yet their economic and political systems were shaped by their subordinate position in a capitalist world system organised around a hierarchical international division of labour [...] These multiple hierarchies (including the racial/ethnic hierarchy), together with the predominance of Eurocentric cultures [...], constitute a global coloniality' between Europeans/ Euro-Americans and non-Europeans. Thus, 'coloniality' is entangled with, but is not reducible to, the international division of labour. The 'colonial' axis between European/Euro-Americans and non-Europeans is inscribed not only in relations of exploitation (between capital and labour) and domination (between Europeans and non-Europeans), but also in the production of subjectivities.

Another myth of decolonization is that of conflating the attainment of juridical freedom with the achievement of popular freedom by the African citizens. The post-apartheid poverty that the black majority experienced in South African is a clear testimony of the dangers of degeneration of liberation movements into emancipatory formations concerned with simple politics of the right to vote and removal of discriminatory legislation from statute books without embarking on systematic and radical restructuring of the apartheid state. Those who fought for the liberation of South Africa from the vicious apartheid colonialism found themselves celebrating not freedom and independence but democracy. Today, one of the most defended things in South Africa is the national constitution mainly by those who benefited from apartheid simply because the celebrated South African constitution officially adopted in 1996 protects the ill-gotten wealth concentrated in the hands of white bourgeoisie and a few black elites. The constitution of South Africa does not facilitate and enable radical redistribution of resources such as land and mines. Ironically, predominantly black the African National Congress (ANC) who fought against apartheid oppression and brought about the new constitution, are now closely watched as a threat to the same constitution by the right-wing and white dominated political formation known as the Democratic Alliance (DA). South Africa is a typical example of a society where myths of decolonization and illusions of freedom are manifesting themselves in broad daylight in a most detestable form.

MYTHS OF DECOLONIZATION AND PROBLEMS OF JURIDICAL FREEDOM

A body of critical literature by such scholars as Tukumbi Lumumba-Kasongo (1994), Claude Ake (2000), Pita Ogaba Agbese and George Klay Kieh, Jr (2007), Mueni wa Muiu (2009) and others have focused attention on the problems emanating from the character and structure of the postcolonial African state, in the process exposing some of the core myths of decolonization and illusions of freedom. Ake emphasized how the postcolonial state was shaped by colonial legacy into an all-powerful and arbitrary political formation that set it on collision course with the citizens.

The triumphant African nationalist leadership continued the colonial legacy of turning against democracy. This was so because the achievement of political independence only changed the composition of the managers of the state but not the character of the state, which remained much as it was in the colonial era. Consequently, the postcolonial state emerged as an apparatus of violence; its embedding within society was very shallow, its rootedness in social forces remained extremely narrow and this made it to rely for compliance on coercion rather than consent (Ake 2000: 35-37). Ake's central argument and observations were also echoed by Lumumba-Kasongo (1994: 58) who depicted the postcolonial African state as 'an institution of domination par excellence.'

In his interrogation of the idea and meaning of freedom in Africa, Foltz (2002) came up with a four-dimensional thesis on the trajectories of the African struggles for freedom. These are: freedom for the African state, freedom from the African state, freedom within the African state, and freedom through the African state system. Used in conjunction with the existing rich literature on the problems of the African postcolonial state, Foltz's intervention provides an ideal entry point for critical interrogation of the core myths of decolonization; how ordinary citizens have responded to postcolonial state's alienating practices, oppression and exploitation; and the pathways taken by ordinary citizens and excluded elites in search of popular freedom.

Scholars like Young (1994) and Mamdani (1996) have studied closely the colonial state which formed the template for the postcolonial state. They noted that the colonial state lacked three essential attributes found in other modern states, namely, sovereignty, nationalism and external autonomy; and crisis emanated from the fact that the colonial state was imposed by force of arms on the African society. At the initial construction level, the colonial state did not even pretend to serve the interests of the colonized African people in terms of provision of services. Coercion became the DNA of the postcolonial state.

As Muiu and Martin (2009: 54) have argued, the colonial state was 'essentially a foreign construct that could not possibly take root on African soil'. It even destroyed existing African indigenous civil society that had taken the form of age-grades and other forms. The postcolonial state was merely a de-racialized colonial state that was never structurally changed to enable it to suit African demands and aspirations. Thus the myths of decolonization and illusions of freedom become very clear if one closely analyses the politics around the transfer of political office from white colonial administrators to black administrators.

In the Francophone Africa, except Guinea, the postcolonial states were born with diminished sovereignty which still remained with France. They had no control over foreign, economic, monetary and defence matters (Mueni wa Muiu and Martin 2009: 56). In the Anglophone Africa, Chinweizu (1975: 167) noted that the African nationalists had to sign agreements to uphold some negotiated neocolonial compromises including safeguarding properties accumulated by white colonialists such as land and mines even before entering new offices. Independence constitutions were written for the African leaders by the departing colonial masters. Muiu and Martin (2009: 56) argued that Duncan Sandys who became Britain's Secretary of State for Commonwealth Relations in 1960, was a notorious expert in persuading African leaders to sign independence constitutions which did not favour the aspirations of the black majority through keeping the participants talking until they signed out of sheer exhaustion. They concluded that:

> Thus decolonization was just a façade barely disguising the continuation of colonization by other means and leading to the mere 'flag' (or juridical) independence of utterly impotent and powerless quasi-states lacking the substance of sovereignty (Muiu and Martin 2009: 56).

Myths of decolonization and illusions of freedom had the negative impact of silencing the ordinary citizens through giving them a false hope that through hard work they would harvest the concrete fruits of freedom that were denied by colonialism. The postcolonial state itself was not free because multinational corporations and the ex-colonized still controlled the economy in league with metropolitan governments that ran African affairs by remote control and through African elites. The difficult question to answer is whether it was really possible for African leaders to pursue an independent political, ideological and economic path without provoking reaction from the ex-colonial powers?

This question is pertinent because Muiu and Martin (2009) and other scholars who argue for the reconstitution and reconstruction of African postcolonial states on the basis of indigenous knowledges and institutions, seem to imply that African founding fathers of postcolonial states had a choice not to ignore indigenous institutions and to alter the states to meet the priorities and needs of the African people. At the same time, they point to the case of such leaders as Patrice Lumumba, Modibo Keita, Thomas Sankara, Mirien N'Gouabi, Samora Machel and Laurent-Désiré Kabila who lost their lives while trying to radically transform the African states to serve the interests of their citizens.

What we see here is a cul-de-sac within which the African leaders operated; a path policed by colonial matrices of power that included CIA operatives, sponsored coup plotters, assassins and all sorts of dirty tricks ranged against those African leaders who tried to transcend the coloniality of power and translate myths of decolonization and illusions of freedom into real African freedom. Even Kwame Nkrumah fell victim to the snares of these forces and was toppled in 1966.

This cul-de-sac meant that the African leaders had to tread carefully including choosing to suppress African people's aspirations and demands than provoke the anger of the Euro-American political league that was capable of disciplining those who deviated from the given script on governance and state management. Instead of delivering services to the people, African leaders engaged in deluding their own people by pretending to be in charge and inviting the hungry and angry population to partake of annual celebrations of flag independence that did not change their well-being.

Having inherited the colonial state together with its repressive apparatus, African leaders presided over a leviathan that was active in suffocating alternative popular struggles for freedom. The first group of people to react against the postcolonial state was the excluded elite who found themselves at the mercy of those who controlled the state. According to Ake (2000: 37), the excluded elite fought for incorporation, manifesting a situation where 'Africa is in constant turmoil from struggles between people who must secure power and those who must access it by incorporation'. It was often the excluded elite that resorted to mobilization of ethnicity to build a political constituency to use in bargaining for power. On the other hand, were ordinary masses of peasants and workers who struggled for economic incorporation and this demand propelled them to seek what became known as 'second independence' not from colonial masters but from the indigenous elite (Ake 2000: 47).

Generally speaking, the ordinary citizen's struggles for freedom took various forms involving disengagement from the state; agitating for internal democratization of the state; supporting opposition parties; trying to take control of the state; outright emigration; mocking the state; trying to influence state policy from within, agitating for secession, and other subtle and softer forms of resistance and engagement such as conviviality and use of music, jokes, comic strips and satire to reveal the vulgarity, debauchery and buffoonery of those in control of state power.

In the face of internal opposition, the postcolonial state evolved various survival techniques. Mbembe (1992; 2001) focused on the ideological production of power within the postcolonial neocolonized African world and how this configuration of political power impinged on the development of relations between the state governors and the governed (state-society relations). But scholars like Mikael Karlström have criticized Mbembe for overestimating the ideological power of the postcolonial state and for 'unjustifiably' creating a pessimistic portrayal of state-society relations in postcolonial Africa 'as terminally mired in inherently dysfunctional political dispositions and practices'

(Karlström 2003: 57). While Mbembe drew his examples from Cameroon and Togo, Karlström studied the rural communities of southern Uganda from a Bakhtinian perspective and discovered 'reciprocity and ritualized "dialogism" between state and society' (Karlström 2003:57).

Karlström spent energy demonstrating that 'the disabling paradoxes of postcolonial politics identified by Mbembe do not arise out of any inherent pathology of the African political imagination, but rather out of the postcolonial state's tendency to deploy local models and practices of the public sphere in ways that evacuate them of much of their legitimating content' (Karlström 2003: 57-8). While Karlström tries to create a positive image of the postcolonial neocolonized world as characterized by harmonious state-society relations based on particular case study of Uganda, there is overwhelming counter-evidence that reveal what Mbembe has uncovered.

The fact was that the postcolonial state was not well embedded in society meant that state-citizen relations were not stable and political elites and ordinary citizens were constantly engaged in struggles since those who did not control the state remained closed out of economic benefits of decolonization. As such the general thesis that postcolonial state-society relations have not been characterized by deep and horizontal comradeships running across interactions of ruling elites and the governed is very plausible. Tensions rather than 'ritualized dialogics' remained a common factor in state-society relations across postcolonial Africa, with minimum achievement of consent in only exceptional cases and on very brief occasions particularly during the first decade of independence dominated by false hopes and euphoria. Myths of Decolonization and Illusions of Freedom

A combination of Foltz's four-dimensional thesis of trajectories of ordinary citizens' struggles for freedom and Mbembe's studies of thematics and aesthetics of power constructions in postcolonial Africa reveals an intricate disjuncture between forces of juridical freedom and those of popular freedom that have a bearing on further understanding the myths of decolonization, illusions of freedom and vicissitudes of society-state relations since the end of direct colonial rule in Africa.

What revealed the myths of decolonization and illusions of freedom was the lack of legitimacy of the African postcolonial state. Ali Mazrui offered a ground-breaking explanation for this legitimacy crisis:

> In situations where the leaders are identified too readily as people who have arisen from the ranks, it is easier for those who remain in the ranks to become envious of the privileges enjoyed by their former peers. Long-established elites are sometimes forgiven luxurious living more easily by 'lower classes' than newly successful members of the privileged classes. Those who have been rich for generations have consolidated their social distance and made it appear natural if not deserved. But the newly opulent are more easily accused of 'giving themselves airs'—and are more easily resented as a result. Resentment arises not from a defined social distance but, on the contrary, from the persistent residual social nearness between these newly opulent and the power fold from whom they spring. The Africa of the first generation of independence was an Africa bedeviled by precisely this close interpenetration between the elite and the masses (Mazrui 1988: 476).

Mazrui's intervention is very important as it challenges the common intellectual wisdom which generally explained tensions between the governed and the governors (state and citizens) in terms of widening distance between the ruling elites and the ordinary citizens. To Mazrui, the issue of postcolonial legitimacy crisis must not be sought in 'social distance' but in 'social nearness' that breeds envy among the ordinary members of society and other elites excluded from corridors of power.

In African studies there is a large corpus of literature which emphasized that despite its ambiguities African nationalism was a positive force which sought to achieve decolonization, nation-building, development, democracy, and regional integration (Mkandawire 1997: 71-107). What is ignored is the reality that once liberated from colonial rule, the postcolonial state went on to deny African citizens freedom within its boundaries on a massive scale, in the process denting the whole agenda of decolonization from a freedom perspective. Celebrated nationalist discourses of nation-building and development of the 1960s became justifications for denial of freedom for citizens as well as authoritarianism. This is confirmed by Ake who emphasized the pervasive presence of the postcolonial state in all walks of African people's lives, making it a phenomenon to be loathed, courted, and even avoided (Ake 1993: 17-25).

Praise-texts that emerged during the independence euphoria of the 1960s were less critical of denials of freedom to citizens by the postcolonial state. The freedom for the African state was celebrated as freedom for the ordinary people. Those people who questioned whether decolonization bequeathed freedom on the ordinary citizens were quickly branded as traitors and enemies of the postcolonial state. They were either forced to flee to exile or were detained, if not liquidated completely. The earliest targets were excluded elites who were trying to create opposition political formations and critical intellectuals who were easily branded as counter-revolutionaries as though decolonization was ever a revolutionary enterprise in the first place.

What has dominated and preoccupied the minds of those who assumed state power at the end of direct colonial administration was coaxing ordinary citizens to celebrate with them what is termed 'Independence Days' each year as the time when freedom was attained. Whose freedom was it that is being celebrated, one may ask? In his studies of how postcolonial power was institutionalized, performed and displayed in his native country Cameroon and Togo, Mbembe revealed how ordinary citizens were forced to celebrate the 'taste for lecherous living' enjoyed by those in control of the postcolonial state and how elites constructed and deployed a particular official discourse that served to maintain the fiction of an African postcolonial society of happy citizens devoid of conflict (Mbembe 1992: 6).

Mbembe (1992: 3-37) introduced the concept of the 'postcolony' which is useful in capturing the mindset of a particular calibre of leadership and a particular configuration of power and unique mode of postcolonial governance (Mbembe 2001). According to him:

> To be sure, the postcolony is chaotically pluralistic, yet it has nonetheless an internal coherence. [...] The postcolony is characterized by a distinctive style of political improvisation, by a tendency to excess and a lack of proportion as well as by distinctive ways in which identities are multiplied, transformed and put into

> circulation. [...] In this sense, the postcolony is a particularly revealing, (and rather dramatic) stage on which are played out the wider problems of subjection and its corollary, discipline (Mbembe 1992: 3).

The postcolony is dominated by tensions between the state and citizens, and the governors and the governed. These tensions were deeply rooted and traceable to the practices and politics of postcolonial power routine, institutionalization, and broadcasting within a terrain dominated by colonial matrices of power. As the postcolonial state and those who manage it try to institutionalize their power, they invariably provoke reaction from those over whom they governed. Mbembe (1992: 4) described the complex postcolonial state-citizen relationship as 'illicit cohabitation, a relationship made fraught by the very fact of the commandment and its "subjects" having to share the same living space'.

What has not received adequate scholarly attention in this scheme of things is how 'subjects'/ordinary citizens fought and resisted being captured, dominated, exploited and being used to indulge in officially imposed postcolonial order that did not benefit them. Worby (1998: 337-354) argued that postcolonial African leaders rarely enjoyed undisputed power, meaning that their hold on power has always been tenuous and contested. This forced them to opt for and try to depend on the performance of quotidian ceremonies underpinned by extravagant dramaturgical and improvisational content, aimed at fostering popular collusion and eliciting citizen consent.

Because the postcolonial neocolonized state lacked strong essence – which forced it to operate through coercion rather than consent - such Western institutions as the World Bank and International Monetary Fund called for 'limited state' and dominance of market forces as a solution to problems of governance and development bedevilling Africa. The postcolonial state became a condemned institution that not only threatened people's freedom but distorted operations of laws of demand and supply. On this situation, Mkandawire argued that:

> For Africa the 1980s and 1990s were a period of wanton destruction of institutions and untrammeled experimentation with half-baked institution ideas. The result was 'unconstructive destruction' in its most institutionally debilitating form. The view by BWIs of African institutions was a jaundiced one borrowing eclectically from both the rational choice and new Weberian view of the state. From either point of view the message was African institutions should be circumvented or simply destroyed often because they were guilty by association (Mkandawire 2003: 10).

The World Bank and IMF recommended the burial of the 'age of intervention' by the African state of the 1960s and 1970s that was blamed for economic and political crises. The postcolonial state was derided as 'a giant theft machine' captured by corrupt and renting-seeking leadership (Mkandawire 2003). But the current economic and political thinking is that the postcolonial state is not only the creator of the desperately needed institutions but also an indispensable engine rather than an enemy of development and freedom if well democratized and made accountable to the people. It is within this context that the notions of using the postcolonial state as an institution that can facilitate the attainment of freedom for the people re-emerged.

This is informed by the metamorphosis of economic thinking from 'getting prices right', through 'getting institutions right' to the current thinking of 'getting everything right' (Mkandawire 2003: 25). In short, the current efforts are focused on building strong institutions, not dismantling the state. Dangers remain though that the state still continues to be captured by certain interest groups that deny others freedom as is the case in Zimbabwe where a nationalist-military oligarchy is keeping the whole nation hostage while looting such resources as land and minerals under the guise of indigenization of the economy (Hammar et al 2003; Ndlovu-Gatsheni 2009).

The question of freedom has always been a central aspiration of the colonized peoples, and decolonization was supposed and expected to bring it to the ordinary people. Freedom in general is linked to the development of human consciousness and was articulated in various languages, metaphors and idioms. As a concept, freedom is often used interchangeably with such other broader ideas in political and social theory, as liberty, development, liberation, emancipation, democracy and even revolution. Robert H. Taylor argues that:

> Freedom is an idea which was not merely discovered once and then spread around the world like a new commodity. Rather, freedom and its institutions emerge and re-emerge out of concrete circumstances of individuals' lives in history. The story of freedom knows no cultural barriers and continues to unfold in unexpected ways (Taylor 2002: 7).

The challenge in studies of freedom is how to define it as it covers a wide spectrum of human aspirations and visions subsumed under both emancipation and liberation. It is a loaded concept. Any attempt to coin a generic meaning of freedom is a futile exercise as it means different things to different people across space and time. R. W. Davis chose to define freedom from a Western modernist, liberal and emancipatory perspective:

> We use freedom in the traditional and restricted sense of civil and political liberty— freedom of religion, freedom of speech and assembly, freedom of the individual from arbitrary and capricious authority over persons or property, freedom to produce and to exchange goods and services, and freedom to take part in the political process that shapes people's destiny (Davis 2002: vii).

But in Africa, freedom can be easily understood in its relationship to those processes that denied it. This is why Crawford Young has argued that for Africa, freedom is generally understood in relation to 'its negative other'. This is how he put it:

> The ultimate sources of unfreedom, in much of the reflection upon it, are external to Africa: the Atlantic slave trade; colonial subjugation; great-power imperial pretensions, globalizing capitalism (Young 2002: 9).

African notions of freedom emerged from the sites of struggle against oppression and exploitation. The sites of struggles for freedom ranged widely from those of one person resisting domination of another person, and one society resisting the domination of another. Karl Marx, for instance, was concerned with oppression and exploitation of one class by another.

Freedom, therefore, is articulated in various forms such as the Marxian class struggles, liberation wars such as the anti-colonial wars, as well as feminist struggles against patriarchal forms of domination and exploitation of women by men. But to gain a deeper understanding of the vicissitudes and tensions within politics of juridical freedom and popular freedom, it is important to briefly analyse the nature and character of post-1945 normative order within which the postcolonial state was born and under which ex-colonized peoples graduated from being subjects into citizens (Mamdani 1996).

The end of the Second World War in 1945 witnessed the birth of a transformed global normative international order. The right of self-government and self-determination was inscribed in the United Nations Charter. By 1948, a Universal Declaration of Human Rights was adopted that codified human rights as another major ingredient of the post-1945 global normative dispensation. For Africa, the post-1945 period witnessed intensified struggles for decolonization.

Decolonization gained a further boost from the fact that the post-1945 international system became dominated not by major colonial powers like Britain and France but by new superpowers, the United States of America and the Soviet Union. Even though these post-war superpowers became engrossed in a complex Cold War rivalry, both of them 'by different logics favoured the dissolution of the colonial order' (Foltz 2002: 28). During this period, African freedom was simplistically defined in relation to colonial rule. The conception of freedom was articulated by Kwame Nkrumah (1962: 175) who said: 'When I talk of freedom and independence for Africa, I mean that the vast African majority should be accepted as forming the basis of government in Africa.' This point is further amplified by Crawford Young who wrote that:

> 'Freedom' as the transcendental political goal, with the rise of anti-colonial nationalism, thus had as primary referent alien rule. Colonial subjects, in this doctrine of protest, achieve standing and rights only collectively as members of a community defined by territorial geopolitics of the colonial partition. [...] The compelling need both for solidarity in anti-colonial challenge and for consolidating the unity of the new state gave a collective cast to the idea of freedom (Young 2002: 31).

What is often missed in studies of decolonization with the exception of the work of Frantz Fanon is that the departure of direct colonial rule resulted in the birth of an undemocratic postcolonial neocolonized states that inherited repressive structures and oppressive institutions created by colonial rule. This is a point well captured by Frederick Cooper who argued that:

> African states were successors in a double sense. First, they were built on a set of institutions--bureaucracies, militaries, post offices, and (initially) legislatures--set up by colonial regimes, as well as on a principle of state sovereignty sanctified by a community of already

existing states. [...] Second, African states took up a particular, and more recent, form of state project of colonialism: development (Cooper 2002: 156).

This means that colonialism deeply interpellated African nationalism and the postcolonial state could not escape the snares of colonial matrices of power. Young captured this point is well by Young when he stated that:

> African nationalists, at the time, sought no other formula; even as they fought colonial power, their own education and socialization had schooled them to hold the institutions of the imperial occupant in high regard as exemplary models of freedom (Young 2002: 29).

Just like colonial administrators, African leaders embarked on state consolidation that privileged the freedom of a clique of people and their clients and patrons rather than expansion of frontiers of freedom for the citizens. A state-centric concept of freedom emerged that ran counter to popular discourses of freedom. Mbembe argued that the postcolonial state soon considered 'itself simultaneously as indistinguishable from society and as the upholder of the law and the keeper of the truth. The state was embodied in a single person: the President' (Mbembe 1992: 5). Cascading from this mentality was a complicated relationship between the state and citizens. Liisa Laakso and Adebayo Olukoshi have an apt description of this development:

> At independence, most African governments set themselves the task of undertaking a vigorous process of nation-building with the aim of welding their multi-ethnic, multi-lingual, multi-cultural, and multi-religious countries into 'one nation'. A central element of this official project of nation-building was the assumption that only the state could constitute it. The nation-building project was, therefore, state-driven from the outset, often relying on a top-down approach that carried far-reaching centralizing implications. In time, the unity project increasingly took on the form of a unitary project which sometimes rested on a narrow ethnic base around which a system of patronage networks was then built linking other groups and their elites. Another element of the nation-building project was the assumption that the diversity of ethnic identities was inherently negative and obstructive and that it was a requirement of successful nation-building that the different identities be eradicated, submerged under or subordinated to the identity of the group(s) that dominated state power (Laakso and Olukoshi 1996: 13).

This conception of freedom by the African elites in charge of the postcolonial state marked the beginning of the crisis of the postcolonial nation-state project. One after another, the postcolonial states 'abandoned the multi-party political framework on the basis of which freedom from direct colonial was attained and adopted single party rule or slid into military rule' (Laakso and Olukoshi 1996: 13-14). Once this process was on course; the state increasingly became predatory and unrepresentative. A majority struggled to free themselves from predatory postcolonial states. Victor Azarya and Naomi Chazan argued that this struggle involved a shift from an 'engagement paradigm' to a 'disengagement paradigm' as the state failed to afford ordinary people material welfare and freedom (Azarya and Chazan 1998: 110-111).

Given the cataclysmic changes of the 1990s, described by Larry Diamond as the 'second wind of change', provoked by the collapse of the Soviet Union, implosion of communist regimes of eastern and central Europe and the fall of the Berlin Wall did not succeed in facilitating the gaining of sovereignty by the ordinary people (Diamond 1998: 263-271). This argument is amply demonstrated by recent political developments that took place in Kenya and Zimbabwe between 2007 and 2008 where political elites continued to display extreme lack of respect for citizens' lives, disdain for ordinary people's choices in elections, and proclivities to use violence to re-assert freedom for the governing elites as opposed to the freedom for the people (Ranger 2008). During a campaign for the March 2008 elections, President Mugabe of Zimbabwe had the audacity to tell the electorate:

> You can vote for them [MDC], but that would be a wasted vote. I am telling you. You would just be cheating yourself. There is no way we can allow them to rule this country. Never, ever! We have a job to do, to protect our heritage. The MDC will not rule this country. It will never happen. We will never allow it (Quoted in Solidarity Peace Trust 2008).

This extreme disdain for the sovereignty of the citizens prompted a leading Zimbabwean opposition leader and academic Welshman Ncube to argue that:

> If all political players were to accept that it is the sovereign right of the people to freely elect a government of their choice no matter how we may disagree with their judgment. Even if we fiercely believe that it is wrong judgment we must accept it as their sovereign choice. If the political parties were to embrace that principle that the will of the people is sovereign [...] in my view that is the problem that faces the country at the moment—the refusal by the major political players that people can make a judgment, which is different from theirs. For as long as there is unwillingness to accept the judgment of the people we will have this crisis where the major political players seek to manipulate the will of the people (Financial Gazette, 22 November 2008).

Both in Kenya and Zimbabwe, citizens have found themselves hostage to the elites in charge of the postcolonial state. For both countries, it became clear how difficult it was to remove from power those elites that had entrenched themselves within the postcolonial state structures. Elections proved to be inadequate as a means used by the ordinary people to reclaim their sovereign power to choose their leaders. In Kenya, the December 2007 elections resulted in the worst form of violence ever experienced since the Mau Mau period; and in Zimbabwe, the post-29 March 2008 harmonized parliamentary, council, and presidential elections were greeted with extreme forms of violence that targeted ordinary citizens (Prunier 2008; Masunungure 2009; Ndlovu-Gatsheni 2009). These examples help to show that juridical freedom cannot be conflated with popular freedom.

STRUGGLES TO TRANSLATE JURIDICAL FREEDOM INTO POPULAR FREEDOM

Since the end of colonization the struggle for freedom has taken complex forms. As noted by Foltz (2002: 40): 'Often, these relations have pitted freedom--or freedom of manoeuvre--for the political elite against the freedom and human rights of the ordinary citizens.' What is beyond doubt is that freedom of the African state entailed among other things admitting it to membership in the international society of sovereign states. The immediate struggle by the elite in charge of the young postcolonial states was to consolidate 'freedom of the state' into 'freedom for the state' (Foltz 2002: 40). This thinking developed within a terrain of emergence of African states as unique 'quasi-states'. Robert H. Jackson defined 'quasi-states' as new polities which were recognized as sovereign and independent units by other states within the international system, but which could not meet the demands of 'empirical' statehood (Jackson 1990).

Empirical statehood is measured by the state's capacity to exercise effective power within its boundaries and ability to defend itself from external attack (Clapham 1996: 15). The crisis of the postcolonial African state was well captured by Christopher Clapham who said: 'African independence launched into international politics a group of the world's poorest, weakest and most artificial states' (Clapham 1996: 15). These realities forced the African leadership to search for 'freedom for the African state' (Foltz 2002: 40). This took various forms including nationalization of the economy making it the domain of elite plunder and introduction of authoritarian one-party-state regimes and other forms of regime security rather than human security.

The postcolonial state assumed the character of the proverbial goat that grazed where it was tethered—preying upon the people, capturing, dominating, exploiting, and squeezing the local citizenry. Examples include Ghana and Guinea under Kwame Nkrumah and Sekou Toure (see Azarya and Chazan 1998: 115). These two West African states were practizing socialism that was used to justify extreme forms of centralization and politicization of every aspect of society.

Youth movements, trade unions, women's movements, and other voluntary associations became integrated within the ruling parties. At the end of it all: 'Every citizen had to be a party member, and every village, neighbourhood, factory, and office had its party committee' (Azarya and Chazan 1998: 115). The underlying logic was to bring larger and larger segments of the population into the state domain of surveillance, repression, domination, and exploitation.

No doubt the search for the freedom to African states in reality became the search for the freedom of those who were in control of the postcolonial neocolonized state and their select clients and cronies. Sooner than later, it became apparent that the immediate benefit of decolonization accrued to the political elites in charge of the state rather than ordinary citizens. The postcolonial state soon became a symbol of repression, oppression, and deprivation rather than a facilitator and guarantor of ordinary people's freedom. Those who felt excluded from the state responded by seeking 'freedom from the African state' (Foltz 2002: 41). This happened when the postcolonial state had undergone a cycle of deliberate circumscription of opposition, closure of the democratic space, squandering of political legitimacy, and increasing failure to deliver public services.

SEEKING FREEDOM FROM THE STATE

The failure by the postcolonial state to deliver material benefits and freedomto the ordinary people resulted in a problematic relationship between the state and the citizens. Those in control of the state became the only full citizens together with their clients and cronies. The majority of the ordinary people became subjects once more after the end of colonial rule (Mamdani 1996). Instead of governing, the elites in charge of the state became rulers in the crudest sense of the term whereby their words became law and they reduced citizens not only to subjects but also to powerless sycophants and hungry praise-singers (Mazrui 1967).

Azarya and Chazan identified four common mechanisms employed by ordinary people to disengage from the state. These are 'suffer-manage syndrome', 'escaping', 'creation of systems parallel to those of the state', and 'self-enclosure' (Azarya and Chazan 1998: 110-135). One can add secession and attempts to seize the state itself as other forms employed by the dominated to attain freedom. The 'suffer-manage syndrome' involved constant adjustment to a deteriorating state performance. It encompasses a coterie of activities of learning to manage life and survive during moments of depravity and crisis. The activities ranged widely from altering diets and adjusting consumption habits to accord with existing meagre food supplies; urban dwellers cultivating vegetable gardens for home consumption and conversion of home craft into cottage industries (Azarya and Chazan 1998: 115-116).

These survival and suffer-management strategies were recently manifest in Zimbabwe where the economy experienced a free-fall from 2000 to 2008 (Vambe 2008). Those groups and individuals that failed to extricate themselves physically from the domain of the malfunctioning state resorted to 'suffer-management' as a mode of survival. Suffer-management is a form of coping with crisis and cannot be seriously considered as amounting to a form of freedom or a form of disengagement from the state. The advocates of active citizenship often blame those people who 'resort to suffer-management 'suffer-management' as passive citizens open to victimization by the state.

But when all avenues of exiting from the predatory state become closed, some citizens rely on resilience and constant adjustment to endure diminishing circumstances (Azarya and Chazan 1998: 117). In Zimbabwe, those responsible for causing deterioration of the economy through corruption and implementation of ill-conceived policies like the fast-track land reform programme, turned around and advised the suffering citizens to persevere in the midst of extreme scarcity of basic commodities. The common 'official jingle' that became banal on Zimbabwean television and radio was a song 'Rambamakashinga' (remain resolute and persevere).

The other common route is that of escaping from the malfunctioning or oppressive state physically. This takes the form of emigration. This option is commonly utilized by those who are better educated such as teachers, nurses, doctors, and academics. This group is usually followed by unskilled and semiskilled groups who also experienced unbearable consequences of socio-economic and political crises. Political activists opposed to those in control of the state form another layer of those who emigrate.

During the crisis years under Kwame Nkrumah, 10 per cent of Ghana's population exited the country while about half of the Guinean population moved to live in countries such as Senegal, Ivory Coast, Sierra Leone, Liberia, Gambia and Mali. Ghanaians were mainly trooping to oil-rich Nigeria (Azarya and Chazan 1998: 115). In the southern African region, too, Zimbabweans have responded to the unprecedented economic and political crisis in their country through emigration. About 3 million Zimbabweans are estimated to be living in South Africa and another 2 million in the United Kingdom and other parts of the world (Sisulu et al 2007: 552-573). Escaping or migrating to another country is one of the oldest strategies that have been employed by Africans to escape political persecution, economic depravity and other forms of oppression.

The main constraint to this form of disengagement is the existence of modern boundaries that are often manned by state functionaries that require such documentation as passports and visas that are issued by the same state they are disengaging from. While in exile and in the Diaspora, some groups organize themselves into various political movements, campaigning for democracy such as the Campaign for Democracy in Ghana that was headed by Boakye Djan in the 1970s. Zimbabweans in exile and in the Diaspora have also formed various quasi-political groups including Mthwakazi People's Congress (MPC) calling for secession of Matabeleland from Zimbabwe as well as numerous welfare associations (Ndlovu-Gatsheni 2008: 167-199).

Secession is another of the routes to freedom that some frustrated constituencies and groups tired of oppression, domination, and expression have attempted. It was the most radical form of claiming political freedom. The idea was to disengage from the state and attain recognition as a new sovereign state. The most commonly cited examples are those of Biafra in Nigeria and Katanga in Congo in the 1960s. Other stirrings of secessionist struggles occurred in Senegal (Casamance), Ethiopia (Eritrea) and Sudan (Southern Sudan). For sometime Eritrea remained the only example of successful secession until recently when Southern Sudan succeeded in breaking away from Arab dominated Northern Sudan.

Foltz (2002: 48) has explained why secessionist movements were few and had limited success in Africa. According to him, Secession 'ran strictly against the African state system's norms of preserving territorial integrity and the inherited colonial boundaries'. This norm was underwritten by the Organization of African Unity (OAU) which institutionalized the principles of inviolability of existing colonially-crafted borders in its Charter. The consequences of this decision by the founding fathers of postcolonial states was that minority groups that were often segregated from employment, excluded from benefitting from the national wealth and whose history, culture and languages were deliberately sidelined, had to endure bondage of boundaries.

The other option that was available to politically motivated military elites was to try and seize state power. This took the form of rebellion and military coups. The earliest examples included that of the Chadian rebellion of 1965. This was followed by other examples that culminated in civil wars in Uganda (1981-1986), Angola (1975-2002); Ethiopia (1974-94); Rwanda (1990-1994); and Mozambique (1980-1993) (Foltz 2002: 48). For several decades in countries like Ghana and Nigeria, military coups became the means of changing government and military strong-men succeeded each other via the barrel of the gun (Austen and Luckham 1975). Monopoly of force rather than elections and other softer forms of political bargaining became a raw material for political power.

The other option available to those excluded from power and its elaborate clientilist and patronage networks was to create alternative if not parallel systems to those of the state as an outlet for human needs that the state failed to fulfil. Examples include informal markets (black markets), smuggling, corruption and the use of alternative methods of justice. The logic behind these alternatives is that they override official channels and skirt the state's laws (Azarya and Chazan 1998: 123).

This form of disengagement involves attempts at beating the state systems and laws. In Zimbabwe, the late 1990s and early 2000, witnessed the mushrooming of flea markets that were not fully regulated by the state. There was also proliferation of informal street money-markets where hard currencies were sold and bought. But as the state became more and more desperate with the national banks running short of money, it had to act through a military style 'Operation Murambatsvina' (Operation Clean-Up) (Vambe 2008). It involved the demolition of structures and displacement of over 70,000 people as the state reacted against overriding cynicism towards official structures and widespread non-compliance with its laws (Tibaijuka 2005).

Azarya and Chazan have also noted that other forms of disengagement from the state have taken the form of conversion to new Pentecostal religious sects and magical cults where the ordinary people seek new spiritual redemption and material security (Azarya and Chazan 1998: 127). John and Jean Comaroff have drawn our attention to the proliferation of 'occult economies' involving ritual killings, use of magic, witchcraft and zombie conjuring in South Africa. They see these developments as an integral element of a thriving alternative modernity (Comaroffs 2000: 310-312). One of the most striving new religious movements in South Africa is the Universal Church of the Kingdom of God whose roots are traceable to Brazil. It has skilfully deployed the protestant ethic and combined it with enterprise and urbanity to link spiritual and material world issues that appeal to the poor.

Within the Universal Church, prayers are deployed in such a way that they speak directly to mundane issues of depression, lack of employment and financial problems (Comaroff 1996: 297-301). Because of this, the Universal Church and other Pentecostal religious movements have become an alternative space where people concentrate their search for material and spiritual deliverance. This is happening alongside with the proliferation of popular cultures with anti-establishment overtones, drawing on both traditional and Western sources. These forms of popular protest take the 'soft' forms of underground press, song, dance, poetry, theatre and literature. Ayi Kwei Armah's widely read novel The Beautiful Ones Are Not Yet Born, was part of protest literature (Armah 1971).

Mbembe (1992: 8) has identified ways by which ordinary citizens used their laughter to 'kidnap power and force it, as if by accident, to examine its own vulgarity'. For Zimbabwe, those in the Diaspora have evolved other forms of doing the same thing by setting up private radio stations and online newspapers. Examples include the British-based SWRADIO Africa and American-based Voice of America's Studio 7 staffed with exiled journalists and DJs. The most popular online newspaper is

Newzimbabwe.com that consistently carries uncensored writings very critical of the state and its leadership.

Disengagement also took the form of 'self-enclosure' (Azarya and Chazan 1998: 128). This involved attempts to insulate oneself from the state, thereby gaining protection from its uncertainties. For example, the white minority groups in Zimbabwe have been using this strategy from as far back as 1987 when the twenty seats reserved for them were scrapped from the voter's roll. They withdrew from national politics and took refuge in their farms, business premises and gated communities located in the expensive suburbs (Muzondidya 2010: 5-38). They only came back to the public political domain when their land ownership was threatened through the Fast-Track Land Reform Programme whose modus operandi was compulsory acquisition of white-owned farms for resettlement of the black people. Only then did they become visible in large numbers in support of the opposition Movement for Democratic Change (MDC).

'Self-enclosure' also took the form of withdrawal: some urban dwellers withdrew to the rural enclaves; medical doctors withdrew from government contracts to establish their own firms; and other professionals loosened their ties with the state as a means of self-protection (Azarya and Chazan 1998: 130). Goran Hyden has argued that even peasants also participated in the evasive 'self-enclosure' technique, particularly those he described as 'uncaptured' ones who opted for a return to an ancestral 'economy of affection' (Hyden 1980).

SEEKING TO DEMOCRATIZE THE POSTCOLONIAL STATE

Some African people still believe that they can attain freedom through fighting from within the boundaries of the oppressive state. The main method has been to deploy post-Cold War global normative values of democracy, human rights, and good governance to contest the basis of state authoritarianism. This strategy became very popular in the 1990s following the collapse of the Soviet Union and implosion of the communist regimes in Eastern Europe.

A convergence of local and global voices called for democracy as the precondition for any economic and military support for African postcolonial regimes. This began in 1990 with the French president, Francois Mitterrand, telling the Franco-Africa Summit attended by numerous heads of state from Francophone Africa that French economic and military assistance would be given to those regimes that were committed to progress towards democracy (Marchesin 1995: 5-24).

Since that time, France has scaled-down on its practise of giving military support to autocratic African leaders, the first casualty being Hissein Habre of Chad who was toppled violently from power while and the French stood aloof because he refused to follow the new path of democratization. The global financial institutions -- notably the World Bank, the International Monetary Fund and even the African Development Bank -- joined the voices of those fighting for democracy and made financial aid conditional on progress towards good governance (World Bank 1995). Foltz concluded that: 'Taken together, these external factors, interacting with domestic pressures, opened a political space in which Africans seeking political freedom could manoeuvre' (Foltz 2002: 53).

The 1990s also witnessed the mobilization and organization of Africans into civil society organizations (CSOs) ranging widely from churches, trade unions, women's movements, student movements, to ethnic-based pressure groups. As the Comaroffs:

> [...]Civil Society has served as a remarkably potent battle cry across the world. During inhospitable times, it reanimates the optimistic spirit of modernity, providing scholars, public figures, poets, and ordinary people alike a language with which to talk about democracy, moral community, justice, and populist politics; with which, furthermore, to breathe life back into, 'society,' declared dead almost twenty years ago by powerful magi of Second Coming [...] (Comaroffs 2000: 331).

African-based CSOs worked closely with Western non-governmental organizations (NGOs) and aid agencies to campaign for freedom. In Francophone Africa, the embers of freedom culminated in what became known as 'the National Conference' phenomenon that began in Benin as a convergence zone of those groups fighting for an end to authoritarianism practised by the one-party regimes (Robinson 1994: 575-610).

Indeed, a few one-party authoritarian regimes that had come to power in the 1960s crumbled under the weight of a combination of civil society and opposition forces' resistance to oppression and exploitation. Ready examples include Mathieu Kerekou of Benin, Mengistu Haile Mariam of Ethiopia, Kenneth Kaunda of Zambia, and Kamuzu Banda of Malawi. These regime changes were celebrated by Samuel P. Huntington as the 'third wave' of 'democratization in the late twentieth century' (Huntington 1991).

Despite the chequered history of the freedom struggles of the 1990s, with some proving to be false starts and others hijacked by incumbent dictators thirsty for relevance and re-birth, they formed a strong background for the current push for transparency, accountability, predictability, good corporate management and good political governance. By 2000, a new continental and global consensus had emerged on the complementarities of democracy and development.

The development of authoritarianism of the 1960s and 1970s was replaced by a strong belief in democratic development of the 1990s and 2000s (Sen 2000). Those fighting for freedom were no longer calling for the death of the state but for its restructuring to serve the interests of the people rather than that of the elites. Issues of corruption, kleptocracy and nepotism were identified as obstacles that needed to be removed if the African state was to serve the interests of the ordinary people. Some of the most corrupt and kleptocratic states like that of Mobutu Sese Seko of Zaire (now Democratic Republic of the Congo) could no longer rest until Mobutu himself was forced to leave the country to die in shame in exile. These realities led Young to conclude that:

> The democratic era of the 1990s, in spite of its disappointments and limitations, situated ideas of freedom in a multiplicity of sites, opened many new debates, and revived older ones on making freedom authentic by rooting it in an indigenous heritage (Young 2002: 37).

The new millennium witnessed the continuing struggles of ordinary people for widened frontiers of freedom consonant with the millenarian mood of hope for new life. The voices range from those of women and girls still pushing the remaining frontiers of patriarchy into the dustbin of history; youths claiming their space as a new generation; ethnic groups flexing their muscles for recognition and calling for decentralized forms of governance; and religious congregations creating a niche for their flock. What is common among these voices is the clarion call for democracy that would free them from the control of the centre and how to make the centre serve the ordinary people.

SEEKING TO RECONFIGURE THE POSTCOLONIAL STATE INTO AN ENGINE OF DEVELOPMENT

Since 2000 increasing voices have been calling stridently for new African states that would serve the ordinary people and promote popular freedom. In some literature, this type of state is described as a democratic developmental state. It is a state that is capable of working to fulfil the democratic and developmental aspirations of the majority of the people within its borders.

The envisaged democratic developmental state is to be defined by its institutional characteristics. The first key feature is that of embedding in African society, that is, a state that has formed strong and broad-based alliances with society and ensures effective and active participation of citizens in decision-making. The second is that of building autonomous institutions free from control by capricious and venal cliques bent of fulfilling personal selfish agendas. Such a state is expected to be totally freed from the trappings of autocracy of the 1960s and 1980s (Mkandawire 2001: 289–314).

Foltz attributed this change in thinking about the state to the impact of normative and historical transformation in the larger external environment. He identified two factors responsible for this normative shift: reduced global and continental tolerance for those leaders who seized power through coups and other violent means, and the questioning of the non-interference in national affairs norm (Foltz 2002: 58). The other contributory factor was the coming to power of a 'new generation of African leaders' that included Thabo Mbeki of South Africa, Yoweri Museveni of Uganda, Paul Kagame of Rwanda, Meles Zenawi of Ethiopia, Isaias Afewerki of Eritrea and Olusegun Obasanjo of Nigeria, who were less authoritarian and less dogmatic unlike the founding fathers of the postcolonial states of the 1960s and the military leaders of the 1970s (Ottaway 1998).

While the 'new generation of African leaders' degenerated into authoritarianism of varying degrees, they remained better than those who presided over one-party and military dictatorships of the 1960s and 1970s. They were committed to the reconstruction of the African state in the direction of the fulfilment of popular demands for economic development and democracy. In combination or as individuals, they engaged and toyed with bigger plans for Africa such as the New Partnership for African Development (NEPAD), Pan-African Parliament (PAP), and the African Peer Review Mechanism (APRM). These pan-African institutions were meant to create a new momentum for Africa characterized by economic development and democratization (Murithi 2005). As Timothy Murithi puts it:

> With the creation of the African Union, African governments and their societies are expressing the desire, as yet unfulfilled, to address the unjust practices of the past which led to the social and economic marginalization of members of their societies. In so doing it is also an expression that Africa wants to play a constructive role in international relations as an equal partner and that the first step towards achieving this is to put its own house in order (Murithi 2005: 166).

The decision to build pan-African institutions as part of the plan to concretize African aspirations for economic development and democracy is happening in conjunction with the return of the state as the legitimate driver of development and democratization. The Nigerian scholar, Eghosa Osaghae, noted that it has dawned on many researchers that the state remains the sole anchor for citizenship. It has also been realized that the state is the only institution that can carry and drive the distribution of resources (Osaghae 2010). The continuing struggle is over the nature and the type of state that will not be a menace to the people but a facilitator of economic development and provider of freedom and security.

CONCLUSION

Decolonization cannot just be celebrated uncritically. Such praise-oriented approaches towards decolonization have obscured the myths and illusions of freedom and tend to ignore the poor and problematic ethical, ideological, and political foundations of this project. Decolonization remained hostage to Western notions of emancipation that did not seriously question the ontological and epistemic essence of colonial modernity from the snares of which it tried to free Africans. Throughout the unfolding of decolonization, the radical liberatory aspects were compromised by the privileging of emancipatory-reformist ideas that did not predict the neo-colonial traps.

On top of unpacking decolonization in general, this chapter also analyzed the complexities of African struggles for freedom transcending those studies that conflated juridical freedom (freedom for the state) with popular freedom (freedom for the people). It has given empirical flesh, expanded and further problematized the pathways followed and pursued by ordinary people in search of freedom beyond Foltz's four-dimensional thesis.

Combining Foltz's thesis and Mbembe's work on dialectics, dynamics and entanglement of the interests of those who command and those expected to obey those commands within the postcolony, the chapter has discussed the complexities of postcolonial constructions of power and hegemony and how ordinary people have ceaselessly satirized, mocked, deflected, contested it; and even exited from the harsh domains of the postcolonial state at its most predatory moments.

The chapter unearthed multiple pathways to freedom pursued by ordinary citizens that transcended the conventional binary categories of domination and resistance, power and passivity, and autonomy and subjection that have shaped conventional wisdom. In the process, such issues as the crisis of legitimacy of the postcolonial state and the supposed redemptive aspects of the decolonization process are cast in new light that expands frontiers of knowledge on constructions of power within the postcolony, struggles for citizenship, and popular sovereignty.

Cinematising the Ghostly Postcolonial Timescape: John Akomfrah & Black Audio Film Collective

by KJ ABUDU

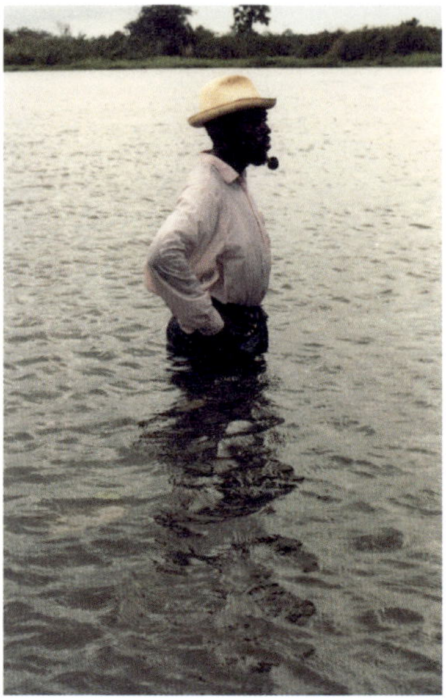

John Akomfrah, *Testament*, 1988.
Colour film, dimensions variable, 79 minutes

"[T]he postcolonial African world exists only as that which is absent."•1
– Sabelo J. Ndlovu-Gatsheni

"[T]his time of African existence is neither a linear time nor a simple sequence in which each moment effaces, annuls, and replaces those that precede it, to the point where a single age exists within society. This time is not a series but an *interlocking* of presents, pasts, and futures that retain their depths of other presents, pasts, and futures, each age bearing, altering, and maintaining the previous ones."•2
– Achille Mbembe

"Without this *non-contemporaneity with itself of the living present*, without that which secretly unhinges it, without this responsibility and this respect for justice concerning those who *are not there*, of those who are no longer or who are not yet *present and living*, what sense would there be to ask the question "where?" "where tomorrow?" "whither?""•3
– Jacques Derrida

In an opening scene from *Testament*, 1988, the first feature film by Black Audio Film Collective (BAFC), an unassuming man gently wades into the Volta river and plunges into its murky depths, thereafter floating, as if lifeless, on its rippling surface. The enigmatic scene, following a wavy film dissolve, opens unto archival footage of newly born conjoined twins on a surgical table. We return to the man in the river, who rises from its surface and sinks back into it, his seemingly ritualistic gesture accompanied by Krzysztof Penderecki's dissonant, threnodic *Magnificat in G*. Following an upward shot of birds circling graciously in the sky, the tropical landscape becomes tinted with an icy blue hue, a frigid visuality further punctuated by Arvo Pärt's melancholic *Cantus in Memoriam of Benjamin Britten*. Soon after, we hear the voiceover of Abena, the film's protagonist, deliver a dictum of poetic and philosophical gravitas: "In the end, history takes all in turns, and in turning is lost to memory."•4

I have begun this chapter with the descriptions above to emphasize the layered aesthetic approach with which BAFC and John Akomfrah (one of the collective's founding members) engages with and materialises the African postcolonial condition, a socio-historical condition that I argue is an inherently spectral condition and which thus requires for its audiovisual explication and meditation, the mobilization of a spectral aesthetics, a "spectropoetics." Throughout this chapter, I will be examining the complex ways in which, through allegory, colour filtering, eerie soundscapes, and visual and textual archival excavation and recontextualization – formal methods clearly elaborated in *Testament*, which BAFC and Akomfrah would go on to refine over many decades – the viewer is keyed into

1 • Sabelo J. Ndlovu-Gatsheni, *Coloniality of Power in Postcolonial Africa: Myths of Decolonisation*, (Dakar: CODESRIA), 2013, 12.
2 • Achille Mbembe, *On the Postcolony*, (Berkeley, Los Angeles, and London: University of California Press), 2001, 16.
3 • Jacques Derrida, *Specters of Marx: The State of Debt, the Work of Mourning and the New International*, trans. Peggy Kamuf (New York and London: Routledge), 1994, xviii.
4 • Black Audio Film Collective, *Testament*, 1988.

a historical space-time of absent-presences, a *haunted* space-time, in which the colonial past has not quite passed and the unfulfilled future promise of decolonisation looms large.

Of particular importance to this text is its exploration of the unique capacity of the film medium – its materiality, conditions of production, and modes of reception – to produce a poetics of the spectral, and how such a structure of poetics critically figures what the theorist, Achille Mbembe, has termed the "postcolonial timescape."[5] Through an analysis of two films, BAFC's *Testament*, and Akomfrah's more recent *Transfigured Night*, 2013, this chapter will think through how both films' related meditations on African postcolonial disillusionment are not just spectral in nature but also how they impose active ethical demands on contemporary viewing subjects through their historical conjurings, through their very ability to *haunt*.

THE POSTCOLONIAL TIMESCAPE

Contemporary postcolonial Africa inhabits a spatio-temporal zone of immense disjointedness. As a continent which has historically been defined from without, projected unto by the European imagination as a site of radical otherness, as Valentin-Yves Mudimbe writes in the *Invention of Africa*, any critical project that centers Africa – its life-forms, politics, and history – as its ground for knowledge production must necessarily contend with centuries of Eurocentric onto-epistemological negation and phantomization.[6] This "Africa," whose identity is in truth heterogenous and internally incoherent like any other continent, remains discursively bound to Western Enlightenment projections, from Hegel's assertion that Africa exists outside of history itself, to Joseph Conrad's writings on Africa as the irredeemable "heart of darkness."[7] By rendering Africa as a screen projection for colonial myths, illusions, and fantasies, a spectralizing process inextricably entangled with the continent's epistemic erasure, such early modern writings only expose the violent colonial underpinnings of Enlightenment modernist thought whose claims to liberty, rationality, and progress (and the capitalist infrastructures birthed therein) depended on the dehumanization and subsequent commodificatory conversion of the African into the Negro during the transatlantic slave trade, this world-historical process (as well as the land dispossession of Indigenous peoples) being the ultimate condition of possibility for the emergence of what we might call a global modernity.[8]

The transatlantic slave trade produced and was legitimated by a plethora of ontological and epistemological structures – the paradigmatic notions of racial and civilizational difference being two core examples – that later enabled the mass colonisation of the African continent by European imperial powers in the 19th century. Both these violent modern/colonial worlding processes, which engendered disparate African diasporic populations in Europe, Asia, and the Americas, and accelerated Euro-America's accumulation of wealth via its rapacious extraction of the continent's natural resources, have in turn eroded and ruptured the very spatial integrity of "Africa." By this, I mean that as a result of centuries of migration, displacement, cross-cultural entanglement, and resource extractivism – all events subtended by the spread of global capital and its attendant colonial, racialising logics – Africa has experienced a historically unprecedented degree of deterritorialisation in the modern era.

5 • Achille Mbembe's presentation as part of the panel in "After Post-Colonialism: Transnationalism or Essentialism?," convened by Gabriela Salgado and Paul Goodwin, including contributions by Kader Attia, Ângela Ferreira, Kiluanji Kia Henda and Zac Ové, at Tate Modern, 8 May 2010. Recordings are available online at www.tate.org.uk/ context comment/video/after-post-colo-nialism-transna-tionalism-or-essentialism-video-recordings (accessed 28/06/21).

6 • V.Y. Mudimbe, *The Invention of Africa: Gnosis, Philosophy and the Order of Knowledge*, (Bloomington and Indianapolis: Indiana University Press), 1988. Achille Mbembe works with and extends Mudimbe's ideas on Africa's epistemic phantomization in *The Critique of Black Reason*, (Durham: Duke University Press), 2017.

7 • See Georg W.F. Hegel, *The Philosophy of History*, 1834, and Joseph Conrad, *Heart of Darkness*, 1899.

8 • As Mignolo and Catherine Walsh argue, "coloniality is constitutive, not derivative, of modernity." See Walter D. Mignolo and Catherine E. Walsh, *On Decoloniality: Concepts, Analytics, and Praxis*, (Durham, NC; London: Duke University Press), 2018, 4. Quijano further agues, "the European paradigm of rational knowledge, was not only elaborated in the context of, but as part of, a power structure that involved the European colonial domination over the rest of the world. This paradigm expressed, in a demonstrative sense, the coloniality of power of that structure." See Aníbal Quijano "Coloniality and Modernity/ Rationality," *Cultural Studies*, Volume 21, No. 2, 174.

Consequently, Africa, being at once a source of cultural memory for its diaspora, a primal extractive site of globally circulating commodities, and the ideological foil against which Western civility is measured, becomes a space that is at once physical and idealised, there and not-there, contained and dispersed, in other words, ghostly and discontinuous.

A related observation can be made regarding Africa's warped historical temporalities. Aníbal Quijano and Walter D. Mignolo refer to the onto-epistemological structures that govern the current geo-political world order as the "colonial matrices of power," the nearly invisible hierarchies and heterarchies of power that, over the last five centuries, have legitimated Euro-American domination of Africa, Asia, and Latin America.[9] It is these (im)material matrices of power, which work along a plurality of axes and through varying levels of abstraction, that gave birth to Africa's colonial states in the late 19th and early 20th centuries, and which subsequently created their awkwardly conjoined postcolonial twin states in the mid 20th century. As Quijano notes:

> "Coloniality is one of the specific and constitutive elements of global model of capitalist power. It is based on the imposition of a racial/ethnic classification of the global population as the cornerstone of that model of power,and it operates on every level, in every arena and dimension (both material and subjective) of everyday social existence, and does so on a societal scale."[10]

Coloniality, as opposed to colonialism, is crucial for theorising the disjointed timescape that postcolonial Africa inhabits. Whereas colonialism denotes a temporally delimited and officialised regime of dominance, coloniality refers to a *relation* of dominance, a transhistorical logic of power, that is maintained and reproduced even after the evacuation of the colonial administration. Colonial matrices of power may thus be, and indeed still are, insidiously operative in the supposed *post*-colonial era. As colonialism's afterlife, coloniality suppresses and perpetually defers the realisation of a truly decolonised and independent African political body.

Referring back to the wave of African decolonisation movements that occurred in the 1960s and 1970s, Sabelo J. Ndlovu-Gatsheni reminds us that, in most cases, only juridical independence was achieved during this period of euphoric liberation while tangible political and economic changes for the subaltern masses were rapidly stalled by the postcolonial elite's consolidation of power. As Frantz Fanon famously argues in *The Wretched of the Earth*, the failure of the postcolonial "national bourgeoise" to deliver on the promise of thoroughgoing decolonisation was driven, among other factors, by the group's psychic and economic identification with the Western bourgeoise, a globally dominant class whose interests, in turn, relied on the continued extraction and exploitation of African labour and land.[11] Ndlovu-Gatsheni gives visceral historical form to Fanon's arguments when he mentions that, in Francophone Africa (with the exception of Guinea), "the postcolonial states were born with diminished sovereignty which still remained with France. They had no control over foreign, economic, monetary and defence matters" and that in Anglophone Africa, "African nationalists had to sign agreements to uphold some negotiated neocolonial compromises including safeguarding properties accumulated by white colonialists such as land and mines even before entering new offices."[12]

9 • Walter D. Mignolo and Catherine E. Walsh, *On Decoloniality: Concepts, Analytics, and Praxis,* 2018, and Aníbal Quijano, "Coloniality of Power, Eurocentrism and Latin America," *International Sociology*, Vol. 15, Issue 2, 2000, 215-232.
10 • Aníbal Quijano cited in Sabelo J. Ndlovu-Gatsheni, *Coloniality of Power in Postcolonial Africa: Myths of Decolonisation*, (Dakar: CODESRIA), 2013, 7.
11 • Fanon writes, "[T]he national bourgeoisie never stops calling for the nationalization of the economy and the commercial sector. In its thinking, to nationalize does not mean placing the entire economy at the service of the nation or satisfying all its requirements. To nationalize does not mean organizing the state on the basis of a new program of social relations. For the bourgeoisie, nationalization signifies very precisely the transfer into indigenous hands of privileges inherited from the colonial period." See Frantz Fanon, *The Wretched Of The Earth,* trans. Richard Philcox, (New York: Grove Press), 2004, 100.
12 • Sabelo J. Ndlovu-Gatsheni, *Coloniality of Power in Postcolonial Africa: Myths of Decolonisation*, (Dakar: CODESRIA), 2013, 75.

Fanon's well-known account of the African postcolonial condition, with its specific focus on the Algerian Revolution, additionally gestures towards coloniality's constitutive subjective expressions (which inevitably have concrete, objective effects), such as the coloniality of knowledge and the coloniality of being.•[13] One might frame these subjective, immaterial dimensions of coloniality as determining factors that prevented many postcolonial elites – often schooled at prestigious institutions in the West or at Euro-colonial institutions in Africa, and who resultingly inherited a colonial onto-epistemological worldview and metric of valuation – from creating completely alternative governing models to the hegemonic Western liberal democratic nation-state in the wake of national independence (and as we will soon see, to those elites that *did* attempt such radical experiments, the coloniality of power, through exercising its economic and militaristic might, kept such dissidents in check either through assassination or political destabilization).

Kwame Nkrumah, the first president of Ghana, famously wrote about this frustrated dream of autonomous African becoming, terming the holdover of colonial economic and political ties after the achievement of independence as "neocolonialism." Nkrumah refers to neocolonialism as "the worst form of imperialism. For those who practise it, it means power without responsibility and for those who suffer from it, it means exploitation without redress."•[14] Neocolonialism, which can be conceived as an adaptative, re-emergent form of coloniality in the late twentieth century, constitutes a dispossessive force that thwarts the radical horizons of anti-colonial liberation movements, and exposes the project of decolonisation, as it was articulated in the mid-20th century, as a myth, as a shadow vision which is incomplete and still waiting to be fulfilled.

Through this kaleidoscopic temporal entanglement, as theorized by Achille Mbembe, of a colonial past that still haunts the African postcolony via the invisible yet deeply felt machinations of the (neo)colonial matrices of power, and of a futural decolonial promise, notably unrealised, that hovers at the horizon of political possibility, akin to a mirage, something of a profound disjointedness emerges that we might refer to as the postcolonial timescape. This timescape, structured by overlapping past-presents and future-pasts, rhymes with Derrida's formulation of the specter as that which throws time (and space) "out of joint."•[15] I would like to extend Derrida's understanding of the specter, which creates a "dislocated time of the present" to understand the African postcolonial condition, in which "time is off its hinges, time is off course, beside itself, disadjusted."•[16]

This "disadjusted" time encapsulates the timescape of the African postcolony, what Ndlovu-Gatsheni, following Gayatri Chakravorty Spivak, richly terms the "postcolonial neocolonized world."•[17] An admittedly wordy term, this phrase, however, aptly describes a complex socio-historical condition in which the postcolonial state does not become conflated with the colonial state, even though the former inherits many of its pathologies from the latter – in other words, the "post" is taken seriously as a temporal analytic of aftermath – while it renders the "postcolonial" as latent with decolonial possibility but stalled by the imposition of a repressive neocolonial paradigm.

As a historical location that lacks spatial integrity and is fundamentally non-contemporaneous with itself, in the sense that it circuitously condenses a multiplicity of "interpenetrating temporalities" from past, present, and future, the African "postcolonial neocolonised world" might then be conceived as an inherently spectral terrain.•[18] To put it another way, contemporary postcolonial Africa, by remaining

13 • Ibid.: 8; For a lengthier account of the coloniality of being, see Sylvia Wynter, "Unsettling The Coloniality of Being/Power/Truth/Freedom: Towards The Human, After Man, Its Overrepresentation - An Argument," *The New Centennial Review*, Vol. 3, No. 3, Fall 2003, 257-337.

14 • Kwame Nkrumah, *Neocolonialism: The Last Stage of Imperialism*, (London: Thomas Nelson & Sons, Ltd.), 1965.

15 • Jacques Derrida, *Specters of Marx: The State of Debt, the Work of Mourning and the New International*, 1994, 1.

16 • Ibid.: 20.

17 • Sabelo J. Ndlovu-Gatsheni, *Coloniality of Power in Postcolonial Africa: Myths of Decolonisation*, (Dakar: CODESRIA), 2013, 12.

18 • Achille Mbembe, *On the Postcolony*, (Berkeley, Los Angeles, and London: University of California Press), 2001, 14

discursively and materially constituted to a large extent by the not-quite-present shadows, illusions, myths, and abstractions of both Eurocentric coloniality and African decoloniality, engenders a warped space-time in which absences, more so than positivist presences, animate life, culture, and politics. As Mbembe maintains, referring to the interlocking temporalities of African social formations, "it may be supposed that the present as experience of a time is precisely that moment when different forms of absence become mixed together: absence of those presences that are no longer so and that one remembers (the past), and absence of those others that are yet to come and are anticipated (the future)."•[19] It is precisely this entangled, hauntological terrain of present-absences that *Testament* and *Transfigured Night* self-reflexively elucidate and materialise through their poetic, docufictional lamentations, which I will now turn to.

A BRIEF INTRODUCTION

Testament and *Transfigured Night* both utilise cinema and its structuring aesthetic logics as formal and allegorical vehicles to convey the complex and spectral spatio-temporal entanglements that characterize the African postcolonial condition. Produced a quarter of a century apart, both works meditate on the devastating "failures" of mid-century African decolonisation movements. *Testament* meanders through the rivers of historical memory like its protagonist, Abena, a TV reporter who returns to Ghana two decades after the 1966 military coup that ousted Kwame Nkrumah from power and which brought an abrupt end to the experimentalist spirit of Pan-African socialism. Abena's return from exile in Britain is prompted by an opportunity to report on Werner Herzog who happens to be filming *Cobra Verde*, 1989, in her West African coastal homeland. Under the auspices of this meta-cinematic, intertextual narrative, Abena visits friends who she had known as fellow activists while at the Nkrumah Ideological Institute. To Abena's frustration, none of her friends want to speak to her; no one forthrightly explains to her what happened to the country after she left. Like a ghost, Abena wanders through emptied Ghanaian landscapes, contending with a traumatic history that refuses to cohere into a singular form, a history of loss that is rather structured by irretrievable, gaping silences – historical absences that have been "lost to memory." Occasionally, the film's narrative is interrupted by a procession of Ga women mourners whose funerary chants cry out to the ancestors (the importance of which I will return to later) and archival fragments from the immediate post-independent period detailing the rise and fall of Nkrumah's leftist political party, the Convention People's Party.

Transfigured Night takes on a similar structure but unfolds via two conversant screens. In the work, about a third of the length of *Testament*, Akomfrah combines archival footage, depicting euphoric independence rallies and street processions as well as ensuing episodes of postcolonial state decay and civil war, with wide-shot angle tableaux of enigmatic Black subjects in a range of pastoral and urban settings staring out into the distance. The Washington Monument and the Lincoln Memorial feature heavily in this work as ideologically loaded icons of postwar global coloniality, oscillating in time between John F. Kennedy's diplomatic reception of newly elected postcolonial leaders in Washington DC in the early 1960s, including Tafawa Balewa (Nigeria's first prime minister), Félix Houphouët-Boigny (the Ivory Coast's first president), and Jawaharlal Nehru (India's first prime minister), and contemporary shot footage of tourists and young Black men populating the National Mall. Titled after Arnold Schoenberg's string sextet composition, *Verklärte Nacht*, 1899, which in turn was adapted from Richard Dehmel's poem of the same name, *Transfigured Night* unfolds over five stanzas mimicking, in an intertextual moment of decolonial détournement, the structure of its fin de siècle literary and musical references. More so, *Transfigured Night* reconfigures, *transfigures*, if you

19 • Ibid.: 16.

will, its European continental sources by adapting the thematics elaborated in Dehmel's poem – of a man's loving acceptance of a pregnant woman who tells him her baby is by someone else – to the postcolonial African context – of the postcolonial subject's euphoric embrace of the postcolonial state, despite its colonial baggage – therefore allowing for a forceful cross-cultural allegorical migration. Subtitled *Five Allegories of the Narcoleptic State*, *Transfigured Night* further allegorizes an observation noted by Fanon, that "After independence, the [national] party sinks into a profound lethargy," to comment on the hindered postcolonial state who, after achieving its independence, falls into a trauma-induced narcoleptic slumber and thereafter suffers from cataplexic episodes of political and social volatility engendered by the state's spectral possession by the colonial matrices of power.•[20] Before I elaborate on the allegorical dimensions of these works, and their spectral underpinnings, I would first like to discuss how both works use montage, the archive, and the ontological specificity of the moving-image to reflect on and materialize the very spectral postcolonial conditions that they signify.

THE ARCHIVE AS FORM, PROCESS, AND GHOST RESIDENCE

Black Audio Film Collective has long been preoccupied by the open-ended possibilities offered by a meticulous attention to and careful deconstruction of the archival image. Emerging in 1980s Britain in the midst of great social unrest stemming from racial antagonisms, BAFC sought to articulate what it meant to be both Black and British in the wake of the country's postwar and postcolonial societal transformations. The seven members of BAFC, including John Akomfrah, Reece Augustine, Edward George, Lina Gopaul, Avril Johnson, Trevor Mathison, and David Lawson (who replaced early member, Claire Joseph) all constituted a distinct social formation in the nation's history, as the first African, Afro-Caribbean, and South Asian population, of an unprecedentedly large size, to have grown up in the UK. BAFC's members were the product of a mass migratory flow of formerly colonised subjects from the imperial peripheries to the British metropole after WWII, a process necessitated by the flailing British economy's need to fill its labour shortages. This migratory process, and the rapid demographic shifts it produced, forced upon the white British population a historical reckoning with Britain's deep colonial entanglements, which said population unsurprisingly reacted to with anxiety-ridden episodes of racial violence and amnesiac disavowal.•[21] BAFC was formed in 1982 in response to this moment of national amnesia, energised by the then-emerging postcolonial and cultural theoretical discourses of Stuart Hall, Paul Gilroy, Homi Bhabha, Kobena Mercer, and others. All art school undergraduates at the time, its members came together in various British cities to pose nuanced, theoretical questions rather than express didactic and reactive political positions.•[22] Mobilizing the "Black" in BAFC as a politicized term to encompass a multiethnic coalition of former British colonial subjects and their descendants – a strategy in line with the British Black Power movement of the 1960s and 1970s – BAFC went on to produce pioneering works, such as *Expeditions I & II*, 1982-84, which sequences 35mm slide tapes, layered with colonial archival imagery, transfer typefaces, and ambient soundscapes, that prod the ideological construction and visual representation of imperial fantasies, and the well-known *Handsworth Songs*, 1986, which challenges the conventional documentary form through its

20 • Fanon, 115. Cataplexy is defined in *Transfigured Night* as a rare condition affecting those who suffer from narcolepsy, whereby there is a "sudden loss of muscle tone often triggered by emotions such as laughing, crying, and terror."
21 • One might recall Enoch Powell's infamous "Rivers of Blood" speech, delivered in 1968, which provoked and legitimated white, anti-immigrant sentiments; the seemingly endless list of racially motivated riots that erupted all over Britain in the latter half of the 20th century, such as the Notting Hill riots in 1958, the Brixton riots in 1981, and the Handsworth riots in 1985; and the litany of 21st century racialised political incidents, one of the most recent being The Windrush Scandal of 2018 wherein nearly a hundred people of Afro-Caribbean descent were wrongfully detained and threatened with deportation by the Home Office.
22 • Zoe Whitley, "Geography Lessons: Mapping the Slide-Tape Texts of Black Audio Film Collective, 1982-84" in John Akomfrah, *Signs of Empire*, (New York: New Museum), 2018, 11.

poetic and multi-perspectival meditation on the 1985 London and Birmingham race riots. The film collective dissolved in 1997.[23]

BAFC's aesthetic approach is animated by a critical awareness of the (post)colonial archive as a systematised *form* structured by mechanisms of power that determine what, where, and who shall be documented, and on what terms. This understanding of the archive, following Foucault, as the "law of what can be said" and as a "system that establishes statements as events and things" encourages an active, process-oriented relationship towards the archive's ideological conditions of possibility.[24] If the archive is conceived in this way, as a material sedimentation of a *selectively chosen* past that attempts to fashion a certain historical narrative in accordance with a set of hegemonic ideological visions, rather than as a neutral document that can be approached at face value, one might better apprehend its inherently spectral dimensions. This is to say that the archive's spectral quality arises from its exclusionary logic of selection whereby for every historical event that is included, another one is excluded, denied, forgotten, ignored, or silenced; and so haunting every archival image is the immaterial shadow of an ideologically suppressed historical event or an absented subaltern subject. Therefore, the archive, like the postcolonial African condition, remains littered with ghostly absent-presences.

These half-absences are further reflected, more generally, in the very ontology of the cinematic image, which as Derrida argues, possesses a "spectral structure."[25] This is because the moving image both (partially) indexes a past event through technological capture and uncannily reanimates it in the present in the form of, say, a character's voice or bodily gestures. By giving a "thereness" to the "no-longer," a living presence that is both actual, in that it constitutes a re-staging of real affects in the material world, and virtual, in that it illuminates a world that is not physically there, moving images resemble and inhabit the "non-sensuous sensuous" character of the specter.[26]

Testament uniquely materializes the (post)colonial archive's gaping absences and cinema's inherent spectrality through its very mode of production. Akomfrah, speaking of the "wall of silence" he encountered in making the work, mentions "When I realized we couldn't do a straight-forward historical account of what happened because of the lack of testimonies or archives, it became clear to me that we needed a guide."[27] This guide ended up being the character of Abena who in failing to definitively know what happened to Ghana in the wake of its post-independence decline mirrors Akomfrah's ambivalent relationship with the archive as both a trace and a negation of the past. In *Testament*, Abena's return to post-independent Ghana is met with a series of absences, not only in the stunted and sparse dialogues with her reticent friends – who symbolise the ways in which trauma, as inflicted on postcolonial subjects, inhibits cognitive faculties of recall – but in the visual absence of monuments and records that could testify to the prior presence of Nkrumah's Pan African socialist regime. Akomfrah, like Abena, experienced this "theft of memory" first-hand when he mentions that, while filming in Ghana, "it was illegal to talk about Nkrumah, one couldn't even mention his name, it was illegal to make a film about the CPP, the party that he led."[28] Akomfrah has relatedly spoken of the "absence of ruins," a term borrowed from Orlando Patterson, to describe the lack of physical monuments to the Black experience in the modern world, which leads Afro-diasporic filmmakers to contend with and obsess over what Derrida calls the "tangible intangibilities" of history.[29] Akomfrah describes this

23 • Following the dissolution of Black Audio Film Collective in 1997, three of its members – Akomfrah, Gopaul, and Lawson – went on to form a film and television company by the name of Smoking Dogs Films.

24 • Anne Laura Stoler, "Colonial Archives and the Arts of Governance." *Archival Science 2*, 2002, 94.

25 • Jacques Derrida quoted in "Cinema and Its Ghosts: An Interview With Jacques Derrida," *Discourse*, Volume 37, No. 1-2, Winter/Spring 2015, 26.

26 • Jacques Derrida, *Specters of Marx: The State of Debt, The Work of Mourning and the New International*, 1994, 6.

27 • Kobena Mercer, "Postcolonial Trauerspiel: Black Audio Film Collective," in *Travel & See: Black Diaspora Art Practices since the 1980s*, (Durham and London: Duke University Press), 2016, 286.

28 • John Akomfrah quoted in an interview with Stoffel Debuysere: "The Politics of Mourning," *Diagonal Thoughts*, 2014: https://www.diagonalthoughts.com/?p=2115.

29 • Ibid. See also Jacques Derrida, *Specters of Marx*, 6.

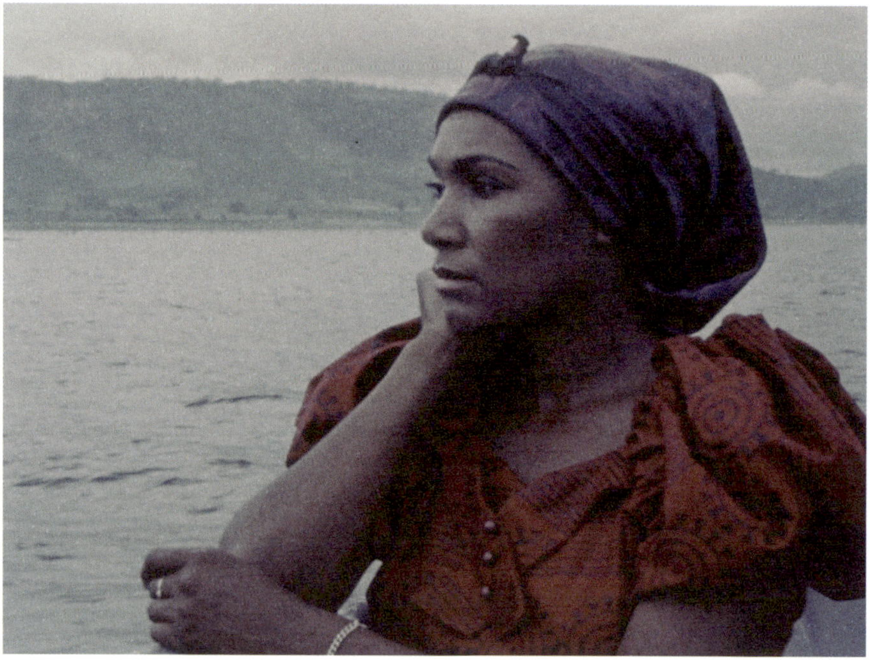

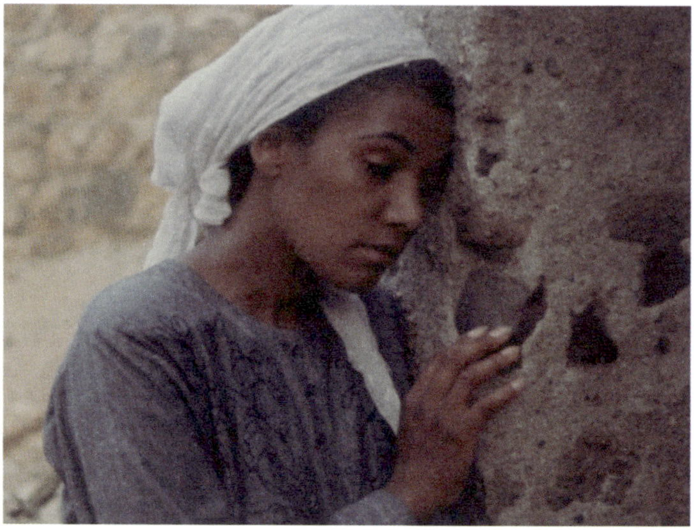

John Akomfrah, *Testament*, 1988. Colour film. Dimensions variable. 79 minutes.

tendency in Black filmmaking and aesthetic practice as a form of "necrophilia" as Afro-diasporic artists continually engage with the dead, the no-longer, the by-gone subaltern subjects who have been erased from history and "lost to memory."•[30]

What one then finds in *Testament* is not an empirical positivist response to the archive's historical absences, which would presume that such absences could simply be filled to assume a prior wholeness, but a formal meditation on the epistemic limits of the archive, and by extension, on the fictive construction of history as well as history's fraught relation to memory. BAFC's deployment of montage is crucial in figuring the complex fragmentation of African postcolonial space-time, which as *Testament*'s evocative subtitle suggests is a "war zone of memories."•[31] By assembling fragments from a multiplicity of archival sources and juxtaposing them with shot footage, akin to the excavation-driven method of the Benjaminian "bricoleur," *Testament* not only represents the irresolvable plurality of collective memory, and thus the impossibility of fashioning a singular perspective of history, but paradoxically gives affective presence to history's irretrievable absences.•[32]

One sees this clearly at play in *Transfigured Night:* while the viewer visually observes three newly elected leaders from formerly colonised territories being received by JFK in Washington DC, the center of the so-called free world, one simultaneously observes a series of textual excerpts, many of which were penned by radical, leftist, Pan-African leaders, activists, and intellectuals, silently opening each of the film's five chapters. We read Nkrumah's galvanizing statement of Third World, Non-Alignment solidarity, "We face neither East nor West: we face forward;" the melancholic words of Amílcar Cabral (the Bissau-Guinean, Pan-Africanist leader), delivered as a speech on the occasion of Nkrumah's death in 1972, "What should we say, because we must speak at this point. If we don't, our hearts may burst;" and Frantz Fanon's sobering, anti-colonial proclamation, "Each generation must, out of relative obscurity, discover its mission, fulfill it or betray it."•[33] Akomfrah's textual orchestration of this polyphony of radical, anti-colonial possibility, loud yet silent, haunts the filmed diplomatic convenings in Washington DC, revealing the invisible machinations of the coloniality of power through the notable corporeal absences of Nkrumah, Cabral, Thomas Sankara (first president of Burkina Faso), Patrice Lumumba (first prime minister of the Democratic Republic of the Congo), Julius Nyerere (first president of Tanzania), and a host of other revolutionary political leaders in the US capital during this period of Cold War ideological contestation. These anti-colonial leaders constituted a threat to the post-war, geopolitical world order given their refusal to align with either the liberal, capitalist West or the authoritarian, communist East.•[34] As *Transfigured Night* carefully "shows," through the incorporation of anti-colonial textual excerpts and visual archival material depicting ensuing civil wars and regime changes in Africa and Asia, such radical dissidence was typically eliminated through militaristic assassination (often, aided by Euro-American intelligence agencies) as was the case with Lumumba, Sankara, and Cabral, or through political depositions, as was the case with Nkrumah.

Testament and *Transfigured Night* thus embody a paradoxical filmic ontology whereby, through their montage-led construction, which draws "affective proximities" between an incommensurable variety of images, texts, and sounds, what is lost to memory

30 • John Akomfrah quoted in an interview with Kass Banning: "Feeding off the Dead: Necrophilia and the Black Imaginary," *Border/Lines*, No. 29/30, July 2016.
31 • Kobena Mercer, "Postcolonial Trauerspiel: Black Audio Film Collective," 2016.
32 • Akomfrah, speaking of his method of bricolage, specifically in relation to *Seven Songs for Malcolm X*, 1993, says "The attempt is to find a solid thing and when you can't find it you begin to literally patch it together which is a process of mummification of ideas in a way:" Kass Banning, "Feeding off the Dead: Necrophilia and the Black Imaginary," *Border/Lines*, No. 29/30, July 2016.
33 • John Akomfrah, *Transfigured Night*, 2013.
34 • This anti-colonial, revolutionary attitude defined an emergent political consortium of newly independent, postcolonial states in Africa, Asia, and Latin America during the Cold War, which came to be known as the Non-Aligned Movement. The Non-Aligned Movement was formally established in 1961 in Belgrade, Yugoslavia, although its history can be traced to a series of internationalist, diplomatic convenings organized throughout the 20th century, stretching from the well-known Afro-Asian Conference held in Bandung in 1955 to the first Pan-African conference held in 1900 in London. Kwame Nkrumah and Jawaharlal Nehru (who both visually feature in *Transfigured Night*) as well as Gamal Abdel Nasser (president of Egypt), Sukarno (president of Indonesia), and Josip Broz Tito (president of Yugoslavia), were responsible for initiating the Non-Aligned movement.

is not visually represented in a frontal manner but comes to haunt the frame, and the viewer, by virtue of a forceful absence.[35] This aesthetic strategy, which surrounds and gives shape to the inarticulable, materialises the workings of the specter which is at once present and absent, dead and live, here and not-here.

A CINEMA OF AFFECT: FROM HISTORY TO MEMORY

While BAFC and Akomfrah engage in the bricoleur's task of burrowing through the filmic wreckages of modernity, composing non-linear, multi-locational filmic assemblages that materialise the spatio-temporal disjuncture of the postcolonial realm, these fragments are additionally re-composed and re-contextualised into altogether new forms that open up latent, repressed and alternately possible historical pathways for the contemporary viewer. Following on from our earlier discussion of the archive as a formalised ideological construction, one might view *Testament* and *Transfigured Night*, and the entirety of BAFC and Akomfrah's oeuvre, as aesthetic attempts to shift the archival image from the fixed, singular, and objective realm of history to the fluid, collective, and affective realm of memory. Pierre Nora writing on the difference between history and memory notes:

> "Memory is life, always embodied in living societies and as such in permanent evolution, subject to the dialectic of remembering and forgetting, unconscious of the distortions to which it is subject, vulnerable in various ways to appropriation and manipulation, and capable of lying dormant for long periods of time only to be suddenly reawakened. History, one the other hand, is the reconstruction, always problematic and incomplete, of what is no longer."[36]

According to Nora, memory is vague and impressionistic, "a phenomenon of emotion and magic," whereas history, being supposedly universal and truth-seeking, calls for "analysis and critical discourse."[37] What Nora's argument seems to imply is that memory is history's unprocessed fodder material, which the historian must then analyse and organise, in other words, discipline, into an objective, factual narration. The political danger of historicisation, however, lies in the historian's non-acknowledgement of the ideological framings that always already shape and determine the conversion process from memory into history. Put another way, the historian risks erasing their own subjective enmeshment and affective investment in the historical account they are attempting to establish, giving rise to a false objectivity that, as BAFC and Akomfrah show, may be induced by the pathological delusions of colonial amnesia. A return to memory, particularly those possessed by marginalised, subaltern subjects – what we might call "counter-memory" – exposes the gaps and fissures in the official historical record, and in doing so reveals history itself to be a fictive, constructed and narrativised process that is, like memory, privy to volatile, ambivalent processes of remembering and forgetting.[38]

In both *Testament* and *Transfigured Night*, the archival image is layered with colour tints and emotive sonorities, and cut into elliptical narrative sequences in a way that dislodges the fixity of its supposedly objective historical meaning. In the latter work for instance, the viewer repeatedly observes a suited-up, middle-aged man who blankly stares out of the window from a corporate office in a skyscraper

35 • "John Akomfrah: In Conversation with Fawz Kabra," *Ocula*, July 2018: https://ocula.com/magazine/conversations/john-akomfrah/.
36 • Pierre Nora, "Between Memory and History" in *Realms of Memory: The Construction of the French Past*, Volume I – Conflicts and Divisions, trans. Arthur Goldhammer, (New York: Columbia University Press), 1996, 3.
37 • Ibid.
38 • According to Foucault, constructing a counter-memory involves the "recording of the singularity of events outside of any monotonous finality." Counter-memories thus constitute a protest against the finitude of homogenizing historicist reason. This resistance to homogeneity, as we will soon see, forms an essential ethical dimension of spectropoetics. Foucault cited in Stoffel Debuysere, "Signs of Struggle, Songs of Sorrow: Notes on the Politics of Uncertainty in the Films of John Akomfrah," *Black Camera*, Volume 6, No. 2, 2015, 61-78.

building located somewhere in the West. As a close up of the man's introspective face appears on the left screen, the viewer witnesses on the right screen the unfolding of a series of historical events, such as a parade in Ghana wherein a car bearing C.P.P. letters makes its way through a busy crowd, and Houphouët-Boigny's stately descent from a private jet that has just arrived in the US. The juxtaposition of these moving images via the dual screens' spatial arrangement re-contextualises the archival fragments as subjective memories being by recalled by the enigmatic man, whose age suggests that he may have indeed witnessed these historical events for himself. Furthermore, the dense urban architecture of International Style skyscrapers that populate the man's highline view – glass-sheathed edifices that house the world's corporations and which, in turn, signify as domineering monuments to the homogenising spread of global financial capital – have been notably coloured with an icy blue tint, affectively alluding to historical registers of social, political, and psychological alienation produced by the coloniality of power and its specifically neoliberal capitalist manifestations from the 1970s to the present day.

One can also observe the memorial mobilisation of colour in *Testament* in Abena's lonely wandering through the tonally washed out landscapes of the Ghanaian coastline – chromatic inversions that subversively challenge depictions of West Africa as a warm, tropical paradise.[39] Also in *Testament*, archival footage showing Ghanaians burning a heap of Marxist books – what better way to demonstrate a collective ritual of forgetting – is followed by clips of protests, imbued with a bloody red tint, of Ghanaians demonising Nkrumah and his allegedly corrupted leftist governance. In these ways, colour manipulation functions as an aesthetic mode to convey inarticulable individual and collective psychic conditions, particularly as they pertain to the ghostly postcolonial space-time of loss – loss engendered by the violence of coloniality and by the ejected political dream of a liberated decolonial future.

These works further punctuate and enliven the archival image with their ambient soundscapes. Given the visceral, vibrational nature of sonic transmission, the viewer of these sensorially immersive films is placed more firmly in an affective relation to history's ambiguous visual traces. For instance, in *Transfigured Night*, as Tafawa Balewa ascends the steps of the Lincoln Memorial with JFK, and their respective political aides, a palimpsestic assembly of ominous sounds fill the frame, deferring any possibly hegemonic celebratory reading of the diplomatic gathering. These spectral sonorities instead *foreshadow* decades of neocolonial economic servitude and imperial political interreference that would proceed from this era of post-independence optimism. Such incorporated sounds, like Schoenberg's dramatic string composition, produce lamentational auditory affects that at once pierce the conventional reception of the archival clips, thereby disrupting their prior chain of signification, and establish sensorial proximities between seemingly disparate filmic fragments, giving form to a melancholic cinematic poem that in turn approximates the fluid, inner workings of memory. Thus, the continuous and elliptical back and forth, in time and place, between the diplomatic pleasantries in Washington DC and the euphoric, night-time celebrations of independence in Ghana in the early 1960s, the explosive scenes of militaristic violence and national conflict that would follow in Africa and Asia in the late 1960s and 1970s, and the luxuriantly shot contemporary tableaux (echoing the European Romantic sublime) of back-facing figures staring out unto the Washington Monument, the Lincoln Memorial, and the moody skies that hover over them, engenders an aesthetics of ambiguity that refuses clear-cut historical answers – the conventional imperative of the documentary genre – and instead embraces the uncertainty of the postcolonial subject's disjunctive relation to past, present, and future.

Through this affective activation of archival fragments, BAFC and Akomfrah produce what Laura Marks, following Deleuze, calls an "optical image"

39 • See "The Otolith Group (Kodwo Eshun and Anjalika Sagar) in Conversation with Naomi Beckwith," *Nka Journal of Contemporary African Art*, No. 34, Spring 2014.

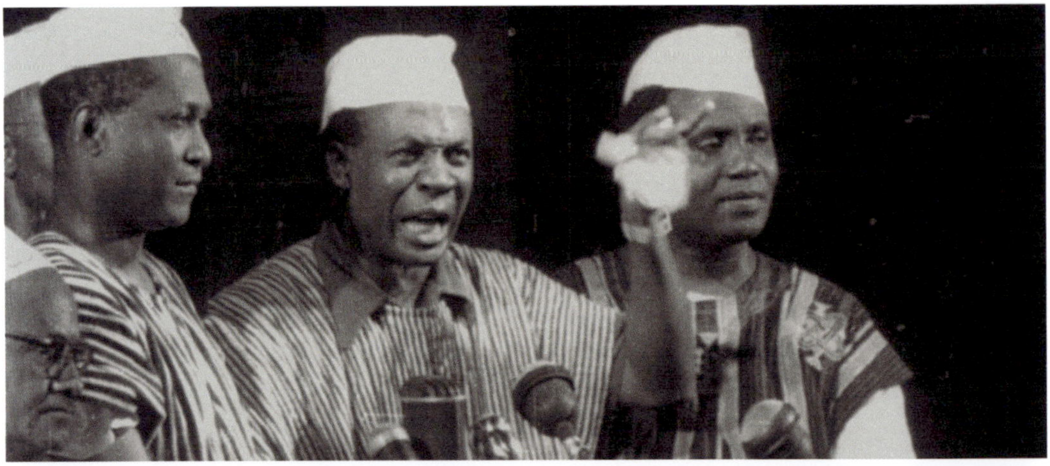

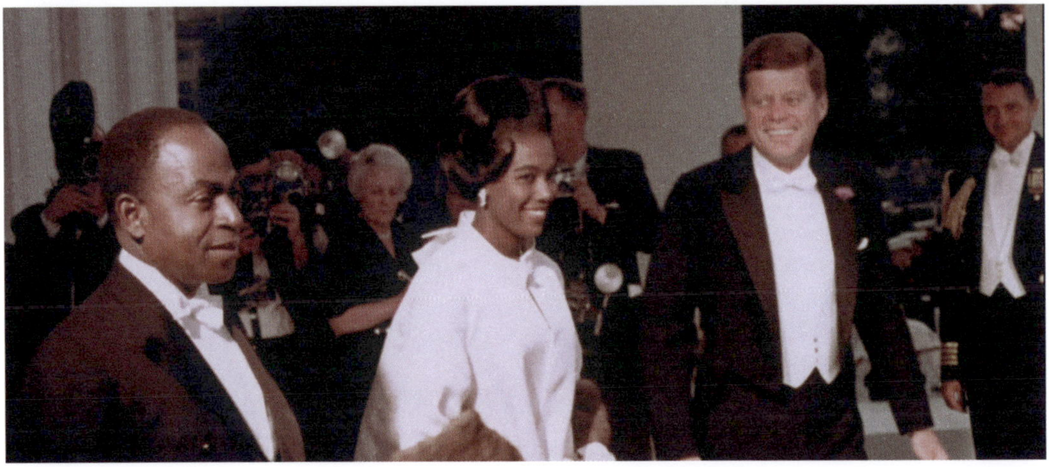

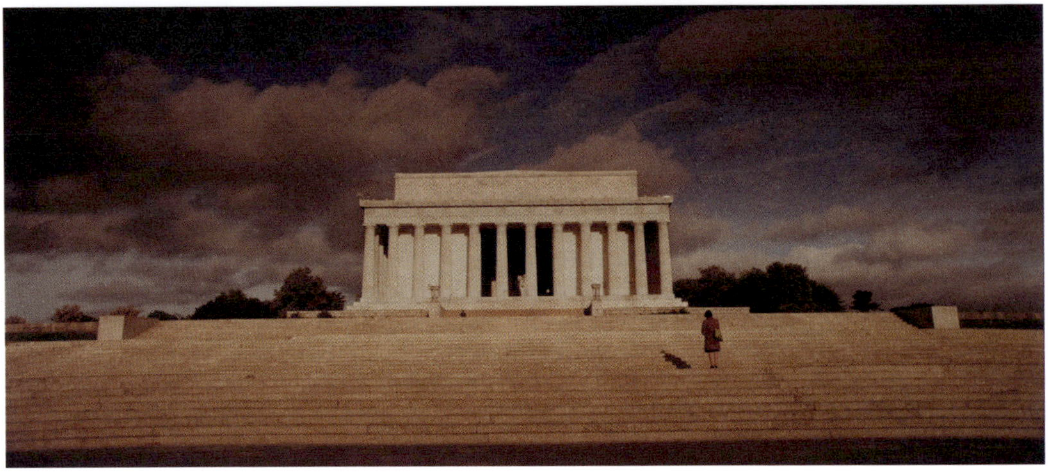

John Akomfrah, *Transfigured Night*, 2013. Two channel HD colour video installation, 5.1 sound. 26 minutes 31 seconds.

which "defamiliarizes the cliché by severing it from its context."[40] Marks essentially argues that optical images free and abstract images from their hegemonic meanings, bleeding them of their overdetermined signs – therefore making them "thin" – which then allows the viewer to generate new meanings by parsing connections between what they see and what they subjectively know or can remember.[41] Optical images therefore necessarily explode singular historical meanings and invite multiple interpretations by opening unto affective planes of colour and sound that exceed orders of the "sayable."[42] This unsayable element of the moving image, which implies a disturbance in the viewer's ordering of knowledge, resonates with what Roland Barthes theorizes as the photograph's punctum, which "pricks" the viewer by constituting an "incapacity to name" and a "subtle beyond" in the photograph's visual texture.[43] The specter, then, as a "non-present present," which following Derrida, "no longer belongs to knowledge" and exceeds knowledge as such – through affect, like the punctum – might be most powerfully conjured through the optical image.[44] Put differently, the optical image's simultaneous semiotic decontextualisation and affective saturation with colour and sound, by respectively approximating the specter's resistive assimilation to knowledge and traumatic memory's inarticulable relation to the past, allows it to become a primal visual site of haunting.[45]

ALLEGORICAL MIGRATIONS: GRIOT AESTHETICS, GA COSMOLOGIES, AND IMAGE AFTERLIVES

Derrida conceives of the occasion of haunting as one that imposes a set of ethical demands on the subject that is haunted. To be haunted by a specter, according to Derrida, is to be made aware of the other within yourself, to be impregnated by the other.[46] Rather than eliminate these othered (non-)presences – these specters – Derrida asks that we live with them and welcome them, rather than bury or exorcise them. The implication of this ethical relation, occasioned by haunting, is a conception of justice that is structured by multiplicity, by heterogeneity: "Guaranteed translatability, given homogeneity, systematic coherence in their *absolute forms*, this is surely ... what renders the injunction, the inheritance, and the future—in a word the other—*impossible. There must be* disjunction, interruption, the heterogeneous if at least *there must be, if there must be* a chance given to any "there must be" whatsoever, be it beyond duty." (italics original)[47]

The violence of homogeneity is enacted when memory is disciplined into history, when rhizomatic entanglements are fashioned as linear, discrete units, when the dead are indeed believed to be dead. *Testament* and *Transfigured Night* forthrightly work against this homogenising logic by inviting the specter's irrepressible and irreducible otherness. We see this in the works' montage construction, which pulls from and reconfigures a multiplicity of visual fragments, archival or otherwise; in the incoherent, overlapping sonic registers that form the works' polyphonic soundscapes, including voices, texts, musical scores, noise, and folk chants; in the layered intertextual, cross-cultural references weaved into the works' cyclical narratives, from Schoenberg's composition and European Romantic painting, to Ghanaian folklore and radical anti-colonial thought; and in the works' unwillingness to come to any firm

40 • Marks interprets Deleuze's understanding of the cliché as a "commonsense, hegemonic image which extends unproblematically into action." See Laura U. Marks, *The Skin of the Film: Intercultural Cinema, Embodiment and The Senses*, (Durham and London: Duke University Press), 2000, 46.
41 • Ibid.: 47.
42 • Ibid.: 30.
43 • Roland Barthes, *Camera Lucida: Reflections on Photography*, trans. Richard Howard (New York: Hill & Wang), 1982, 51 & 59.
44 • Jacques Derrida, *Specters of Marx*, 1994, 5.
45 • T.J. Demos theorises a concept related to the optical image, which he calls a "cinema of affect." Demos uses this term to describe the work of Zarina Bhimji, another Afro-diasporic British artist that, like Akomfrah, emerged in the context of the 1980s British Black Art movement. Demos notes that the "emotional expression" and "informational negation" in Bhimji's works (which are of a greater degree than in Akomfrah's works, one might argue) reflects the psychoanalytic observation that "shocking events [which are responsible for traumatic experience] tend to overflow the language of comprehension, interrupting its ability to communicate." See T.J. Demos, "Ghostly Affect: Zarina Bhimji's Yellow Patch" in *Return to the Postcolony: Specters of Colonialism in Contemporary Art*, (Berlin: Sternberg Press), 2013.
46 • Tyson Stewart, *Cinema Derrida: The Law of Inspection in the Age of Global Spectral Media*, (New York: Peter Lang), 2020, 19.
47 • Jacques Derrida, *Specters of Marx*, 1994, 42.

conclusions – *Testament* ends ambiguously with Abena seeing a skull in a opened grave while *Transfigured Night* ends without really ending, with its final chapter titled "The Beginning." Through these considered aesthetic gestures – of which their meticulous attention to the filmic archive and its repressed spectral energies is most crucial – BAFC and Akomfrah create an open, indeterminate space for the specter to inhabit.

Such heterogenous openings are generated by these works' rich, allegorical structures. At certain points in *Testament,* the multivalent question of whether two bodies can be one is posed. The same question seems to haunt *Transfigured Night*, and the fin-de-siècle poem after which it takes its name. Dehmel's poem narrates the story of a man and woman walking through the woods at night under a radiant moon. The pregnant woman tells the man "I am carrying a child, and not by you. I am walking here with you in a state of sin." The man assuredly says to her "Do not let the child you have conceived be a burden on your soul ... there is the glow of an inner warmth from you in me, from me in you. That warmth will transfigure the stranger's child." Akomfrah uses this poem's thematisation of fraught romance to capture the postcolonial subject's acceptance of the vexed postcolonial state, an acceptance tacitly signified by the cheering masses seen at the many African independence ceremonies in the 1960s, which like in Dehmel's poem, often occurred at night. In the beginning of *Transfigured Night*, we observe archival footage of Nkrumah addressing his (juridically) liberated countrymen, stating "We must change our attitudes, our minds. We must realise that from now on, we are no longer a colonial but a free and independent people."[48]

If, as was argued earlier on, that the postcolonial state inherited many of its repressive pathologies from the colonial state, then the postcolonial state may be figured here as the pregnant woman in Dehmel's poem. In other words, one might say that the African postcolonial state, which was brought into being on the eve of independence, was pregnant with the specter of coloniality – a specter that frustrates and thwarts its achievement of decolonial liberation. This symbolised understanding returns us to a related early sequence in *Testament*, described at the beginning of this chapter, where we see conjoined twins on a surgical table, and who later in the film undergo a procedure of separation. Given what comes before and after this archival footage, the scene is recontextualised as a fitting metonym for the postcolonial subject's desired separation of the postcolonial state from the colonial state, its shadow twin. As Okwui Enwezor notes when analysing this scene, it is unclear whether the surgery succeeded, whether one of, both, or none of the twins survived the procedure.[49] Similarly, one is led to ponder whether such separability is possible, if in fact, two bodies – in this case, the postcolonial subject and the postcolonial state – can be one.

In approaching these historical questions through the use of dense, multivalent allegories, I would like to argue that Akomfrah mobilises the aesthetic sensibilities of the West African griot, and in the process becomes a "griot of the image."[50] Griots are traditionally responsible for the intergenerational transmission of memory and employ a variety of oral storytelling strategies to fulfil their vital societal function. Imbued with an irreducible orality, the griot's narrative mode is structured by performative "conventions of voicing (singing, recitation, and the vocalization of everyday speech forms)," "the deployment of traditional motifs," "the use of mythological symbols," and "the strategic inclusion of panegyric".[51] Akomfrah, like many African artist-filmmakers who have preceded him, such as Ousmane Sembène and Souleymane Cissé, draws on the griot's art as a way to decolonise cinema's objectifying gaze and narrativizing logics. Given that filmic technology is a Western modern invention that is inextricably bound up with the ideological conceits of the imperialist project – the

48 • John Akomfrah, *Transfigured Night*, 2013.
49 • Okwui Enwezor, "The Wreck of Utopia: Alienation and Disalienation in John Akomfrah's Postcolonial Cinema" in John Akomfrah, *Signs of Empire*, (New York: New Museum), 2018, 89.
50 • Peter Hitchcock, "Risking the Griot's eye: Decolonisation and Contemporary African Cinema," *Social Identities*, Volume 6, No. 3, 2000, 264.
51 • Ibid. 265.

camera's function of visual *capture* being the condition of possibility of the colonial administration's representational, and thus epistemological, domination of the racialised Other – film's very materiality becomes ambivalent aesthetic territory for artists and filmmakers of African descent who must contend with its historical and ongoing role in colonial violence and dispossession. BAFC and Akomfrah mindfully work with and against cinematic technology, not only through formalist avant-gardist methods of montage, colour filtration, and sound scoring that forensically deconstruct and dislodge the epistemic orderings of the imperial filmic archive, but also through détourning these very artistic methods by locating their methodological affinities with indigenous African griot aesthetics. Put another way, BAFC and Akomfrah's decolonial critique of the cinematic image is both immanent and external, deconstructive and reconstructive.

Peter Hitchcock, paraphrasing N.F. Ukadike, notes that griot aesthetics involves "shifting points of view across time and space, digressions, a story-within-a-story narrative progression, a search or journey, and the juxtaposition of mythological symbols or figures between the past and present." These are all aesthetic strategies that are present in both *Testament* and *Transfigured Night*. Speaking on *Testament*, Akomfrah expressed "this is one of the few films I've made, that when you show it to a ten year old in Ghana they'll know exactly what the film is about!"•[52] Akomfrah is referring to *Testament*'s visual, sonic and narrative engagement with Ghanaian folklore. For instance, the film's colour tints, while they perform an affective punctuation of the cinematic image, doubly refer to Ga colours of mourning: "You're either, in [the] case of red, angry, black, you're resigned to, white, you're definitely very depressed, and blue, you feel a mixture of anger and depression. So every color in the film is coded in the folk psyche."•[53] Similarly, *Transfigured Night*'s soundscape is littered with the fleshy, oral presence of West African folklore songs from the 1920s and 1930s, which oscillate between melodic chants and breathy glossolalia. Through a multi-sensorial, cinematic textualisation of these folkloric cultural references, Akomfrah's works extend the legacy of the griot who must, out of social, ethical, and historical responsibility, speak to his or her society, in this case, Ghanaian society.

Like the griot, Akomfrah's works do not rely on a singular, dogmatic form of story-telling but rather draw on "tenacious contextualization" and the "art of embellishment" to suit the historical moment of postwar, postcolonial disillusionment.•[54] As Hitchock writes "The main interest for the royal griot was not the historical facts surrounding a hero, but the lively and compelling way in which the narrative could be delivered. The lessons of the story produce a historical lineage even if a particular history itself cannot be proved."•[55] While BAFC and Akomfrah have purposively strayed away from delivering any kind of straightforward moral lesson, therefore diverging from the ethico-political directives of prior anti-colonial film movements like Third Cinema in the 1960s and 1970s, their films have consistently relied on allegory to blur the boundaries between history and fiction – a strategy that reveals and reflects on the fictive construction of history. (Allegory might be conceived as a spectral form of narration given its use of motifs and symbols as screen signifiers to point to visually absent historical people and events.) Akomfrah explains that the move away from moral and political directness (which was what imbued Third Cinema with its militant urgency and sense of certainty) reflected an attitudinal shift amongst disillusioned leftist filmmakers in the 1980s who were living through the aftermath of post-independence state failures and the (re) consolidation of global coloniality: "'third cinema' is a certainty which simply cannot be spoken anymore. A certainty of place, location and subjectivity. What now characterizes the 'truths' of cinema, politics and theory is uncertainty."•[56]

52 • John Akomfrah quoted in an interview with Stoffel Debuysere: "The Politics of Mourning," *Diagonal Thoughts*, 2014: https://www.diagonalthoughts.com/?p=2115.
53 • Ibid.
54 • Peter Hitchcock, "Risking the Griot's eye: Decolonisation and Contemporary African Cinema," 2000, 265 & 279.
55 • Ibid. 279.
56 • John Akomfrah quoted in an interview with Stoffel Debuysere: "The Politics of Mourning," *Diagonal Thoughts*, 2014: https://www.diagonalthoughts.com/?p=2115.

Such uncertainty is not inherently pessimistic and does not close off the desire for and achievement of utopian, decolonial possibilities. Conversely, I argue that Akomfrah's multivalent, heterogenous method entails the opposite by maintaining an "open door policy" with the dead.[57] At certain moments in *Testament*, a procession of Ga women mourners enters into the frame, momentarily decentering Abena's protagonistic search for the absent ruins of Ghana's Pan-African socialist past. These oral mourners, known as Adowafoi in Ga society, are invited to funerary ceremonies by families of the recently deceased to communicate with the spirit ancestors through lamentational, aestheticised speech and song.[58] However, in *Testament*, the mourners do not lament the death of an individual subject but rather an abstract, collective loss engendered by the arrested utopian aspirations of mid-century decolonisation and the ongoing infliction of colonial trauma. At one point, the mourners sing, in harmony, "We are calling on history today," and after invoking some ancestors' names, "Reveal to us your spirit of defiance. Your kinfolk are dying. Did you forsake us before dying? Had we already lost at the time of your death? What pact did you make with the foreigners? That they now control our lives?"[59]

These performative funerary chants reflect the cosmological structure of Ga (and many other West African) systems of thought, which take as a given the ontological suturing of the material and immaterial worlds. Whereas mortals inhabit the material world, deities and ancestors reside on an adjoining spiritual plane and possess the ability to interfere in the affairs of the physical world, not unlike the spectral interferences of coloniality. More specifically, ancestral spirits maintain a greater proximity to the material realm, and act as mediators between their mortal descendants and the gods and the Supreme Being[60] Through rituals and evocations, such as those performed by the mourners, humans call on their ancestors for divine intercession, in order to preserve the well-being of the living and of the society. These funerary rites are held to allow the spirit of the recently deceased to cross over from the physical realm into the spiritual realm where the ancestors reside. What Ga systems of thought offer, I argue, is a decolonial understanding of spectrality – an alternative, indigenous mode of conceiving of the non-separability of the living and the dead, the material and the immaterial, the here and the not-here.

In *Testament*, BAFC and Akomfrah cleverly inflect Ga cosmologies through critical theoretical conceptions of spectrality, as elaborated by European philosophers like Derrida. For example, the phrase, "rivers of memory" – visualised in the first scene as the Volta River – may at once allude to the fluid, uncontainable multiplicity of collective memories and to the divine knowledges of the Ga river gods. What this allegorical, cross-cultural modality offers is not only a critical historiographical reflection on the postcolonial African condition – what I have argued is a spectral condition – but an epistemological shift in how that condition is *understood*, a shift that (re)centers subjugated African indigenous ways of knowing and being.

Consider BAFC's grafting of the mourners' ritualistic orality unto the modern cinematic apparatus. According to the Ga, these funerary chants reaffirm the unity of the spiritual and physical worlds, and reflect their beliefs that the death of the deceased is not indeed a termination of their existence but the beginning of a new life.[61] What if we viewed the cinematic image in this manner? What ethical possibilities would such an understanding offer us? Following T.J. Demos, who seemingly riffs on Giorgio Agamben's ideas of potentiality, one might argue, as Akomfrah does, that every cinematic image possesses an "afterlife," an immanent futural possibility of a "viewing-time-to-

57 • John Akomfrah, "Memory and the Morphologies of Difference," in *Politics of Memory: Documentary and Archive*, eds. Marco Scotini and Elisabetta Galasso, (Berlin: Archive Books), 36.
58 • Barbara L. Hampton, "Music and Ritual Symbolism in the Ga Funeral," *Yearbook for Traditional Music*, Vol. 14, 1982, 76.
59 • Black Audio Film Collective, *Testament*, 1988.
60 • Barbara L. Hampton, "Music and Ritual Symbolism in the Ga Funeral," 1982, 86.
61 • Ibid. 86. The mourners are additionally seen pouring libation on the ground which is a ritualistic gesture that in many West African contexts signifies the acknowledgment of the (spiritual) presence of the dead.

come."[62] Therefore, even though the moving image – archival or otherwise – indexes that which is no longer (and thus contains latent, spectral energies), its ontological capacity for endless re-stagings – in different spaces and times, and with different audiences – entails an immanent resistance to finality and closure, to homogeneity. This is to say that every moving image, at the moment of its making, embodies a "semantic surplus" that exceeds its original use and intent.[63]

This resistance to closure, entailed by an ethical willingness to feed and attend to the ghosts of history, rather than bury or ignore them, lends *Testament* and *Transfigured Night* their unique affective power and structures their appeals to decolonial justice. Through these works' irreducible unfinishedness, the viewer is keyed into a melancholic space of present-absences that characterises the postcolonial African condition. The affective transfer of melancholic unease from the screen to the viewer, spurred by an audiovisual encounter with the specter – either in the form of a historical revenant or a troubled ancestral spirit – produces an ethical imperative of a "something-to-be-done."[64] To be haunted by these works is to be made aware of the non-presentness of the (postcolonial) present. More so, it is to be impregnated with an unyielding desire to dismantle coloniality's ongoing domination and bring about the as-yet-unrealised dream of African decolonisation.

62 • Demos, on the "afterlife of the image," writes, "This imaging and viewing-time-to-come define a utopian dimension intrinsic to image making, a virtual futurism embedded in cinema as a political ontology of endless materialization and anticipation." See T.J. Demos, "Feeding the Ghost: John Akomfrah's Vertigo Sea" in *Beyond The World's End: Arts of Living At The Crossing* (Durham and London: Duke University Press), 2020. For a theoretical engagement of the cinematic image's afterlife with Agamben's theory of potentiality, see A.S. Grønstad, "Archival Ghosts or the Elsewhere of the Image: John Akomfrah" in *Rethinking Art and Visual Culture: The Poetics of Opacity,* (London: Palgrave Macmillan), 2020, 77-101.
63 • A.S. Grønstad, "Archival Ghosts or the Elsewhere of the Image: John Akomfrah," 2020, 89.
64 • I am borrowing this phrasing, of the ghost's incitation of a "something to be done," from Avery F. Gordon. See Avery F. Gordon, *Ghostly Matters: Haunting and the Sociological Imagination*, (Minneapolis and London: University of Minnesota), 1997, 202.

BOUCHRA KHALILI and KJ ABUDU in CONVERSATION

What does it mean to inherit? Who speaks when someone speaks? These are just some among many other thought-provoking questions that the French-Moroccan artist, Bouchra Khalili, asks during our rich discussion. I have been fortunate to include Khalili's formally rigorous, historically saturated, and gracefully poetic works in both the first and second iterations of *Living with Ghosts*. During our conversation, we unpack Khalili's varied critical impulses, conceptual methodologies, and aesthetic influences, covering a fifteen-year span of the artist's focused, accumulative practice, from *The Mapping Journey Project*, 2008-2011, to *Foreign Office*, 2015, to the recently produced *The Magic Lantern,* 2022. These film-based installation works sensitively explore subterranean histories of (post)colonial worldly entanglement, moving effortlessly between the mid-20th century era of Third World revolutionary struggle, the contemporary Mediterranean migration crisis, and constellative genealogies of lens-based media technologies. Without doubt, what we find here – via our discussion of montage, orality, historiography, political solidarity, and filmic ontology – is a committed art practice that speaks on, with, through, and beyond the thematic concerns of *Living with Ghosts*.

KJ ABUDU In our prior conversations, you've spoken at length about your interest in montage, as concept, as form, and as methodology. Montage, at its basis, involves the suturing of multiple, disjunctive fragments to form a filmic whole. One could therefore say that montage speaks a cinematic language of irreducible heterogeneity. In *Specters of Marx*, 1994, Derrida argues that such heterogeneity is a necessary condition for the conjuring of specters in so far as the spectral encounter bears the trace of a radical foreignness that disturbs linear conceptions of time – relatedly, the singular "voice" of hegemonic historical narratives – and the spatial fixity of geographic coordinates.[1] Your works, such as *Foreign Office*, 2015, and *Garden Conversation*, 2014, cleverly orient montage towards a poetics of the spectral via their visual, textual, and lyrical evocation of Third World

1 • Jacques Derrida, *Specters of Marx: The State of the Debt, the Work of Mourning and the New International,* trans. Peggy Kamuf (New York and London: Routledge), 1994, 42.

internationalist histories – we move imaginatively from Algeria and Morocco to Palestine and Cuba, from Guinea-Bissau and the United States to Oman and Mozambique. The haunting gaps and slippages that arise between these montaged times, places, and the figures therein, point to the paradoxical (im)materiality of the specter's absent-presence, to its *haun(on)tology.* You've similarly spoken of the fact that many of your works are constructed from a "missing image," in other words, they take their shape from an archival lack, from the impossibility of fashioning a complete historical account of a particular era from a particular point of view. Could you speak more about the function of montage in your work and the multiple levels through which it operates in your practice?

BOUCHRA KHALILI I'm essentially interested in the "unarchived." In his writings on the image, Pierre Reverdy provides a potential definition of montage: "The image is a pure creation of the mind. It cannot be born from a comparison but from a juxtaposition of two more or less distant realities. The more the relationship between the two juxtaposed realities is distant and true, the stronger the image will be—the greater its emotional power and poetic reality."[2] This potential definition of montage as a conceptual, intellectual, and poetic practice has ever since haunted filmic approaches that conceive moving-image-making as the production of constellations formed of varied material across media, genre, time, and space. It echoes Walter Benjamin's conception of the "constellation" where he states that "image is dialectics at a standstill. For while the relation of the present to the past is purely temporal, the relation of what-has-been to the now is dialectical: not temporal in nature but figural. Only dialectical images are genuinely historical."[3] From that perspective, montage is indeed the "tool" as much as the method for excavating the manifestastions of the "unarchived" as it can potentially bear witness to a future. Using the word "tool," I also refer to montage as a manual labour. When editing, it is indeed the hands that "think." Many of my works, including *Foreign Office*, show young non-actors performing their "selves" while simultaneously "editing" heteregeneous fragments with their hands. These fragments are mostly photographs printed on basic paper or pictures on cellphones and video monitors, as in *Twenty-Two Hours*. Using their hands, they quite literally embody the function of the *passeur*. In French, a *passeur* can refer to a ferryman, a smuggler, or someone who passes something with their hands unto someone else. Within a cinephilic context, shaped by cinematheques as free film schools, the *passeur* is the one who transmits the transhistorical "promise of a world." I'm here referring to the seminal film critic, Serge Daney, whose work is unfortunately still little translated into English. Daney popularised the use of that word for defining the role of film programmers, critics, and movie lovers as knowledge disseminators. The late Nourredine Saïl exemplified the function of the *passeur* in Morocco in the 1970s – an era of fierce repression – during which he established the National Federation of Film-Clubs, smuggled films into Morocco, and even organised secret screenings of radical cinema that animated debates on the future of postcolonial cinema in the region. In that sense, Saïl strongly believed that the *passeur* of images contributed to disseminating a "decolonial promise" that is still yet to be achieved.

2 • Pierre Reverdy, "L'image," *Nord-Sud*, Issue 13, March 1918, 3.
3 • Walter Benjamin, *The Arcades Project*, trans. Howard Eiland (Cambridge, MA: Belknap Press/Harvard University Press), 2002, 462.

In *Foreign Office*, *Twenty-Two Hours*, or *The Magic Lantern*, the protagonists pass images to each other, thus forming constellations, in order to examine how to excavate that promise, and therefore how to inherit and transmit it. That's why within my practice, what could be labeled as "the archive" is only a deceptive presence of it. Such material – from its absence – is only made present to generate gestures of montage. Inès, Fadi, Quiana, and Vanessa – the featured non-actors in these works – do not wear gloves when handling the archival material, as is common when touching such items. On the contrary, they are all performing a "manual work," the work that comes with thinking with one's hands in the vast editing suite that is history-writing, which, for them, equals reclaiming it from the hands of power.

Within this configuration, the progatonists are constellation-makers: assembling with one's hands the traces, signs, marks, and words left of a potential unarchived future still yet to come into being. Thus, the "constellations maker" is the one who can hear and speak the voices of ghosts, provided that the manual labour of making constellations is performed on the assembling/dis-assembling/re-assembling line of montage.

KA Montage, as you suggest, carries with it the formal possibility of materialising an anti-colonial chrono-politics, that is, a differential relation to time, memory, and history that unsettles the organising logics of (neo)colonial historiography. Many of your works embody this historiographic transgression through their cool destabilisation of past, present, and future. Although the works often address seemingly bygone events from the mid-20th century – Algiers as a revolutionary mecca between 1962 and 1972 or Jean Genet's secret visit to the United States in 1970 at the invitation of the Black Panther Party – they are typically narrated, interpreted, or one might say, resurrected, by young searching figures in the contemporary moment. In bringing elapsed decolonial futures from the no-longer to bear on the now, your works articulate the spectral co-presence of past, present, and future within the fractured realm of the postcolonial. You've spoken about this persistent hauntological thematic – of ghosts calling from a colonial past that is not past, and also from a decolonial future that has not yet arrived – in relation to Pasolini's proposal for film as "free indirect speech." Could you elaborate further on Pasolini's ideas, who I'm aware is a very important figure in your practice, and how his philosophy of film has influenced your approach to time?

BK I've been a reader of Pasolini's poetry for more than two decades now. Since then, I have been meditating on his unachieved proposal for a "heretical" film semiotics. But it is one of his most famous poems that comes first to my mind: "I'm a force of the past. My love lies only in tradition ... I see the twilights, the mornings over Rome, the Ciociaria, the world, as the first acts of Posthistory to which I bear witness, for the privilege of recording them from the outer edge of some buried age."

Pasolini, the poet, positioned himself as a witness to the haunting force of a past calling for, and from, a future still yet to come into being. He calls that future "posthistory," which to me sounds not too far from Benjamin's messianic conception of history.

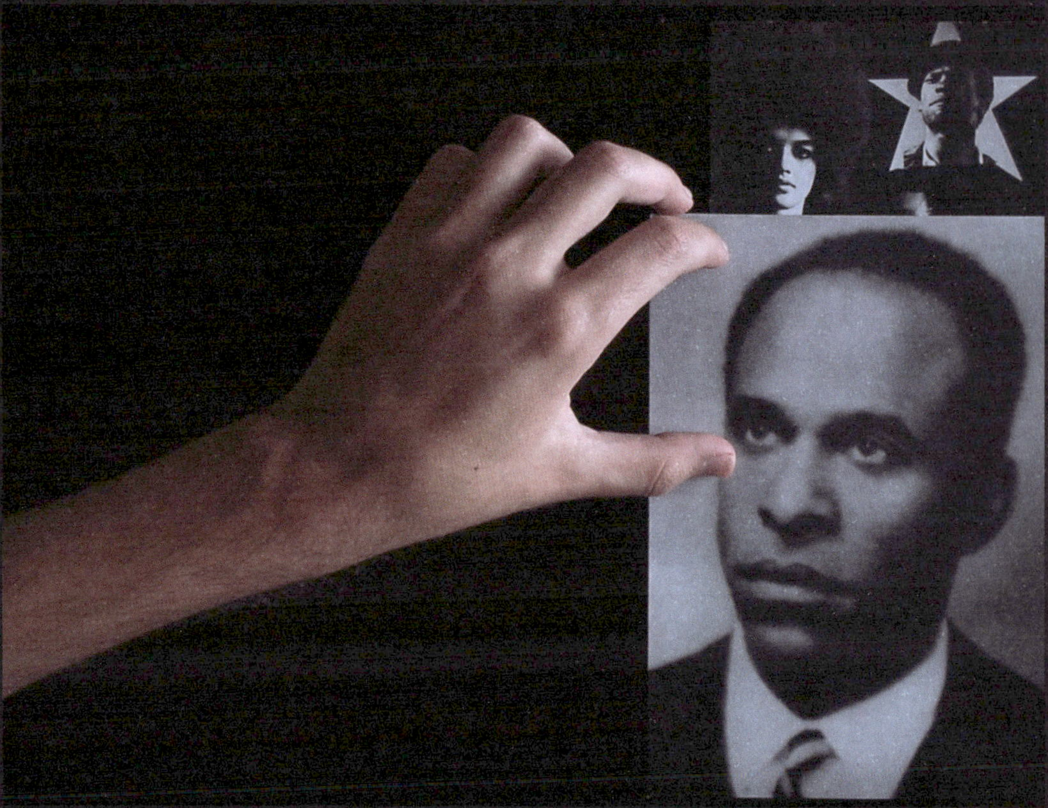

Bouchra Khalili, *Foreign Office*, 2015, video still

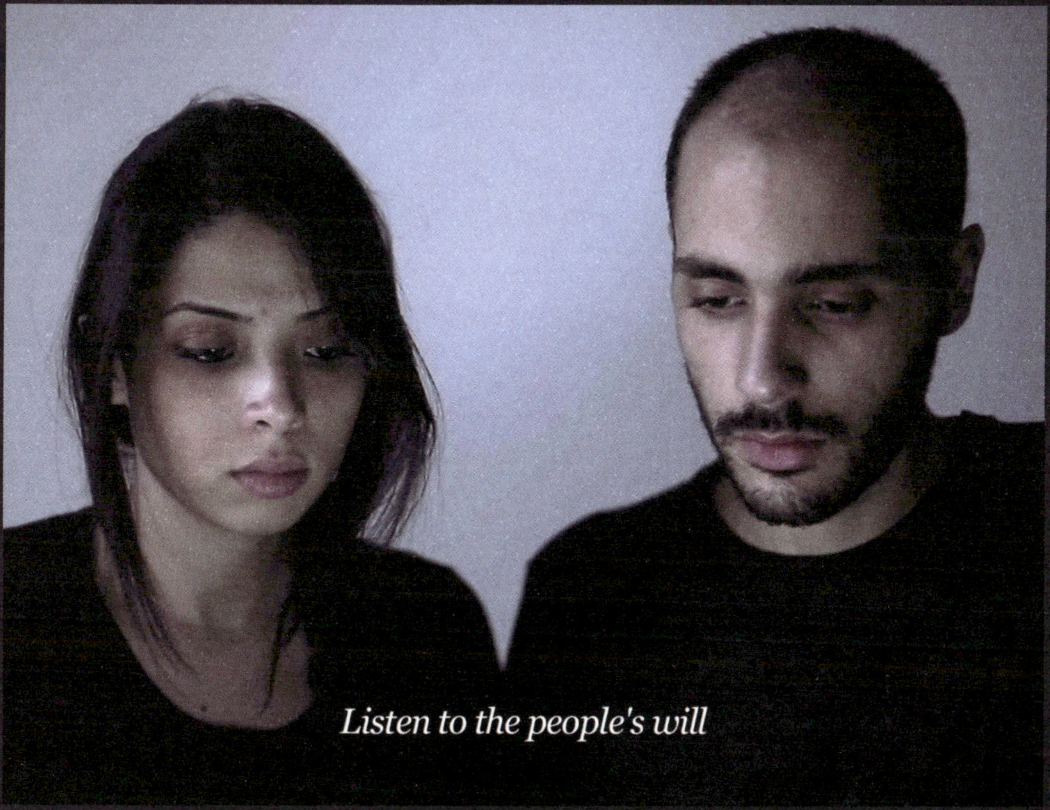
Listen to the people's will

Similarly, in his film semiotics, Pasolini envisions a "cinema of poetry" shaped by the use of "free indirect speech" in film. Free indirect speech is an operation of linguistic and stylistic contaminations that allows multiple voices and languages to come together. In his two volumes on cinema, Gilles Deleuze extensively examined Pasolini's ideas. Deleuze openly addressed the many difficulties that Pasolini's concepts involve: they remain nebulous both because Pasolini left only a few essays behind and also because these concepts are nowhere to be found in Pasolini's own films. However, Deleuze decided to take seriously Pasolini's proposals and use them to identify markers of radical modernity, based on examinations of speech-acts in film: "The speech-act becomes an act of story-telling ... 'the flagrant offence of making up legends' [*légender*], and which takes on the political dimension of the constitution of a people."•4 What Deleuze understands of a Pasolinian free indirect speech in film is how it manifests the form of a "missing people" (*le peuple qui manque*) as a potential community to come into being.

So to answer your question, my interest in free indirect speech as a technic of equality for speech-acts in filmic works relies on its promise that it can allow us to picture a community to come into being. In my films, the protagonists may be alone; nevertheless, they are speaking/spoken (by) a multitude of voices across time and space.

KA As you've just hinted at, Pasolini's meditations on speech are clearly related to your work's deep sensitivity to language. In all your works, from the *The Mapping Journey Project*, 2008-2011, to the more recent *Magic Lantern*, 2022, the narrators or witnesses speak a multiplicity of languages that include English, French, and multiple Arabic dialects. The subject of speech is also made unstable as the work sometimes begins with an individual voice which then gradually morphs into a collective voice. At first, because of the work's demonstrated concern with language, not to mention its quasi-theatrical staging of young narrators, as well as its internal division by "chapters," I took its textuality to be primarily literary in spirit – hence my initial proposal to re-print the dialogue from *Garden Conversation* in this publication. In this work, you fabulate a dialogue that purportedly took place in Cairo in 1959 between Che Guevara and Abd el-Krim Khattabi, drawing on these figures' writings, interviews, letters, and speeches. In responding to my proposal, you warned that the dialogue should not be accessed merely textually – it had to be *voiced*, orally performed. Your emphasis on a verbalised mode of reception reminded me of the fraught relation between written and oral forms of recording history and producing testimony (the latter of course being rather dominant within many regions on the African continent). Relatedly, I'm thinking about your works' meta-performative qualities. In *Garden Conversation*, *Foreign Office*, *Twenty-Two Hours*, and also in *The Magic Lantern*, the narrators, by reading out writings penned by past revolutionaries, typically in a very passive, unaffected manner, appear to be uncannily ventriloquised by the wandering ghosts of these unresolved histories. I'd love for you to offer some insights into your interest in speech, orality, and performance, and what relationships they bare on the connections between aesthetics and politics, between poetry and revolution.

4 • Gilles Deleuze, *Cinema 2: Time-Image*, trans. Hugh Tomlinson and Robert Caleta, (University of Minnesota Press, Minneapolis), 1989, 243. First published as *Cinema 2, L'image-temps*, (Paris: Edition de Minuit), 1986.

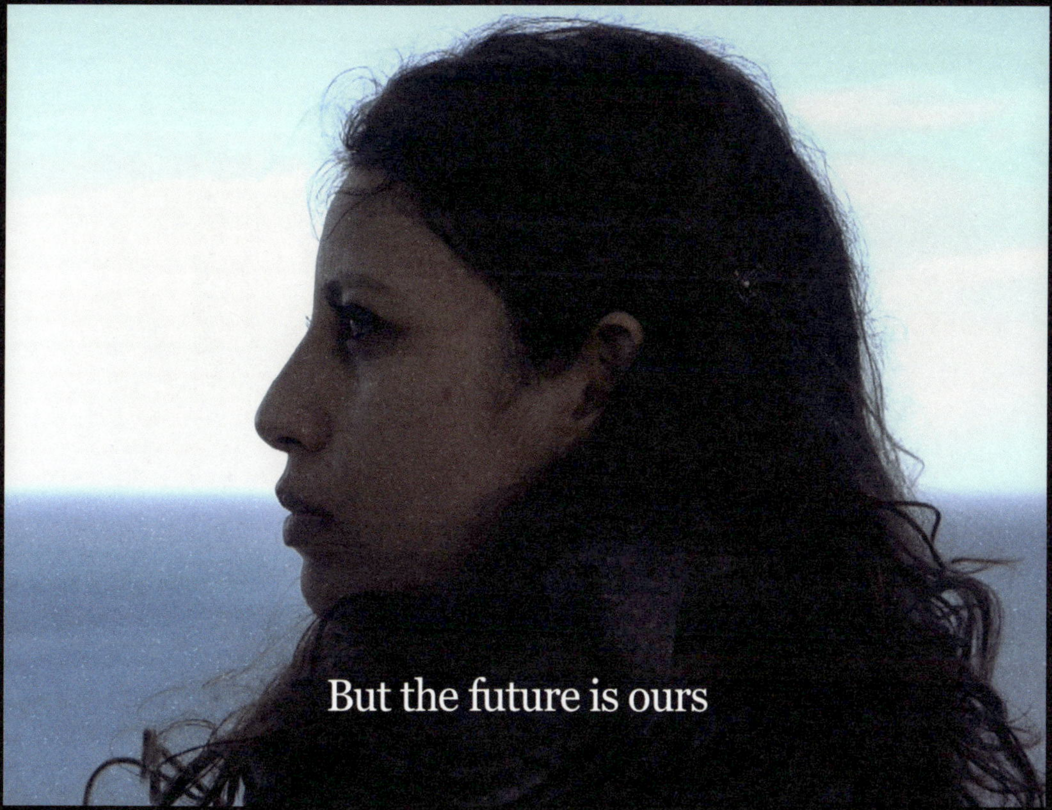

Bouchra Khalili, *Garden Conversation*. Digital film. 2014. Color. Sound. 18'.
Courtesy of the artist and mor charpentier, Paris

BK To clarify one point, in *Garden Conversation*, *Foreign Office*, *Twenty-Two Hours*, and also *The Magic Lantern*, the protagonists don't read but have memorised their own speech-acts, which they then recite. What you call meta-performance originates for me from a question: in a film, *who speaks when someone speaks*? It's exactly the question underlying the notion of "free indirect speech" – allowing a multitude to speak. For *The Mapping Journey Project*, memorisation was not involved. It instead involved long conversations that lasted weeks, during which I did not ask questions, but rather listened. This formed the space and time required for survivors of perilous journeys of forced illegal migration to appropriate their own voice and story. This methodology is the subject and core of my trilogy, *The Speeches Series*, 2012-2013, which examined speech acts and language as a form of resistance and agency.

For *The Mapping Journey Project*, I called that method "Writing without writing." But even for works such as *Garden Conversation*, *Foreign Office*, *Twenty-Two Hours*, *The Tempest Society*, or *The Magic Lantern*, the logic is not that different. First, the protagonists of those works are not professional performers. Secondly, the protagonists perform their selves although they are very much conscious that their own voice articulates multiple ones. They very well know that they don't speak alone: others are speaking through their body, their voice, and through the multiple languages that are woven together.

This specific type of performance is at the intersection between the "Brechtian" distancing effect and the old tradition of Al Halqa, the most ancient form of public storytelling in Morocco, which is very similar to the tradition of the Djelli or Griot in West Africa. The performer of Al Halqa moves freely between registers and languages, blending ancient poetry, oral tales, episodes of the Sunna of the Prophet (delivered in classical Arabic), and jokes narrated in oral forms of Arabic and/or Tamazight, the native language of North Africans. The performer is at once "ventriloquised" by a tradition and embodies the voice of the living archives of the people. However, there's in my practice a refusal of the performative as commonly conceived. This cool distancing effect is meant to create a dialectical tension between identification and "opacity," as defined by Édouard Glissant.[5] One could also speculate even further that opacity is part of the spectrality you referred to earlier. The refusal of the performative can then be conceived as a form of resistance to appropriation through identification.

Finally, if I'm reluctant to print the "scripts" of my filming work it is essentially because I do not dissociate words and sound from images. In film, sound is also image. I make a point at recording synchronised sound and not using voice-over precisely because I approach sound and spoken words as integral parts of the moving image. For that reason, I cannot conceive spoken words in my filmic work as a literary material: its "aurality" cannot be dissociated from the experience of watching the films.

KA Let's talk about the specificity of the moving image, about the technological predicates of the cinematic apparatus and its structural relation to the conjuring of phantoms, spirits, and ghosts. Referring back to Derrida once more, in a 1998 interview in *Cahiers du Cinema*, he argues that the cinematic image possesses an inherently spectral structure: "The cinematic experience belongs thoroughly to

5 • Édouard Glissant, *Poetics of Relation*, trans. Betsy Wing, (Ann Arbor: University of Michigan Press), 1997, 189-191.

spectrality, which I link to all that has been said about the specter in psychoanalysis—or to the very nature of the trace. The specter, which is neither living nor dead, is at the center of certain of my writings, and it's in this connection that, for me, a thinking of cinema would perhaps be possible."•6 Derrida speaks of the cinematic theatre (and we might extend this to the art gallery) as a hauntological site in which ghosts appear and speak on and through the screen; they are "projections" that are at once actual and illusory, liquidating the temporal borders between a past recording and a contemporary re-staging.

Your most recent work, *The Magic Lantern*, not only meditates very precisely on this collision of hauntology and lens-based technology, but interpolates this *spectrological* juncture through histories of revolutionary action. Contrary to, though not in total disagreement with those who posit lens-based technology as *inherently* colonial and anti-Black, this work instead traces an emancipatory genealogy of such technology through modernity's *longue durée*. The work looks at the camera's prehistories as the "magic lantern" and the "fantascope" in Western Europe from the 17th to the 19th centuries, showing how these devices were used to allow audiences to mourn and dialogue with the ghosts of revolutionaries. We're then thrusted into the short 20th century with figures such as Carole Roussopoulos who employed the video camera as a witnessing tool in many sites of Third World struggle, from Algeria to Jordan and Palestine. Weaving in various historical narratives from your prior works, we learn of Roussopoulos' entanglement with radical figures such as Eldridge Cleaver, of the Black Panther Party, who viewed the video camera as a "revolutionary tool" that could liberate the masses in Africa, and around the world. How would you position your practice in relation to these histories of lens-based media? Might one approach your work as a spectrological vehicle of melancholic mourning? As harbouring hope in the emancipatory potential of film and video? To what extent do you remain wary of the camera's darker, more violent histories, and how have such histories influenced the kinds of cinematic images you make?

BK The notion of spectrality in film is as old as cinema itself. Maxime Gorky, in a famous article about his first encounter with cinema, described the screening he attended as a visit to "the Kingdom of Shadows." George Méliès' movies were also populated by ghosts and were at the same time dream-like speculations on a promising future shaped by technological progress. In his famous essay, *Ontology of the Photographic Image*, André Bazin attempted to define an ontology of lens-based media shaped by our obsession for "embalming" time. He proposes that such media offer a technology for preserving life from a second death. And I won't even mention the tradition of spirit photography and its long cohort of ghosts, which still continues today with pictures produced by cell phones. If we go even further back, Fantasmagorias and Magic Lantern performances were popularised as a "spectrology" as early as the 18th century.

But I need to clarify one point here: in *The Magic Lantern*, the transition from the late-18th century's fantasmagorias to Carole's use of a portapak comes with a depiction of a series of historical events throughout the 19th century. These events shifted the use of magic lanterns from a "revolutionary technology for revolutionaries"

6 • Jacques Derrida quoted in "Cinema and Its Ghosts: An Interview With Jacques Derrida," *Discourse*, Volume 37, No. 1-2, Winter/Spring 2015, 26.

to mainstream forms of entertainment that served in popularising colonial expansion. In its first part, *The Magic Lantern* historicises the reactionary appropriation of this technology as well as attempts to "resurrect" its original emancipatory vocation. The apparition of Carole and her Portapak is thus contextualised within this conflict between the colonial continuum and a tradition of resistance.

A second point I would like to address is an aspect of my method. The works you mentioned – *Foreign Office*, *Twenty-Two Hours*, and *The Magic Lantern* – were developed simultaneously and in parallel although it took years to produce each of them. One could also easily consider that Carole herself is a ghost that haunts my work as she and her camera already appear in the first two works even though they do not seem to relate directly to an ontology of lens-based media. However, in these three works, images – printed and/or displayed on screens – are the tools par excellence for excavating an unachieved promise, for "calling the ghosts of the future."

To clarify another point, Cleaver did not view video technology as a tool to "liberate the masses" but as a tool to "produce our own information." Producing one's own information may sound like a very modest goal for a revolutionary, but it captures a potentially profound transformation: destroying dominant and oppressive representations that contributed to fostering the colonial gaze, and therefore colonial and imperial domination as much as white supremacy.

My deep commitment to the notion of opacity in representation can seem paradoxical as opacity implies a refusal of transparency. But from where comes the injunction to become transparent? Essentially from power and its technologies of control. As an image-maker, I nevertheless remain suspicious of the mythology of the image "revealing" a truth. Who defines this truth, and for what purpose? The fact is that most of the images to which we are exposed are pre-existing ones, pre-conceived ones. To give you an example, in the early 2000s, I was spending a lot of time between Northern Morocco and Southern Spain. I remained deeply shocked by what I witnessed in the South of Spain: each time a "patera" was landing, a cohort of Spanish reporters would show up, holding their video cameras, ready to capture the images of the survivors. I remained haunted by the symbolic violence of such behavior and the resulting media reports.

Most of the reports aimed at documenting these forced illegal journeys included images of silent and suffering Black and brown women and men, with no other voice than the one of the reporter, the presenter, or a voice-over. To quote the words of sociologist Patrick Champagne, who refers to the representation of minorities in media: "They are spoken of more than they speak."[7] Following Glissant, I believe that respecting the opacity of otherness opens us up to a decolonised conception of universality. And even when faces are shown in my works, there's still a sense of opacity that is preserved, relying on the "distancing effect" on which I've elaborated earlier.

KA I would like to return to something I briefly elaborated on at the beginning of this conversation, which is the sense of geographic flux one gets from your work. Because your works are often dealing with leftist internationalist movements and figures, they often become impressed with a transgressive migratory logic, one that has little

7 • Patrick Champagne, "The View of the Media," in Pierre Bourdieu's *The Weight of the World: Social Suffering in Contemporary Society* (Stanford, CA: Stanford University Press), 1993.

regard for national borders or essentialist affiliations. Whether it's Jean Genet's involvement with the Black Panther Party and the Palestian Fedayeen or Amílcar Cabral's meetings with Eldridge Cleaver and other Black Americans, what we can observe in these historical moments is, to borrow Édouard Glissant's term, a "poetics of relation," put to practice.•8 Glissant famously speaks of a poetics of relation as a way to relate to and be with the Other without losing oneself, as a method of remaining situated in local conditions while maintaining an openness to the world. One could argue that such radical praxes of transnational, multiracial solidarity have come under attack in recent years, not only due to the debilitating effects of global capitalism, but also as a result of the ossification of so-called "identity" based politics and its attendant logics of cultural/racial homogenisation, ownership, and "representation." Further, such myopic and reductionist logics have only been exacerbated by binaric algorithms on social media platforms, which disallow any sort of messy, nuanced discourse – the stuff of imaginative, transformative politics. I wonder what solidarity looks like to you in the 21st century and how we might practice it, not just in our critical and artistic work, but also in our everyday lives?

BK You're asking a question I could answer only if my job as an artist were done. The basic truth is that if I still produce works, it is to ask questions to myself in the first place. And once I can phrase the question for myself, I can share it with others.

I can start with summarising the question that probably informs my practice from the very beginning: why have several generations of North Africans since independence been forced into exile? And from there, comes another question: why did anti-colonial struggles, engaging with international solidarity, consider that liberation would be achieved with the establishment of new nation-states? If we accept the idea that nation-states define citizenry by exclusion, what then is the horizon of international solidarity if these struggles settle for a form of citizenship shaped by colonial states? It may sound like a polemical question but it is this very question that prevents me from developing a sense of nostalgia or melancholia with regard to the internationalist era.

In our conversation, you have at several occasions quoted Derrida and his notion of "hauntology." His theory poses a question that we have not discussed yet: what does it mean to inherit? One can understand Derrida's hauntology as the inheritance of what is still yet to come. Within that context, inheriting is not a passive gesture but involves looking backwards in order to identify what/who is the specter to come. As such, hauntology can be understood as a proposal for a politics of memory that allows us to envision a collective future. Of course, it is not by chance if many of my works situate at their core transgenerational transmissions of suppressed histories or investigate the position of the "witness" to emancipatory ideas. And if young women and men populate my filmic works it is because they endorse a heritage, and from the position of the "heir," they can bear witness to the future.

I can't predict the future of international solidarity and certainly not at a moment when nationalism and racism are reaching new heights in recent history. What I see now is an urgency to think a politics of memory that allows us to face the question: how can we fully achieve equality?

8 • Édouard Glissant, *Poetics of Relation*, 1997.

Lives of the Past: Annotations on Abraham Oghobase's CONSTRUCTED REALITIES

by EMMANUEL IDUMA

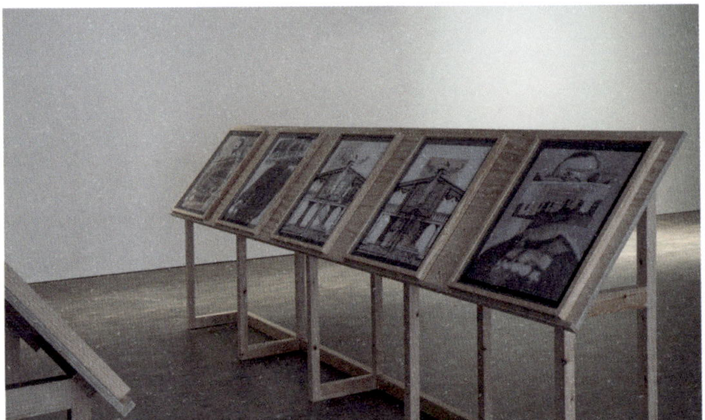

Living With Ghosts, Installation View
Pace Gallery, London

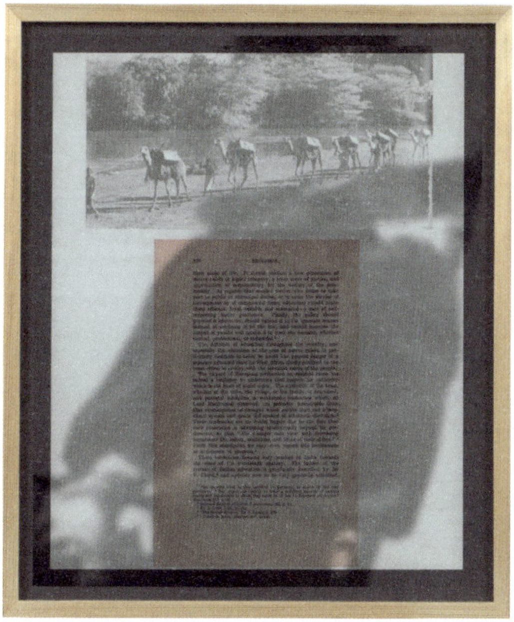

One.

As a thirty-one-year-old I was a connoisseur of ambition. I know this by the journey I undertook two days after my birthday, as a gift to myself. I defined my itinerary through a map I'd found in Alan Burns's *History of Nigeria*. Eight towns in all, along the Niger River: Onitsha, Asaba, Idah, Lokoja, Baro, Jebba, (New) Bussa, and Yelwa. I went in search of a man I read about, in whose company on the page I felt a jab of curiosity, and a prick of rage. And so, I set out, looking for traces of this "merchant adventurer," preceded by the trail he'd left 121 years earlier, a trail more speculative in character than practical. I suppose this is what he might have felt, too, at the height of his exuberance.

The merchant adventurer's name was George Goldie. He'd also been thirty-one when he first arrived in 1877, when he was more "adaptable to climatic conditions than a younger man," as stated in a eulogy published after his death. The writer was Fred Shelford, and he continued to praise Goldie as follows: "The fact that he chose West Africa as the field upon which to wrestle with the fickle goddess of Fortune speaks volumes of the cool courage of the man."

The cool courage of the man. What a line, I thought. And so, I went in quest of glimpses of Goldie's world, this man who had founded the Royal Niger Company, the first to obtain a Royal Charter from Great Britain, which granted him the legal right to commercially exploit everywhere from Sokoto to Lake Chad. And who, at the end of the 13-year term, was said by Frederick Lugard to have amalgamated "all European interests on the Niger." I was eager to swim in this Niger of conquered length, so to speak. Even if, as I say, I was a connoisseur of ambition, I wasn't sure for certain what I hoped to find, which made my weekslong journey torturous with the strain of moving from place to place and the humdrum of inactivity.

Images:
Abraham Oghobase
Constructed Realities, 2022
Wood, inkjet on fibre paper, inkjet on silk organza
130.6 cm x 373.5 cm x 226 cm (depth variable)

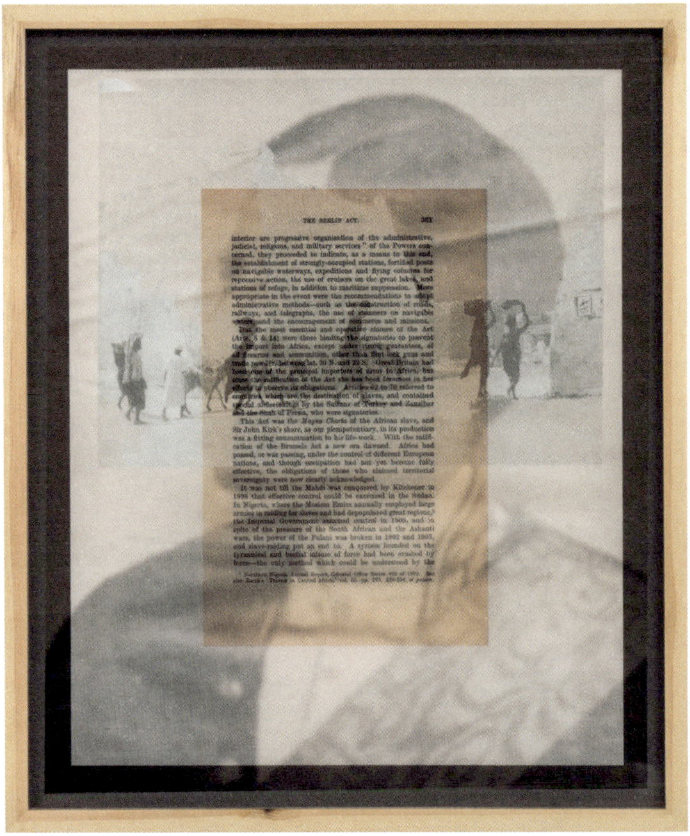

Two.

At twenty-one, I lived alone for the first time. I was desperate to be my own man. I experienced a great blast of fortune. My roommate was moving out. He and I were unequally linked: he was a teaching assistant in my university, and I was a final year student whose parents were friends of the professors who gave me a room in their boys' quarters, one he already occupied. Before he moved out, he cleared the room we shared of nearly everything practicable, all of which he had bought. The pots and the rug and the TV, even buckets. I had two months to leave university, but I went in search of furnishings, things as useless as a rug, things I wouldn't need in the new life I was headed to, the regimented world of law school. Yet to draw from my austere savings was a price I was willing to pay for self-determination, a tax on maturity.

Living with Ghosts:

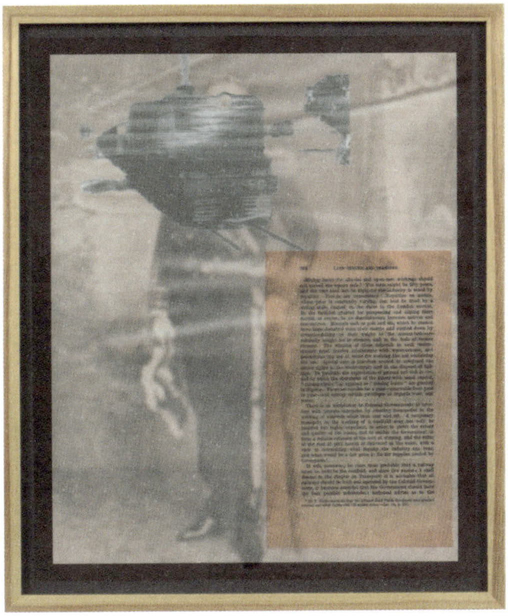

Three.

In law school, some students had received large amounts of money from their state governments as bursaries. As far as I could estimate, they were natives of states in the oil-producing Niger Delta or hailed from northern states with historically low rates of aspiring lawyers. It was also possible to tell, by cursory observation, those who were flush with cash. They drove cars, paid for the meals of strangers, walked around with a retinue of mild-smiling tagalongs, and, if they were men, made confident passes at women everyone considered pretty.

Less than a year later, when I'd graduated law school, I traveled to the office of my local government, prompted by a schoolmate from my hometown who had friends in high places. I produced papers that identified me as an indigene of the state. Then I was taken to a corner office, where I was handed several bills of naira, tens of thousands in all. It was more money than I thought I could receive gratis from my government. And I left with a thrilled mix of gratitude and shame, knowing by then that I was unlikely to ever practice law, which made the bursary laden with misdirected value. Like my peers before me, I spent it for certain on items with diminishing returns, a BlackBerry phone for instance.

Four.

During my years in boarding school, I was considered to have a beautiful handwriting. This meant that, for both my classmates and seniors, I could help with copying out "notes" – dictations by our teachers during lessons, which formed the basis of assessments. If you missed a class, you could ask a classmate to lend you their notebook and write out that day's notes. Sometimes, if you had missed several classes, the notes amounted to half an exercise-book of pages. So it was with Alexander, my senior in class by a schoolyear, but in age by up to a decade. He asked me to help with his notes and gave me a deadline. He and I were friendly – we attended the same church group, and he'd adopted me as a kind of younger sibling, occasionally getting me the outlawed hot water for a bath. When I missed his deadline, he shoved me into a corner of the hostel and began hitting me. I lay in a daze for the first ten minutes, then broke into intermittent yelps.

His reasoning, as he struck me, was that I'd taken him for granted. No mind I was doing him a favour. But this was the world in which we lived: most seniors responded to grievances, justified or imaginary, with the full weight of sticks and belts, and many were famed for the extent to which they meted punishments. "That senior is wicked," we'd say.

All these years later – perhaps since my handwriting has devolved into an elegant scrawl – I am yet stunned by the deliberate viciousness of the assault.

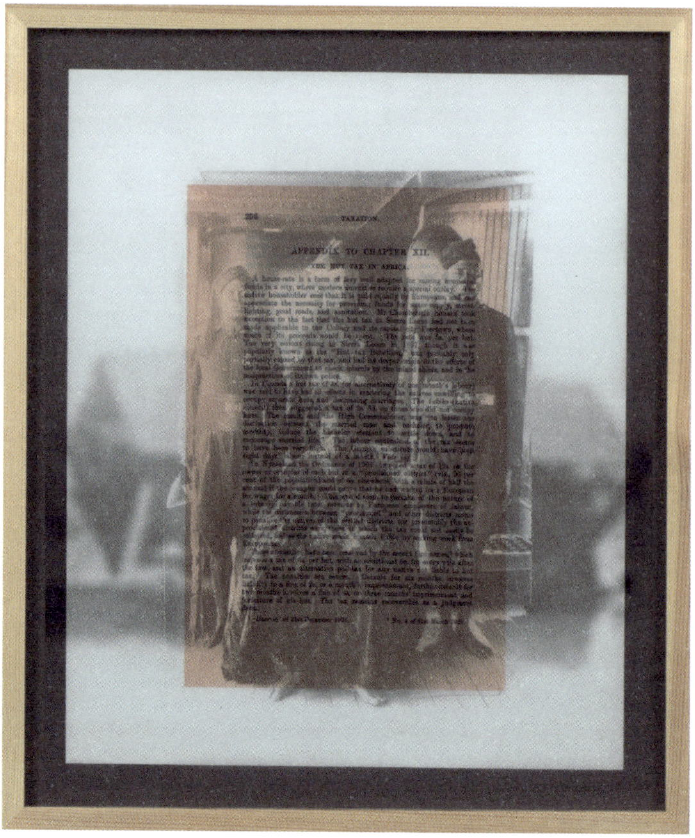

Living with Ghosts:

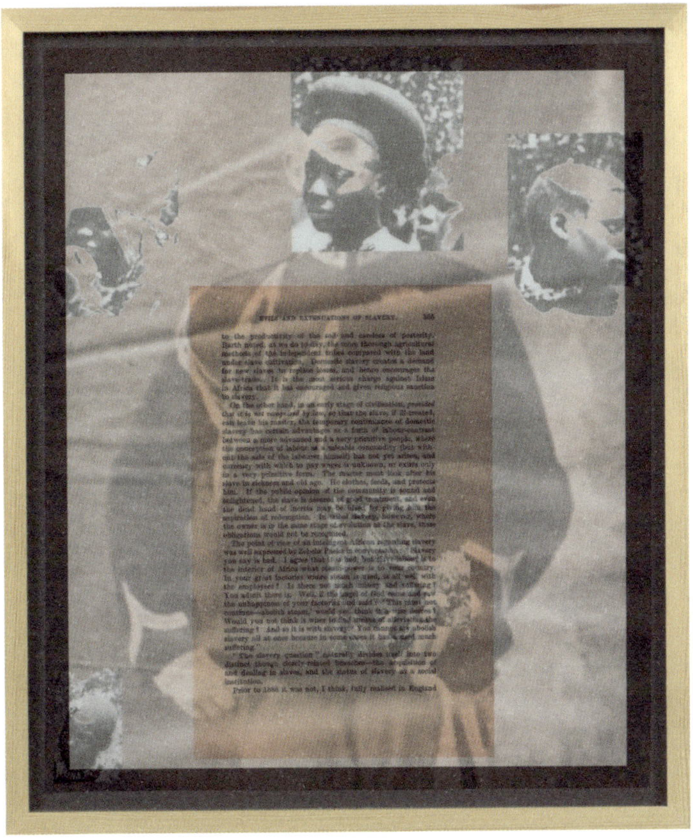

Five.

In the aftermath of her life, a woman long suspected as a witch was buried above ground. Her body was placed on a raised slab and left uncovered in the open. As the story is told by eyewitnesses, burial of that sort was punishment for the evil life she led. Suspended in that manner, her spirit, it was believed, had been banished neither to heaven nor hell, not even purgatory. Wandering forever, she had become a placeless and rootless being.

There is something laughable about the esoteric claims of those who claimed victory over the alleged witch, a victory they could only claim following her death. But what struck me when I heard the story – from two women in Enugu who claimed to be eyewitnesses – was the connection I found between the treatment of the woman's body and my conception of time. How curious, it seemed, that she was punished with neither mortality nor immortality. As if in and out of time at once, an endless present.

Six.

The day I returned to Uncle Moses in Port Harcourt, I found him silhouetted by the evening light, his sleep belabored by heavy breathing. Before I touched him, I glanced at the amorphous shadow his body had cast, a small head resting on a stringy frame. Even when doubled he still seemed weightless.

I sat on the arm of the settee and placed a hand on his neck. "Uncle," I said. My voice was as slight as a hairline. Yet he heard me and grunted. I noticed his eye reorienting to the evening light. He placed a hand on mine. Our hands rested on his shaved, shrunken head like a lifebuoy. Only when minutes had passed did he acknowledge me in words. "My boy, you are here." Within the duration of that silence, I'd begun to weep for, I suppose, all the time I pushed his face to the base of my mind.

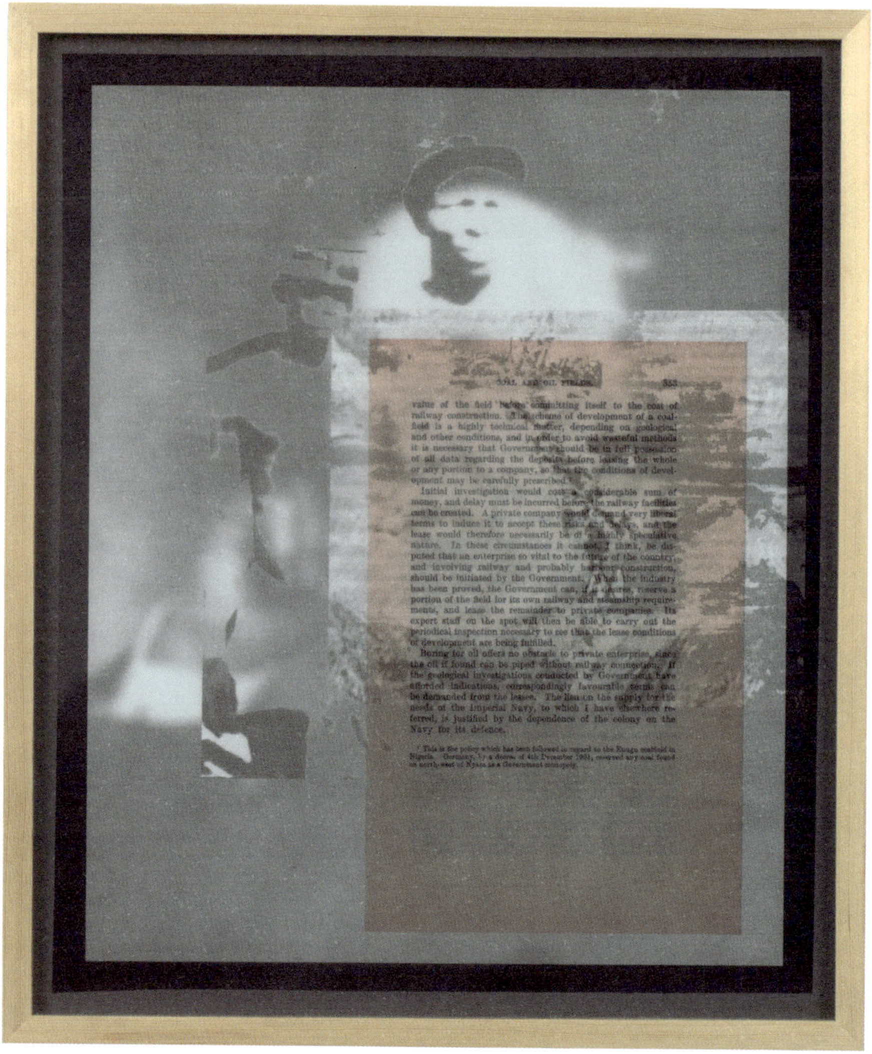

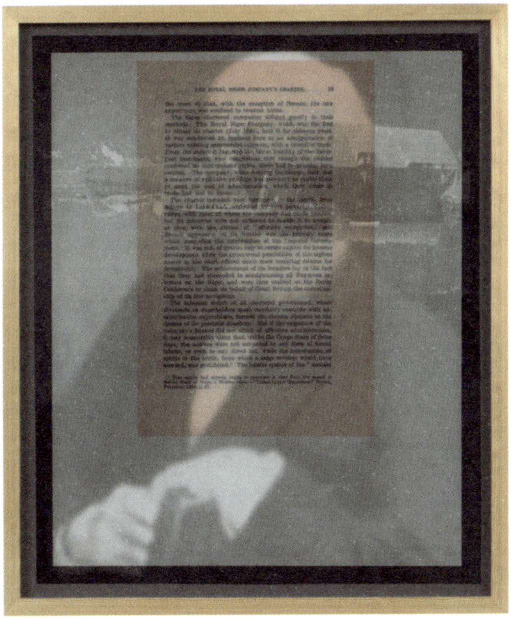

Seven.

History looms. How can I write about George Goldie, whose trail I attempted to follow? [1]

I begin by making a distinction between history as event and as consciousness. In the former, time is linear, and facts are sacred. In history as consciousness, time erupts and is disrupted, and facts are only the first version of truth. The distinctions are broad but hold promise.

Much scholarship exists on colonial-era photographs. Like Abraham Oghobase has done in *Constructed Realities*, my work here was to find complimentary, perhaps alternative vibrations by annotating the images and texts produced during that period. I am writing on the margins of the lives of these shadowy figures, considering their lives as it enters mine. How audacious. If I proffer my memories and encounters and anxieties, it is not to explain away identities I know nothing about. To see, instead, how the historical becomes not just personal, but personable. These annotations are also reverberations and resonances, as well as recollections, which in turn is a process of recoupling an event.

While we discussed *Constructed Realities*, Oghobase told me: "It is difficult to think about history visually without referencing photography." He assembled photographs from images he found in colonial-era books. Each collage consists of a photograph layered on another, printed on chiffon, then framed. The resulting image is placed beside a page excerpted from F. D. Lugard's *The Dual Mandate in British Tropical Africa* – ten works in all, alternating between frames of text and image. Oghobase seems to illustrate what is historical without need for the certitude of fact, as though to revise the record by pointing to the elasticity of the incidents found in it.

The empire is relentless, and so is resistance to it. Neither statement is any truer today than in 1914, when Nigeria was amalgamated into a single colony from two protectorates. What has changed is the language in which we express our fortitude, and with which we console each other.[2]

1 • Some of the accounts in this text are fictional, and I will let each stand undifferentiated. But the ethos – to be "in history to my barest marrow," as Édouard Glissant wrote – is true and uncompromised.

2 • In a conversation with Abraham Oghobase, he told me he felt Lugard wrote *The Dual Mandate in British Tropical Africa* "as though colonialism would never end," a statement that distills in precise terms the degree of arrogant exhaustiveness with which the 600-page book (available in the public domain) was written. And now that colonialism has ended, Oghobase also clarifies his intention in juxtaposing image and text: "The playfulness inherent in the material," he said, "is an act of resistance."

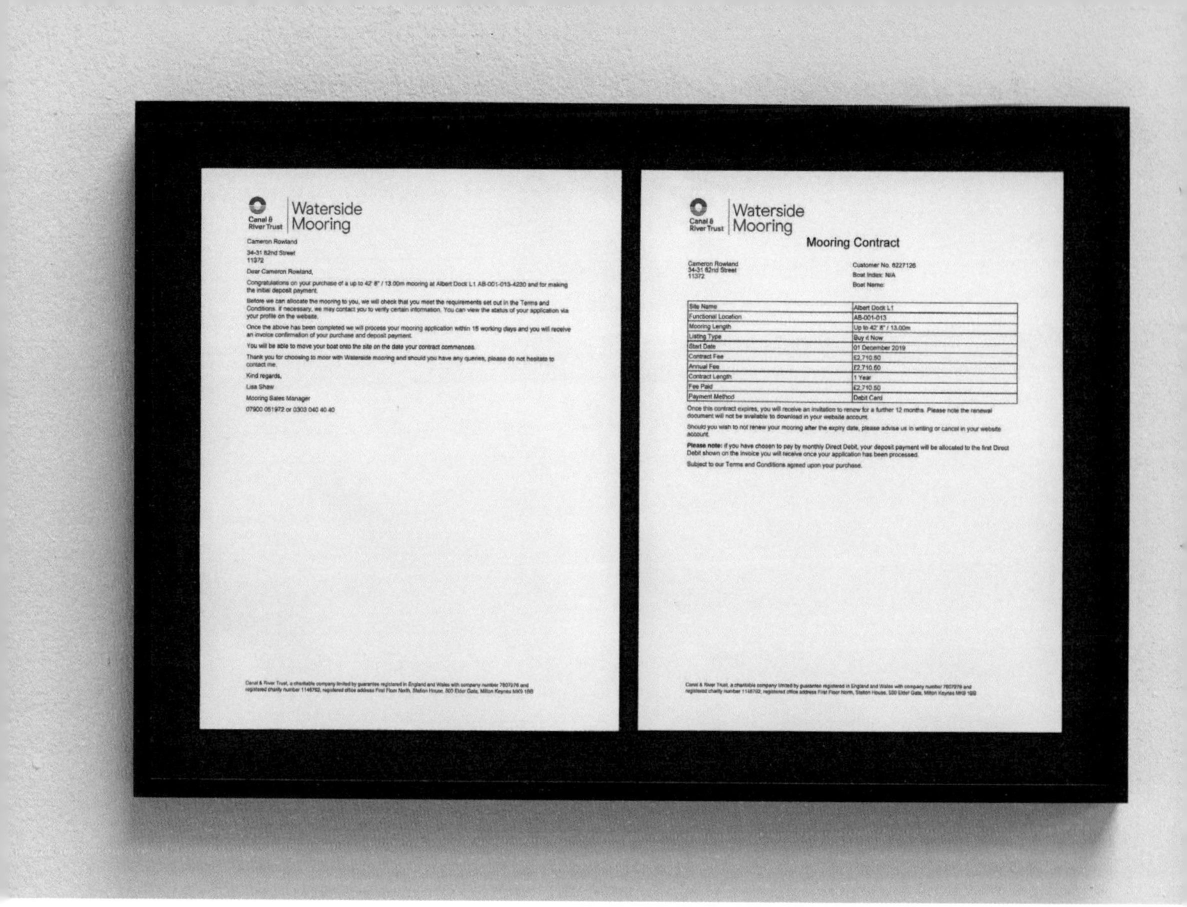
Canal & River Trust
Waterside Mooring
Cameron Rowland
34-31 82nd Street
11372
Dear Cameron Rowland,
Congratulations on your purchase of a up to 42' 8" / 13.00m mooring at Albert Dock L1 AB-001-013-4230 and for making the initial deposit payment.
Before we can allocate the mooring to you, we will check that you meet the requirements set out in the Terms and Conditions. If necessary, we may contact you to verify certain information. You can view the status of your application via your profile on the website.
Once the above has been completed we will process your mooring application within 15 working days and you will receive an invoice confirmation of your purchase and deposit payment.
You will be able to move your boat onto the site on the date your contract commences.
Thank you for choosing to moor with Waterside mooring and should you have any queries, please do not hesitate to contact me.
Kind regards,
Lisa Shaw
Mooring Sales Manager
07900 051972 or 0303 040 40 40
Canal & River Trust
Waterside Mooring
Mooring Contract
Cameron Rowland
34-31 82nd Street
11372
Customer No. 6227126
Boat Index: N/A
Boat Name:
Site Name Albert Dock L1
Functional Location AB-001-013
Mooring Length Up to 42' 8" / 13.00m
Listing Type Buy it Now
Start Date 01 December 2019
Contract Fee £2,710.50
Annual Fee £2,710.50
Contract Length 1 Year
Fee Paid £2,710.50
Payment Method Debit Card
Once this contract expires, you will receive an invitation to renew for a further 12 months. Please note the renewal document will not be available to download in your website account.
Should you wish to not renew your mooring after the expiry date, please advise us in writing or cancel in your website account.
Please note: if you have chosen to pay by monthly Direct Debit, your deposit payment will be allocated to the first Direct Debit shown on the invoice you will receive once your application has been processed.
Subject to our Terms and Conditions agreed upon your purchase.

Cameron Rowland
Mooring, 2020
AB-001-013

William Rathbone and Sons was a timber merchant company founded in Liverpool in 1746. "[T]he foundation of the Rathbone fortune and business was built on the Africa slave trade."[1] During the 18th century, they imported timber felled and milled by slaves in the West Indies and operated a number of trading ships that sailed to West Indian colonies as well as the Southern States of America.[2] Rathbone and Sons' yard occupied a large portion of the Liverpool South Docks.[3] Rathbone and Sons supplied timber for slave ship builders in Liverpool until at least 1783.[4] These ships carried enslaved black people who were sold in the West Indies and in British North America. Ships built in Liverpool also carried the slaves who were sold on Negro Row at the Liverpool South Docks.[5]

Liverpool built the world's first wet dock in 1716, allowing cargo ships to dock directly at the port. By 1796, Liverpool had built 28 acres of docks.

> Liverpool's proximity to Ireland also not only facilitated a profitable trade, but provided a relatively safer route that allowed Liverpool ships less chance to be captured by French privateers. Additionally, the copper and brass manufactures in Lancashire and Ireland allowed for local companies that manufactured African trade goods such as manillas to carry on a prosperous export trade, further giving Liverpool a competitive edge. The relationships forged with nearby merchants not only helped secure trade goods, but also valuable credit terms.[6]

In 1784, Rathbone and Sons imported the first consignment of raw cotton to England from the United States.[7] From this point, they became stated abolitionists and free trade advocates.[8] The abolition of the "West Indian monopoly" on the import of goods to the British Isles would allow for the expansion of U.S. cotton trading. Liverpool became the primary port of 19th-century cotton importation to England. Rathbone and Sons imported American cotton to Liverpool through the American Civil War.[9] The company continues to operate as the investment and wealth management firm Rathbone Brothers Plc.

The mooring at the Albert Dock: AB-001-013 is on the former location of the Rathbone warehouse.
This mooring has been rented for the purpose of not being used. It continues to be rented for this purpose indefinitely.

1 – Jehanne Wake, *Kleinwort Benson: The History of Two Families in Banking* (New York: Oxford University Press, 1997), 15.
2 – Wake, 16.
3 – Adam Bowett, "The Jamaica Trade: Gillow and the Use of Mahogany in the Eighteenth Century," *Regional Furniture* 12 (1998): 22.
4 – Wake, 16.
5 – Eric Williams, *Capitalism and Slavery,* 2nd ed. (1944; repr. Chapel Hill: The University of North Carolina Press, 1994), 52.
6 – Katie McDade, "Liverpool Slave Merchant Entrepreneurial Networks, 1725–1807," *Business History* 53, no. 7 (2011): 1094.
7 – Eleanor F. Rathbone, *William Rathbone: A Memoir* (London: Macmillan and Co. Limited, 1905), 11.
8 – Wake, 15, 31.
9 – Sheila Marriner, "Rathbones' Trading Activities in the Middle of the Nineteenth Century," *Transactions of the Historic Society of Lancashire & Cheshire* 108 (1956): 118.

WALTER D. MIGNOLO

Sylvia Wynter: What Does It Mean to Be Human?

Duke University Press, 2014

THE ISSUES

Following in the steps of Frantz Fanon, Humberto Maturana, and Francisco Varela, Sylvia Wynter's works have been pursuing a cognitive shift that in this essay I characterize as decolonial. Why decolonial? Why not postmodern or postcolonial? Wynter's work has consistently called into question whether the "post"—in poststructural, postmodernity, postcolonial—is a useful conceptual frame, thus putting it aside in order to understand, instead, how particular epistemologies are unthinkable and/or unarticulated within hegemonic Western categories of knowledge and philosophy of knowing. Wynter is a radical thinker. She powerfully explores the roots of Western and colonial knowledge systems and uncovers the otherwise veiled link between racial, gendered, and sexual belonging, differential ways of knowing and imagining the world, and the overarching governing codes that have created, maintained, and normalized practices of exclusion. She is not looking to change or supersede epistemic categories and established knowledge, but rather seeks to undo the systems through which knowledge and knowing are constituted. At the same time, Wynter is not proposing to contribute to and comfortably participate in a system of knowledge that left her out of humanity (as a black/Caribbean woman), but rather delink herself from this very system of knowledge in order to engage in epistemic disobedience. Under the rules of the epistemic canon, and according to its racial mandates, if you have been classified in/as difference, then you are required to submit and assimilate to the canon *or* remain outside. Wynter does not follow either of these pathways. She instead engages what I call the decolonial option, a practice of rethinking and unraveling dominant worldviews that have been opened up by Indigenous and black and Caribbean thinkers since the sixteenth century in América (with accent) and the Caribbean. The decolonial option does not simply protest the contents of imperial coloniality; it demands a delinking of oneself from the knowledge systems we take for granted (and can profit from) and practicing epistemic disobedience.

Wynter's decolonial project calls into question the concept of the Human and its epistemological underpinnings.[1] Her work draws on the research of Chilean scientist, philosopher, and intellectual Humberto Maturana (in collaboration in an early stage with Francisco Varela) and black and Caribbean intellectuals and social theorists. Wynter draws on Maturana's insights, in particular his work on autopoiesis, which uncovers the interconnectedness of "seeing" the world and "knowing" the world: specifically, he shows that what is seen with the eyes does not represent

1 • I have capitalized "Human" and "Humanity" here to draw attention to what Wynter refers to as the descriptive statement that reinvented Man-as-Human under the colonial-biocentric model. See Wynter, "Unsettling the Coloniality of Being," 263–264.

the world outside the living organism; rather, it is the living organism that fabricates an image of the world through the internal/neurological processing of information. Thus, Maturana made the connection between the ways in which human beings construct their world and their criteria of truth and objectivity and noticed how their/our nervous system processes and responds to information.

It is across both neurobiological cognition and decolonial practices that Sylvia Wynter's work and her intellectual disobedience emerge. Wynter suggests that if we accept that epistemology gives us the *principles and rules of knowing* through which the Human and Humanity are understood, we are trapped in a knowledge system that fails to notice that the stories of what it means to be Human—specifically origin stories that explain who/what we are—are, in fact, narratively constructed. Wynter's commentaries on Man1, Man2, and the making of the Human should thus be understood alongside historical and epistemological epochs (medieval, classical) that present humanness through intelligible cosmogonies that, as Denise da Silva argues in this collection, require a juridical-economic colonial presence. To study "Man" or "Humanity" is therefore to study a narrativization that has been produced with the very instruments (or categories) that we study with. In short, it is precisely the practice of *accepting* the *principles and rules of knowing* that produces narratives that naturalize, for example, evolution and dysselection and thus biocentric Human origin stories. It follows that we fail to notice that evolution, dysselection, and biocentricity are *origin stories with an ontological effect*. Put simply: we tend to believe our cosmogonies as natural truth(s); this belief system is calcified by our *commitment* to this belief system; the schema self-replicates, as we continually invest in its systemic belief qualities. In this way, Wynter's writings on the Human and who/what we are are reflective of Maturana's autopoietics.

Wynter refuses to embrace the entity of the Human independently of the epistemic categories and concepts that created it by suggesting instead that our conceptualizations of the Human are produced within an autopoietic system. The problem of the Human is thus not identity-based per se but in the *enunciations* of what it means to be Human—enunciations that are concocted and circulated by those who most convincingly (and powerfully) imagine the "right" or "noble" or "moral" characteristics of Human and in this project their *own* image-experience of the Human into the sphere of Universal Humanness. The Human is therefore the product of a particular epistemology, yet it appears to be (and is accepted as) a naturally independent entity existing in the world.

Implicit in this epistemological framework are the worldviews of those who have been cast as non-Human or less-than-Human: Frantz Fanon's *les damnés*, imperial constructs who can only be understood as the difference outside. Les damnés are the *anthropos* in relation to *humanitas* as *humanitas* is defined by those who conceive of themselves as Human. Here, clearly, imperial epistemologies emerge alongside the widespread coloniality of knowledge: Christian theology, secular philosophy, and sciences that were formed and shaped under European geographic monarchies and nation-states (which also provided the unification of Western knowledge systems in six modern/imperial languages grounded in Greek and Latin). This is the belief system that Wynter's work unveils: the naturalization of and thus a steadfast belief in modes of thinking—

the principles and rules of knowing—that calcify a commitment to an epistemological tract that profits from replicating itself. By unveiling this system, she draws attention to the conditions through which the epistemologies of *les damnés* are made. The epistemologies of *les damnés* do not seek to arrive at a perfect or true definition of the Human, for there is no Human "out there" beyond the Western imperial concept of Man/Human from the Renaissance on.

VITRUVIAN MAN AND 1492

Sylvia Wynter's decolonial project understands that the European Renaissance stamped a concept of Man that brought together the colonization of time, the colonization of space, and the perfection of geometric forms that have been immortalized in the famous *Vitruvian Man*, drawn by Leonardo de Vinci circa 1487–1490. The correlations in this image between the Human body and the universe hide the fact that the body depicted and the experience upon which Leonardo was relying was a Greco-Roman concept of the human figure. The complicity between colonization of time (specifically detaching Man/Human from a Christian medieval idea of human dependency from God) and the colonization of space (specifically the emergence of "Indians" in the European consciousness coupled with the image of Africans, as descendants of Ham, already embedded in the consciousness of European Christians) prompted a system of categories to emerge: derived from Greek and Latin, this system disqualified Africans from Humanness (thus rendering them appropriate for enslavement) and excluded Indians from the proportions, rationality, and knowledge of God.

Wynter's writings demonstrate that Western epistemology built itself on a concept of Human and Humanity that, in turn, served to legitimate the epistemic foundation that created it. That is, Human and Humanity were created as the enunciated *that projects and propels to universality the local image* of the enunciator. The enunciator assumes, and thus postulates, that his concept of Human and Humanity is valid for every human being on the planet. However, once the universality of the Human has been postulated— and we encounter this formulation in many official documents telling us that humans are "all born equal"—hierarchies are needed and put into place to establish differences between all who were "born equal." Indeed, after we are born, we inhabit a world made of inequality. The discourse that "we are all born equal" is inflected with practices of inequity that shape how we live in the world differentially. The mirage of totality—of epistemic totality that is laden with seeming egalitarian open-mindedness entrenched in our various birthrights—is the trap that Wynter has not only recognized but also struggled against.

Columbus's arrival in the Americas in 1492 and other voyages outside of Europe are landmarks of the moment in which the concepts of Man and of Human became one and the same and, at the same time, came to be understood in relation to race and racism. The epistemology from which Indians were observed and described was, of course, not the epistemology of the Indians. And, given that the arrival of Columbus and his contemporaries did not, in fact, correspond to the worldview of the Indians (and the rest of the non-European world), New World subjects did not imagine that they were being classified by a structure of knowledge that will soon become both hegemonic and dominant. With this in mind, racism and epistemology become part of the package whose point of reference is Man-as-Human—a reference point that corresponds to Wynter's project to move "beyond Man, toward the Human," which can be found across her works. By uncoupling Man (the Vitruvian Man) as a model of Humanity, the point is not to find the true and objective definition of "what is Human," but to show that such projects are filled with an imperial bend, a will to objectivity and truth—a truth that, as Maturana explains, bolsters the belief system that supports such an epistemology.

The year 1492 is, for many, a turning point in the history of the world. Sylvia Wynter and many black intellectuals (such as C. L. R. James, George Lamming, Wilson Harris, Aimé Césaire, Frantz Fanon, and so forth) draw attention to the significance of plantations and *palenques* and *kilombos*, colonization, nationalism, and independence, gender, and the state in relation to fifteenth-century global processes. The fundamental issue underlying this intellectual tradition of rereading European encounters in the Americas is not class or hegemony or subalternity but rather the question, What does it mean to be human? The year 1492 is also a turning point for the Indigenous populations of the Americas and for South American Jews—as has been recently strongly and convincingly argued by Santiago Slabodsky.[2] Indeed, Jewish history intersecting with 1492 underlines the significance of this fracture in world history. Indians and Africans were, so to speak, absent from written, printed, and distributed history at the time—certainly, toward the end of 15th century, each coexisting civilization had its own ways of documenting and dealing with the past. But "history" (Greek *istorein* translated into Latin as *historia*) became an anchor word of Western civilizations, including the narrative of the origins told in the Old and New Testaments. Thus, the triad of *istorein*, translated into *historia*, was coupled with the origin narrative embedded in the Bible *and* the consequent secularization of knowledge. In other words, both the sacred and secular, in Hegel's canonical lesson in the philosophy of history, set the stage for the belief that the *facts* narrated were ontologically independent of the narrative itself.[3]

Why is this important? Because in 1492 there is a bifurcation of history that is particularly clear in the case of enslaved Africans, aboriginals (named "Indians"), and Jews. It is the moment, as Carl Schmitt explains, in which "global linear thinking" is defined and linked to the creation of international law.[4] This moment also created and implemented external and internal colonial differences: Indians and blacks were cast as inferior beings outside of Europe; they were deemed without religion and at the mercy of the Devil. "Global linear thinking" traced the lines in land and sea *and* racial lines. Within these geographic and racial paradigms, and due to the logic of internal colonization within Christian Europe, Jews were portrayed as suspicious beings with the wrong religion. In 1492, Jewish history took a detour and became entangled with the history of Indians and enslaved Africans in the New World: in 1492, Spanish Jewish communities were forced to convert, were expelled, or were killed under the Edict of Expulsion, enacted by Ferdinand and Isabella. Thousands of Jewish exiles fled to South America. This is a point that Slabodsky clearly understood and that, surprisingly, Jonathan Boyarin—in a concerted effort to undermine the turning point that 1492 was for Indians (who described

2 • Slabodsky, "De-colonial Jewish Thought and the Americas," 269–290.
3 • Hegel, *Philosophy of Right.*
4 • Schmitt, *The Nomos of the Earth in the International Law of the Ius Publicum Europaeum.*

it as *Pachacuti*/the world turned upside down)—failed to see.[5] For these populations, including the populations of European descent in South and Central America and the Caribbean, 1492 is the date that marks history, memory, and being in the modern/colonial world order. While such narratives and experiences are certainly diverse, given the very different homelands of Europe, Africa, the Caribbean, and so forth, 1492 unfolds into a series of meaningful and interlocking moments: it is the date that marked the expulsion from paradise, it is the date that prompted the advent and the formation of coloniality or the colonial matrix of power and modern / colonial racism and contemporary articulations of race and racism, and it is the date through which the invention of the modern/colonial Other ascended.[6]

Wynter's contribution to the rethinking of 1492, coloniality, race, and humanness is radical in that her work demonstrates how one can perceive the world with one's eyes (a Western imperial weapon) as one feels the weight of the modern-colonial world in the body as that body dwells in the legacies of colonial histories. If Wynter took from Maturana his radical epistemic shift, and called into question the aims and scaffolding of philosophy and science, she turned to C. L. R. James to meet him in the same struggle: the Afro-Caribbean epistemic revolution against the Eurocentric concept of "Man" and its role in the construction of racism.

WYNTER'S EPISTEMIC SHIFT THROUGH JAMES'S COUNTERDOCTRINE

Sylvia Wynter's long, well-researched, and highly insightful articles form a network, wherein her ideas and writings are in conversation with and refer back (and forth) to one another. You can enter the network through engaging with any of her articles and essays, and I will enter through her article on C. L. R. James, "Beyond the Categories of the Master Conception: The Counterdoctrine of Jamesian Poiesis."[7] One of the reasons I am interested in this work is that C. L. R. James has been read, particularly in the United States, as primarily a Marxist thinker due to his *Notes on Dialectics* (1948) and his *State Capitalism and World Revolution* (1950)—even though his allegiance to Marxism is only partial.[8] Wynter unravels the complexity of the ways in which James's thought is anchored in the history and experience of the slave trade—and thus the 15th and 16th centuries—noticing that his sole preoccupation is not with the emergence of the proletarian consciousness and the Commune and the coup of 18 Brumaire. Wynter puts it in this way:

> The starting point for James's displacement/incorporation of the labor conceptual framework is his insistence on the seminal importance of the trade in African slaves. In particular, he wants to end its repression in normative Western conceptual frames ... what Wallerstein has called the world system was constituted by James as above all a single network of accumulation. This network can be divided into three phases: (1) circulation for accumulation; (2) production for accumulation; and (3) consumption for accumulation. In each of these phases ... the source of extractive value ... [are] different. In the first, it was the African slave, in the

5 • Boyarin, *The Unconverted Self.*
6 • Murena, *El pecado original de América*; Quijano and Wallerstein, "Americanity as a Concept," 549–557; Dussel, *The Invention of the Americas*. In terms of racism and its contemporary articulations, I suggest along with others that "racism" as we sense it today emerged in 1492. Greek and Aztec cultures differentiated between themselves and "foreigners" (the barbarians, the Chichimecas) for example, thus drawing attention to ethnic classifications. But racism, as we sense it today, goes hand in hand with the historical foundation of capitalism (which neither Greeks nor Aztecs knew). See Mignolo, "Racism as We Sense It Today," 1737–1742.
7 • Wynter, "Beyond the Categories of the Master Conception," 63–91.
8 • James, *Notes on Dialectics*; James, *State Capitalism and World Revolution*. It would be helpful for the reader to also remember Antonio Gramsci's work. It is clear that the problems that James and Gramsci have with Marxism —rather than with Marx—are related to their respective embodied histories: a white from southern Italy who writes about "the Southern Question" and a Black Caribbean for whom "the Human Question" and racism are of primary concern. Both kinds of experience were off the Marxists' radar.

second, the working class, and in the third and current phase, it has been the consumer.[9]

These three stages are the core of what Wynter describes as James's counterdoctrine. Yet James's counterdoctrine, she argues, also emerges from his willingness to view and think theoretics and aesthetics *together*. A Jamesian aesthetic and theoretic doctrine emerges, then, in the questioning of "the dictatorship of the master conceptions of Liberalism and Marxism."[10] To understand the Jamesian doctrine, "it is necessary to look at the semiotic foundations of bourgeois thought, the monarchical system of power it delegitimated, and the liberal state it helped to establish."[11]

Wynter's analysis of the Jamesian doctrine runs parallel to the arguments advanced by the collective workings of modernity/coloniality/decoloniality.[12] Wynter argues that in order for power to be effective, it has to have, within it, discursive legitimization. As we have learned from Michel Foucault, and Wynter follows suit, discursive formations go hand in hand with institution-building: "Cultural conceptions, encoded in language and other signifying systems, shape the development of political structures and are also shaped by them. *The cultural aspects of power* are as original as the structural aspects; each serves as a code for the other's development. It is *from these elementary cultural conceptions that complex legitimating discourses are constructed*."[13] Thus, the complicity between institution-building and legitimizing discourses allowed an ethno-class (Wynter's term), the European bourgeoisie, to displace the monarchy and the hegemony of aristocratic classes. And Wynter explains: "It was not enough to gain politico-economic dominance. It was also necessary to replace the formal monarchical system of signification with a cultural model that 'selected' its values as normative. The elementary cultural conceptions upon which the monarchical system of signification rested can be designated as 'the symbolics of blood.' "[14]

Wynter focuses on the paradigmatic change, in the internal history of Europe, between the monarchic and the bourgeois ethno-classes, and brings into focus the ways in which broad intellectual, social, and geographic shifts—during the Renaissance, between the European Middle Ages and the Renaissance monarchic system—are due, in great part, to the emergence of sixteenth-century Atlantic commercial circuits and the changes this generated in Europe itself. More specifically, she underscores the first moment of accumulation as it is tied to the exploitation of labor and the initiation of the modern/colonial slave trade Atlantic triangle. Here Wynter's argument recognizes the ways in which the massive exploitation of labor corresponds to the massive appropriation of land. The colonization, expropriation, and violence directed at lands and peoples engendered a new type of economy based on the reinvestments of gain and the impulse to increase production that would create and satisfy a global market. In Wynter's analyses, "capitalism," as we know it, is revealed to be *one* economic *aspect* of the emerging colonial matrix of power; this framework, in turn, challenges analyses that focus solely on the capitalist underpinnings of the slave trade and land exploitation by delineating features, particularly those brought into view by non-Europeans, that are not simply driven by economic matters (cultural practices, social exchanges, political shifts).

9 • Wynter, "Beyond the Categories of the Master Conception," 81–82.
10 • Wynter, "Beyond the Categories of the Master Conception," 65.
11 • Wynter, "Beyond the Categories of the Master Conception," 65.
12 • For an overview, see Mignolo and Escobar, *Globalization and the Decolonial Option*.
13 • Wynter, "Beyond the Categories of the Master Conception," 65 (emphasis added).
14 • Wynter, "Beyond the Categories of the Master Conception," 65.

Wynter's analysis thus seeks to think through the nuances of colonial encounter with and beyond a capitalist frame. Indeed, she reveals that the economy of colonialism, alone, analytically belies a much broader narrative of coloniality and encounter. This framework lends to her reading of C. L. R. James. Wynter removes James from Marxists' co-option and describes his thinking by reading his life through a "pieza conceptual frame."[15] But what is the "pieza conceptual frame"? The "pieza," Wynter tells us, was the name given by the Portuguese during the slave trade to the African who functioned as the standard measure. A pieza "was a man of twenty-five years, approximately, in good health, calculated to give a certain amount of physical labor value against which all the others could be measured—with for example, three teenagers equaling one pieza and older men and women thrown in a job lot as refuse."[16] Wynter suggests that in the "Jamesian system, the pieza becomes an ever-more general category of value, establishing equivalences between a wider variety of oppressed labor power."[17]

The "pieza," then, can be seen as the anchor, the reference point for a sensibility that emerged in the sixteenth century alongside the conquest of the Caribbean islands, Anáhuac, and Tawantinsuyu; it is a measure, furthermore, that did not exist before conquest and that set in motion what today we call "capitalism." This specific sensibility was the facility through which the ruling class, the merchant class, and conquistadores could build an institution and a legitimating discourse that made certain human lives were dispensable vis-à-vis differential categories of value—from the symbolic of blood (the monarchic moment) to the symbolic of skin color (the secular moment whose foundation was established in the Spanish colonies in the sixteenth and seventeenth centuries).[18]

The metaphoric and methodological uses of "pieza" trouble Marxist oriented analyses that suggest that slavery and racism play a secondary role in the constitution of capitalism. For this reason, Wynter argues that "the pieza frame" requires a repositioning of the mode of production in relation to the mode of domination in which the former becomes a subset of the latter. Connecting this framework to James's theoretics—noticing James's system as a remark on the significance of the pieza system—is a way of rethinking European analyses of capitalism. As Wynter writes, "economic exploitation only follows on, and does not precede, the mode of domination set in motion by the imaginaire social of the bourgeoisie. Consequently, the capitalist mode of production is a subset of the bourgeois mode of accumulation which constitutes the basis of the middle-class hegemony."[19]

Here is precisely where the Afro-Caribbean analysis set in motion by C. L. R. James and the modernity/coloniality perspective set in motion by Aníbal Quijano join forces, with both outlooks maintaining their respective local histories in the modern/colonial world *with* the broader singular experiencing of the colonial wound. A black in the Caribbean and a mestizo in the Andes are not the same "rank" in the modern/racial classification, yet they are sensitive to and aware of the colonial wound; they are cognizant of the simple fact that one does not see and feel capitalism in the same way across time and space and thus across different colonial settings. Instead, what you see and feel from different and differential colonial places is the colonial matrix of power of which the economy is only one component: domination

15 • James, *C. L. R. James and Revolutionary Marxism*; Wynter, "Beyond the Categories of the Master Conception," 73.
16 • Wynter, "Beyond the Categories of the Master Conception," 81.
17 • Wynter, "Beyond the Categories of the Master Conception," 81.
18 • Castro-Gómez, *La Hybris del Punto Cero*; Mignolo, The Idea of Latin America, chapter 2.
19 • Wynter, "Beyond the Categories of the Master Conception," 81 (emphasis added).

precedes accumulation, and domination needs a cultural model or a colonial matrix that legitimizes and naturalizes exploitation. The mode of production is a subset of the mode of domination. And, the mode of domination has been set, transformed, and maintained in the colonial matrix. In the colonial matrix, the legitimizing discourse encompasses authority, gender, and sexuality, knowledge and subjectivity, authority and economic organization. In short, Wynter shows us that the Marxist analysis focuses on economic organization, while the pieza frame and the colonial matrix focus on the layered workings of colonial praxis—with the "cultural model" of Europeanness overriding (although not erasing) the perspective of those it marginalizes.

WYNTER'S EPISTEMIC SHIFT THROUGH FANON'S SOCIOGENESIS

To delink and decolonize means to adumbrate what was hidden and ignored—and to do this is to recognize, extend, and invent new concepts. In nineteenth-century Europe, where the "capitalist" economy was dominant, Marx's "surplus value" and Freud's "unconscious" became concepts that were firmly embedded in the internal organization of Europe itself. While both proved to be inadequate descriptive statements, Frantz Fanon utilized them concomitantly to work through the complexities of coloniality, subjectivity, and liberation. It is through Fanon—and his now much cited statement that "beside phylogeny and ontogeny stands sociogeny"—that Wynter develops the sociogenic principle.[20] The sociogenic principle is the process of languaging and knowing. It uncovers the differential workings of power embedded in the ranking of languages in the modern/colonial world order. As Fanon writes: "To speak means to be in a position to use a certain syntax, to grasp the morphology of this or that language, but it means above all to assume a culture, to support the weight of a civilization.... The Negro of the Antilles will be proportionately whiter—that is, he will be closer to being a real human being—in direct ratio with his mastery of the French language. A man who has a language consequently possesses the world expressed and implied in that language.... Mastery of language affords remarkable power."[21]

Sylvia Wynter extends and enhances Fanon's sociogenic principle by envisioning a *scientia* (and I write it in the Renaissance style to distinguish it from the concept of *science* that unfolded from Galileo to Newton and from Newton to Einstein; and from Buffon and Linnaeus to Darwin). Or, more aptly, this area of her work can be posited as *decolonial scientia* based on Fanon's sociogenic principle. Fanon's hypothesis, Wynter argues, is groundbreaking because it is derived from his awareness of reporting in the *third* person, his own experience in the first person ("Look, a Negro"!).[22] The experience he tracks, in other words, is of *Being* through the eyes of the imperial Other. Here he uncovers the *experience* of *knowing* that he is being perceived, in the eyes of the imperial Other, as not quite human. Thus, the *decolonial scientia* is the *scientia* needed not simply for progress or development but for liberating the actual and future victims of knowledge for progress and development. This does not reveal a case for *studying the Negro problem* from the perspective of any of the already established social sciences or humanities—for, if

20 • Fanon, *Black Skin, White Masks*, 11.
21 • Fanon, *Black Skin, White Masks*, 17–18.
22 • Fanon, *Black Skin, White Masks*, 109.

that were the case, sociogenesis would become an *object* of study rather than *being the historical foundation and constitution of future and global loci of enunciation*. This *scientia*, built upon the sociogenic principle (in this case the lived experience of the black man, although this is not the only colonial experience or colonial wound that would sustain the emerging *scientia*), makes clear from the start that the mind/body problem (or the soul/body if we take a step back from secularism to Christian theology) *only makes sense in the domain of ontogenesis*. Put differently, the sociogenic principle reveals what the ontogenesis principle hides: that race is not in the body but rather is built in the social imaginary grounded on colonial differences. Wynter follows Fanon by setting the limits of ontogenesis: ontogenesis is an imperial category while sociogenesis introduces the perspective of the subject that ontogenesis classifies as object.[•23] It is from sociogenesis that concepts such as "double consciousness" and "border epistemology" come into clear view. The concept of sociogenesis underlines that: I am who I am in relation to the other who sees me as such; and, in a society structured upon racial hierarchies, becoming black is bound up with being perceived as black by a white person (as Fanon understood that he *was* black, according to the child's and the mother's eyes, in the oft cited train scene in "The Fact of Blackness"). This process of being seen and seeing oneself is sociogenesis or DuBoisian double consciousness. The sociogenic principle is not introduced as an object of knowledge but rather as a locus of enunciation that links knowledge with decolonial subjective formations.

If modern/imperial epistemology (in its diversity, but always imperial diversity) and *scientia* were spatially, chronologically, and subjectively located vis-à-vis the sociogenic principle, the project of *decolonial scientia* would emerge and recontextualize our global nodes of space, time, and subjectivity. To recast space, chronology, and subjectivity through sociogeny and think about *decolonial scientia* can be imagined as follows:

a) Spatially: *decolonial scientia* is located at the borders (territorial as well as linguistic, subjective, epistemic, ontological) and created by the consolidation and expansion of the modern/colonial epistemic matrix. This matrix emerged in the sixteenth century and was guided by theology and attendant imperial/colonial connections between Atlantic Europe and the Americas. These processes folded and unfolded, in the hands of England and France, and were projected into / onto Asia and Africa, from the late seventeenth century to the mid-twentieth century. This framework was later taken up by the United States and evidenced the ways in which the basic principles and structures of knowledge were expanded by the use of the English language and the meteoric enlargement of scientific knowledge and technology. Consequently, *decolonial scientia* is literally all over the globe, in the same way that modern/imperial science is, and it moves constantly from the "third" to the "first" world, and from the latest Western imperial countries to the "emerging empires."[•24]

b) Chronologically: *decolonial scientia* regionalizes—on the one hand— the chronological line of the imperial matrix of knowledge. This reveals the ways in which Europeans themselves conceived,

23 • Wynter, "Towards the Sociogenic Principle," 30–66.
24 • Such as China, Russia, and perhaps in the near future, India and the Islamic Middle East; further in the future, one can see that in the Andes, under the leadership of Bolivia, the model of Tawantinsuyu will interact with the model of the liberal/colonial state as well.

narrated, and practiced their own conception of knowledge. And, *decolonial scientia* reorganizes—on the other hand—chronology into global space. In imperial scientia connections through time, including epistemic breaks and paradigmatic changes, followed one another in a linear fashion. *Decolonial scientia* links the space of colonial and decolonial struggles around the world to recent large-scale migrations of the "barbarians" to the "civilized regions."

c) Subjectively: *decolonial scientia* draws attention to colonial subjects or modern subjects that detach themselves from imperial knowledge and subjectivity. Contrary to the male, Christian, and Eurocentric subjects and subjectivities that dominated the structure of modern/imperial knowledge systems, the decolonial subject is at the border of non-European languages, religions, epistemologies (and thus subjects that have been categorized, through imperial knowledge, as racially subordinate, sexually deviant, economically disadvantaged, and so forth), and imperial subjects who, instead of "saving the colonial Other" through themselves, join and accept the guidance of the decolonial subjectivity.

Decolonial scientia puts forth three types of tasks. First, it reimagines rather than denies the links between geo-history and knowledge and between biography and knowledge. Second, it explores the consequences that Western expansion (today called "globalization") had and continues to have for the population and the environment (exploitation of natural resources, for example, as *needed* by imperial economy). This emphasizes the ways in which both particular lands and peoples have been and are targeted for conversion to Christianity, conversion to civilization, to development models, and, most recently, *for* human rights and democracy. With this in mind, it is necessary to look at responses globally and avoid the imperial trap that looks at *local responses* to *global designs*. Third, *decolonial scientia* generates knowledge to build communities in which life (in general) has priority over economic gains, economic growth, and economic development. This is knowledge that will subject economic growth to human needs rather than submit human needs to economic growth and development.

WHAT IS IT LIKE TO BE HUMAN? SOCIOGENESIS AND COLONIALITY OF BEING

In her rehistorization of the human, Wynter distinguishes between two kinds of histories. One is the history of the emergence and spread, on planet earth, of living organisms (and, with this, the overrepresentation of Man-as-Human in postmedieval and modern epochs). The second history is that of the sociohistorical *conditions* that made it possible for the elite of European Man to construct such an idea—of Man-as-Human—and to be successful in implementing it. As she notes, the *idea* of Man at a particular moment of world history, the European Renaissance, was also the foundational step for building racism as we sense and know it today.•[25] This rehistorization of the human shifted the geography of reason. Instead of accepting that there is a universal perspective provided by Man's consciousness and imploring it to be recognized in

25 • Mignolo, "*Racism as We Sense It Today,*" 1737–1742.

the house of Humanity, Wynter shifts the perspective, thus rehistorizing what it means to be human from within the perspective of sociogenesis, double consciousness, and, I would add, *la conciencia de la mestiza*. In her work there is not a claim for recognition *within* the hegemonic concept of Humanity but a claim for recognition that the imperial (racist and patriarchal) concept of Man/Human is no longer sustainable. In Wynter's words, outlining the inventions of Man should be accompanied by the history of living organisms of the human species and alternative stories:

> It is the story in which the idea of humanism, of its de-godding of our modes of self-inscription first erupts, where Man and its human Others—that is, Indians, Negros, Natives (and I would add, Jews and Muslims)—are first invented. And this history is the history of the expansion of the West from the fifteenth century onwards, and an expansion that is carried out within the terms of its own cultural conception of its own origins. And you see, it is this ethnoculturally coded narrated history that is taught both in a now global academia as well as in all our schools, while it is this history in whose now purely secular terms we are all led to imagine ourselves as Man, as purely biological and economic beings. The *history* for Man, therefore, narrated and existentially lived as if it were the *history-for* the human itself.[26]

Crucial in Wynter's statement is her concept of *history-for*. It is through this concept that she is able to show the ways in which the local concept of Man/Human and its imperial universality puts out of consideration any other self-conceptualization in languages and civilizations that were not Greek and Latin and thus based in Western Christendom. What Wynter calls "human" (without capitals) and the attendant story of the spread of the human species around the planet from their originary site of becoming—what is now known as Africa—are complemented by Iranian philosopher Ali Shari'ati's assertion that in the Qur'an a distinction is made between *Bashar* (being) and *Ensan* (becoming). In this conceptualization we (humans in noncapitals) are all Bashar; we are collectively that species of living organisms thatspread around the planet from times immemorial, thousands of years ago, many centuries before the elite of the European Renaissance classified themselves as Man/Human and disregarded those who fell outside of this category. *Bashar* (being) and *Ensan* (becoming) are explained by Shari'ati as this: "The difference between Ensan, Bashar and all the other natural phenomena such as animals, trees, etc., is that all are 'beings' except Ensan who is 'becoming.' . . . But man in the sense of the exalting truth, towards whom we must constantly strive and struggle in becoming, consists of divine characteristics that we must work for as our ideal characteristics. . . . Mind you that becoming Ensan is not a stationary event, rather, it is a perpetual process of becoming and an everlasting evolution towards infinity."[27]

I am not offering this definition as a replacement for the Christian humanist definitions. I am just noting that Shari'ati has the same right to be wrong as the European humanists. In other words, I am underscoring that each definition is *truth-for* and moving toward pluriversality and thus seeks to delink from the belief and expectation of universality.

26 • Scott, "The Re-enchantment of Humanism," 198.
27 • Shari'ati, "Modern Man and His Prisons," 47.

And this assertion cannot be made from the perspective of *humanitas* if it is maintained as the point of reference to which one has to aspire. Decolonial thinking and living are not to assimilate but to deny the universal pretense of *humanitas*.

The problem Wynter and all of us face is that we (and I mean all those who are not fully incorporated in the Western construction of Man/Human, that is, all of the "we" who do not identify as Human because "we" have been placed outside of it) have to work through, confront, and engage the concept of Man/Human in order to crack the Vitruvian circle in which Leonardo has depicted the visual image of Man/Human. This working through, confrontation, and engagement require border thinking or border epistemology. Now we (you, reader, and me) must be ready to go into Wynter's *truth-for* and its theoretical, political, and ethical implications. Notice first the Western conditions in which Man/Human emerged. Wynter puts it as follows:

> The issue of race as the issue of the Colonial Question, the Nonwhite-Native Question, the Negro Question, yet as one that has hitherto had no name, was and is fundamentally the issue of the genre of human, Man, in its two variants. The clash between Las Casas and Sepúlveda was a clash over this issue—the clash as to whether the primary generic identity should continue to be that of Las Casas's theocentric Christian, or that of the newly invented Man of the humanists, as the rational (or ratiocentric) political subject of the state. . . . And this clash was to be all the more deep-seated in that the humanists, while going back to the classics and to other pre-Christian sources in order to find a model of being human alternative to the one in whose terms the lay world was necessarily subordinated, had effected their now new conception and its related "formulation of a general order of existence" only by transuming that of the Church's matrix Judeo-Christian conception, thereby carrying over the latter's schematic structure, as well as many of its residual meanings.[28]

Truth-for is a crucial piece of Wynter's argument, and it is the hinge that connects the two stories through the racial contours of colonialism: the global story of the human species and the local story of the European Renaissance Man/Human that appropriated and universalized the first. The starting assumption in her thinking is that "every form of life, every living species would now be able to know its reality only in terms of its specific *truth-for*."[29] This premise *already* questions the assumption that there is a *truth-for* someone who can know the *truth-for* everyone else. For Wynter the premise that every living species has its own truth-for applies to the particular species we are now referring to as humans: the species that can semiotize, that is, translate into audible or visible signs, its own conception of its own being as a species and its place among other species:

> For example, before the voyages of the Portuguese and Columbus we can say that all geographies, whatever their great success in serving human needs, had been ethnogeographies—geographical *truth-for* a genre of human. Before Copernicus, the same—all astronomies

28 • Wynter, "Unsettling the Coloniality of Being," 288.
29 • Scott, "The Re-enchantment of Humanism," 196.

by means of which humans had regulated and legitimated their societies had been, in their last instance, ethnoastronomies. Before Darwin, again, the same thing. Knowledge of biological forms of life had been, in spite of their great value for human needs, ethnobiologies. And now the rupture with these forms of *truth-for* is going to be made possible only by means of the two intellectual revolutions of humanism, the first which took place in the Renaissance Europe, the second which took place at the end of the eighteenth century in Great Britain. . . . Or to put it more precisely, in our case, an ethno-class or Western bourgeois form of humanism, whose *truth-for* at the level of social reality is truth for Man cannot be truth for the human.•[30]

The main task of Sylvia Wynter during the past thirty or more years, at least since the publication of "Ethno or Socio Poetics" (1976), has been to erode the foundation of the Western imperial (racial and patriarchal) concept of Man/Human.•[31] Two pillars in her conceptual genealogy of thoughts that clearly stand out are her analyses, rethinking, and utilization of the ideas advanced by C. L. R. James and Humberto Maturana. From James, and the black and Caribbean intellectual tradition (see also Eudell in this volume), she calls into question the white, post-Renaissance concept of Man/Human. From Maturana, she posits that "creation" of the image of the world is the result of autopoietic (self-generating) processes and links this to the work of Frantz Fanon and the repetitive constitution of Man-as-Human. What she proposes, overall, is a shattering of the imperial concept of Humanity based on the ideal of White Man, and to reconceptualize it not by providing a new definition or image but by starting with the question: What does it mean to be Human? Wynter follows this by thinking through that which we have inherited from imperial Europe, the possibilities and limitations of purely Western science and knowledge systems, and how humanness can be recognized as connective and interhuman. With this, it is crucial to take away the right that an ethno-class attributed to itself to "possess" or embody the truth of what Human is and means. Wynter's argument calls for a radical delinking from that myth and the urgent need to move in a different direction. Wynter summarizes this project in a famous sentence: "Towards the Human, after Man."•[32]

30 • Scott, "The Re-enchantment of Humanism," 196 (emphasis added).
31 • Wynter, "Ethno or Socio Poetics," 78–94.
32 • Taken from Wynter's article title "Unsettling the Coloniality of Being," 257–337.

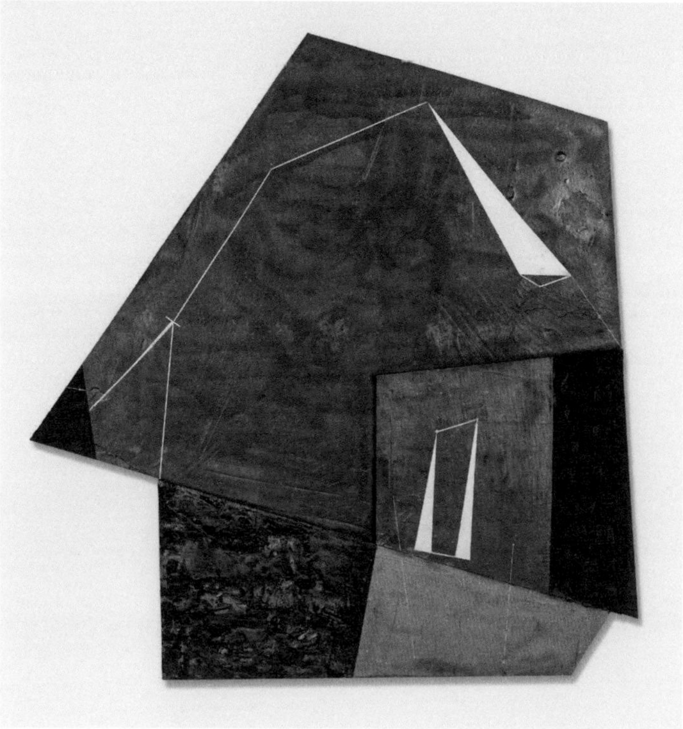

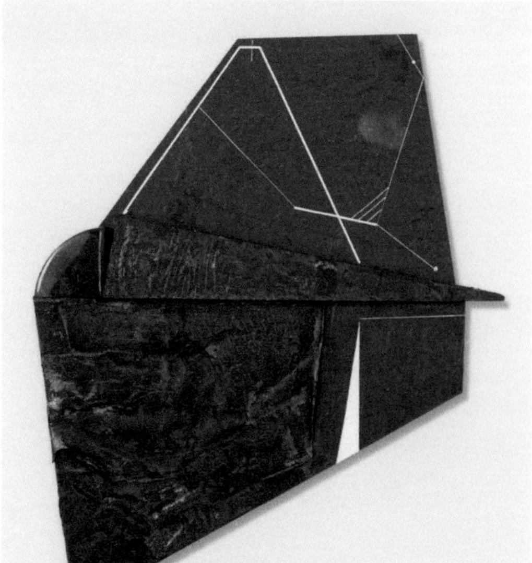

Torkwase Dyson
Black World Building, (Hypershape), 2022
Wood, graphite, acrylic
111.8 cm × 112.4 cm × 3.8 cm

Torkwase Dyson
Symbolic Geography #1, (Hypershape), 2022
Wood, graphite, acrylic, glass
49.5 cm × 58.4 cm × 8.9 cm

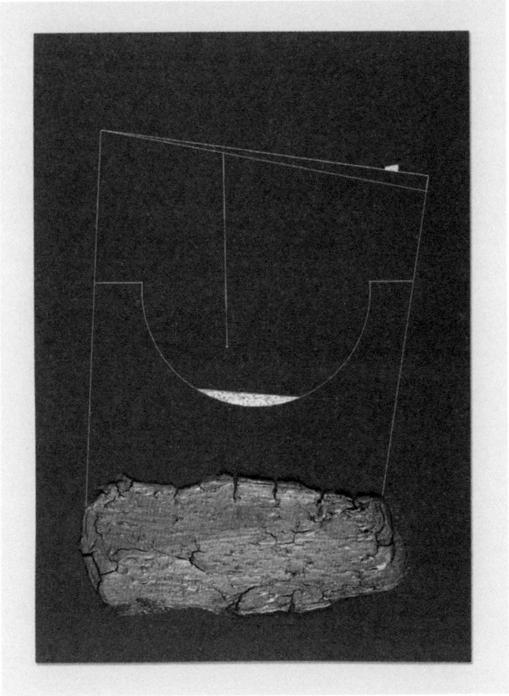

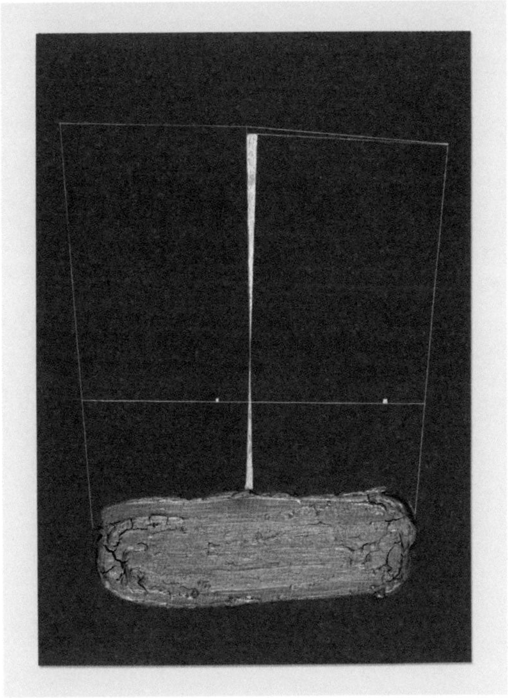

Torkwase Dyson
Enclosure/Encounter – Studies #4 (Hypershape), 2022
graphite and pen on paper
29.7 cm × 42 cm

Torkwase Dyson
Enclosure/Encounter – Studies #5 (Hypershape), 2022
graphite and pen on paper
29.7 cm × 41.9 cm

Avery F. Gordon: Excerpt from *Haunting and thinking from the Utopian margins: Conversation with Avery F. Gordon*

Ghostly Matters was published in the middle of the 'trauma turn' in the memory field. In that context, your language of haunting offered an alternative to trauma in order to reckon with violence and suffering. Rather than focusing on individual experiences of dissociation that could also be medicalized through post-traumatic stress disorder (PTSD), you draw attention to the idea of haunting, thinking through repressed forms of violence that bring 'something to be done' in the present. What is the relationship between haunting and the something to be done? How do you conceptualize the political and ethical effects, traces and demands of the ghost in the present?

Avery F. Gordon: *Ghostly Matters* has an uneasy relationship to psychoanalysis and in fact begins with a story of its limits, a story of my failure to find the answers in it to the questions I had, prompted by Sabina Spielrein's absence in a photograph of a meeting in which she ought to have been present. Analytically, the book leaves psychoanalysis behind, although it reappears in the chapter on the *desaparecidos* in Argentina, where it also fails dramatically and dangerously to help *He Who Searches*, Luisa Valenzuela's protagonist in her novella *Como en la Guerra*. I wasn't engaged in what you call the trauma turn when I was writing the book. I went back and checked: there is not even an index entry for the word trauma in it. The reason is because I was intellectually engaged primarily in African American Studies, Marxism, and cultural studies (in the Stuart Hall tradition), trying to understand, as I said earlier, racial capitalism and state violence, and the paradigmatic referent in the early work of trauma studies was the Holocaust. What broadly goes under the rubric of critical trauma studies or critical trauma theory today is a much broader and more comparative field than the one just starting when I was researching and writing the book, and it is one that both of you know better than I do.

Haunting, in the specific way I used the term, which is not the only way it is or should be used, is an animated state in which a repressed or unresolved social violence is making itself known, sometimes directly, sometimes not. Haunting raises spectres and it alters the experience of being in linear time, the way we separate the past, present, and the future. There were two aspects of what I was trying to say about haunting that relate to your question. The first is that the ghost is not, as I see it, the invisible or the unknown or the absent per se. Ghosts appear when the trouble they represent and symptomize is no longer contained or repressed or blocked from view. In other words, haunting is a way we're notified that what's been suppressed or concealed is very much alive and present, interfering with us and with the systems of repression that produce concealment and blockage. Much of the book was taken up with detailing the experience of this animation or emergence, with the moment when the repression isn't working anymore and the scene shifts. The second aspect is, as you said, that I was using the term haunting to refer to a sociopolitical–psychological state when something else or something different from before feels like it must be done and prompts a something-to-be-done. I described haunting as that moment–long or short–when things are not in their assigned places, when people meant to be invisible or absent or dead show up without any sign of leaving, when the present seamlessly becoming the future gets jammed up, when cracks in the whole infrastructure of repression are exposed. In this sense, haunting in the way I was using the term produces a something to be done.

Haunting is an emergent state: the ghost arises, carrying the signs and portents of a repression in the past or the present that's no longer working. The ghost demands your attention. The present wavers. Something will happen. What will happen is not given in advance, but something must be done. I think this emergent state is the critical analytic moment: when the repression isn't working anymore the trouble that results creates conditions that demand re-narrativization. What's happening? Why now? What does it mean? When the repression isn't working anymore, the trouble that results creates conditions that also invite action. What do I do? Who will help? How to make things better?

In this sense, haunting, in the way I was using it, is different than trauma or inconsolable mourning or various forms of disassociative repetition. I tried to describe the difference between trauma and haunting in an article, 'Some Thoughts on Haunting and Futurity' and also in *The Hawthorn Archive: Letters from the Utopian Margins*, in the latter with reference to the work psychologists must do in occupied Palestine where, as they say, there is no 'P'(ost) in PTSD, so I won't repeat all that here. I will say that while it limits the scope to define haunting in this way, the something to be done directs us to the requirements of individual, social, and political movement and change – and the question of political consciousness and social change is the driving one for me. One of those requirements is that the ghost and its needs must be treated respectfully, and not ghosted or disappeared again in the act of dealing with the haunting.

–

Underlying *The Hawthorn Archive*, your most recent book, is the concept of utopia, which has had various trajectories during the twentieth century, and after a moment of being discredited, it seems that we are attending to a form of rebirth, in new forms. Why thinking about utopia now? Why do we need to (re)think about utopia?

After I finished *Ghostly Matters*, I started a research project that I thought would result in a normal academic book whose purpose was to redefine what utopian thinking and practice had meant and could mean if, for example, slavery and prison abolition or the Jubilee anti-debt movement were examples of it. The impetus for the book was twofold. One was to challenge the twinned triumphalism of the Right's 'End of History' claim and the left's claim that the political universe had closed shut after the failures of 1968. Both seemed completely out of touch with the remarkable wave of anti-capitalist resistance by diverse peoples across the globe, which remained invisible to many until first the Zapatistas and then more widely the Seattle WTO protests woke them up. And both used the utopian as a rejectionist epithet: 'That's not realistic, that's utopian!' The other impetus was a desire to pick up where *Ghostly Matters* ended, with those 'historical alternatives' that 'haunt a given society', as Herbert Marcuse (1969) wrote; to find the place where, as Patricia Williams (1991) put it, our 'longings' are 'exiled'. Both prompts suggested the need for a more capacious language suitable for what seemed to me a significant historical moment of political–economic retrenchment and resistance to it.

I was interested to see if the term utopia could be made to mean something more than the future perfect no-place imagined as a little white nation. When I started the project, the term was still in its 'discredit' phase, as you put it. The discourse of utopia had been roundly criticized for its idealism and futurism, but not much for its deeply racialized historiography and its narrowly exclusive set of literary, aesthetic, philosophical, historical, and sociological references. This became very clear in 2000 when, as the academic field of utopian studies was gaining ground, the New York Public Library and France's Bibliotheque nationale organized a large exhibit, online archive and publication program in 2000 entitled *Utopia: The Search for the Ideal Society in the Western World*. This project, characteristically, established the genocidal settler colonialism that founded the so-called new world as a successful utopian enterprise by absenting entirely what Peter Linebaugh and Marcus Rediker call 'the many-headed hydra of the seventeenth century revolutionary Atlantic', those slaves, maids, prisoners, pirates, sailors, heretics, indigenous peoples, commoners and so on who challenged the making of the modern world capitalist system. I went in search of the utopian thought and practice in this zone of exclusion – what I called the other utopianism – with its distinct onto-epistemological affects and its historical roots in slaves running away, marronage, piracy, heresy, witchcraft, vagrancy, vagabondage, rebellion, soldier desertion, and other often illegible, illegitimate, or trivialized forms of escape, resistance, opposition, and alternative ways of life.

I did find this other utopianism, for sure, but as a living tradition, not as an academic object or subject. When, over time, there was a sea change in the term's fortunes, and a mini academic industry developed around it, all interesting and to the better for the concept, we at the Hawthorn Archive were somewhat far away from all that. New arrivals sometimes brought an enthusiasm for the term that old-timers no longer had, but if they stayed it dissipated out of lack of need for it. In other words, the now in your question is everything. Thinking in utopian terms is important and necessary for social struggle, for remembering what one fights for, for giving it language and form. Once you're already living in what I call in-difference, you don't need that language in quite the same way.

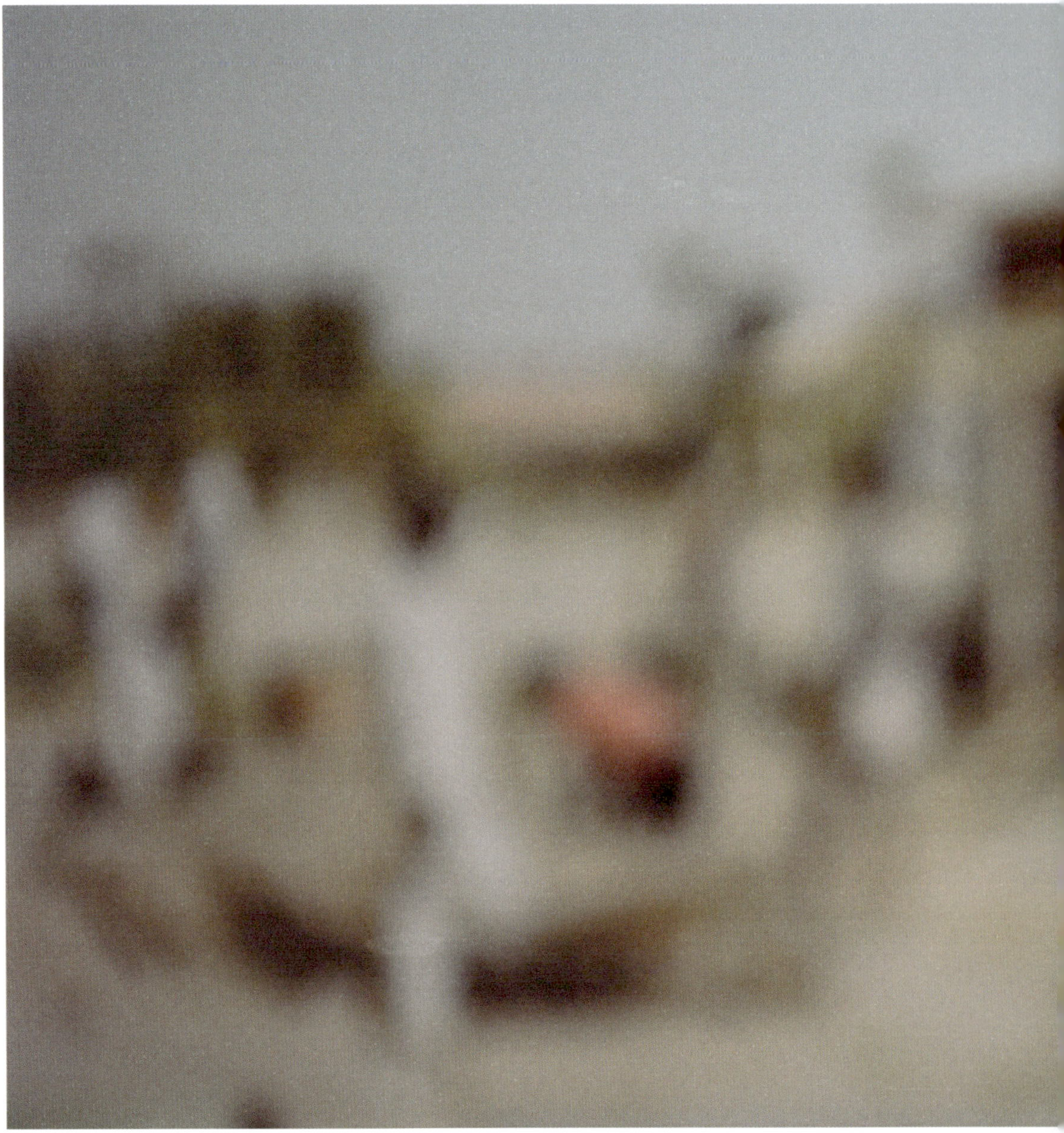

Tako Taal, *I fa mo ketta* (It's been a long time), 2017. HD Video, no sound, 9 minutes 27 seconds

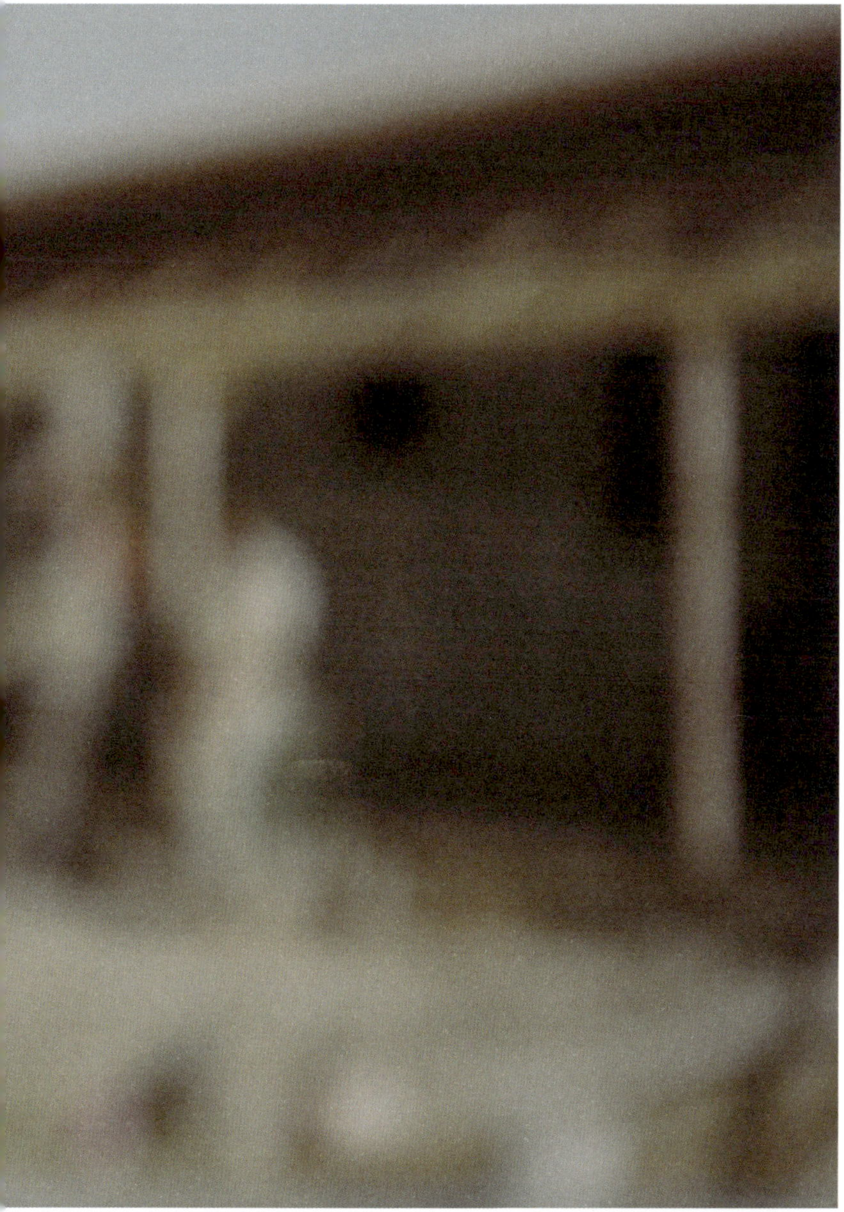

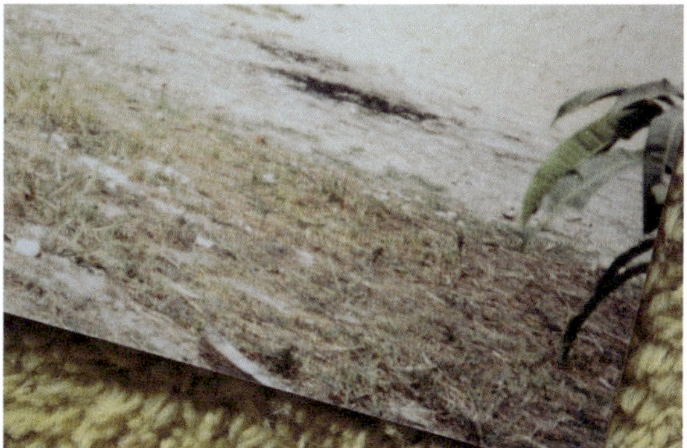

Towards African and Diasporic Futures: The guidance of ghosts and that which animates

by ADJOA ARMAH

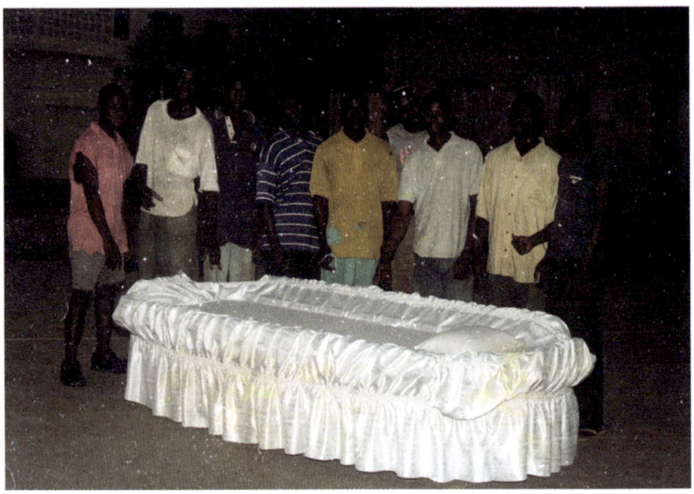

Men gathered around a funeral bed outside workshop. Courtesy of Saman Archive, 1990s, Anloga. Photographer: Photocity Archives

“In our language, we refer to the negative as *saman* - meaning ghost, an unseen object. You see the human being [in] negative! People have the idea that a photographer has to track down the spirit of the one. Some fear their last *saman* may fly away! But *saman* also refers to the spirit of the dead.”•[1]
– Phillip Kwame Apagya

“Writing is one thing and knowledge is another. Writing is the photograph of knowledge but is not knowledge itself. Knowledge is a light that is in man. It is the heritage of all that our ancestors have known, and it is in the germ they transmit to us, just as the baobab tree is potentially in its seed.”•[2]
– Tierno Bokar

This journey began with an encounter with the *saman* of the Akan language. They, the ghosts and photographic negatives, changed the trajectory of my practice. The *saman* offered me spatio-temporal, onto-epistemological and relational modes that traversed what I thought to be my limits and have come to be the centre of my research and artistic sensibilities. The ghostly qualities of the negatives propelled me towards an alertness, signifying an uncanny presence that attuned me to seeing the “life that exists beyond the life on top.”•[3] The life on top here being the world as built by the project of modernity, the *scientific*, the one that had schooled and disciplined me before gathering ghosts and making myself responsive to haunting became my life's work.

Returning to Ghana, my country of birth, for the first time as an adult in 2015, I discovered the common practice amongst studio and itinerant photographers of destroying photographic negatives.•[4] Having no real plan about what I'd do with these objects, I began asking photographers to donate any negatives they still had in their possession to me. At that point, my focus was on accessing the photographic image through digitising the negatives. I wanted to see a life that *could-have-been*: in the images of church services, festivals, weddings, funerals, in studios, on beaches, and so on, were glimmers of experiences foreclosed by the distance of a life lived in the diaspora. In conversations with photographers in Accra, I began to recognise a familiar word, though its meaning was not readily available to my mind.

mewɔ saman ma wo.
saman aseɛ kyerɛ sen?
aseɛ kyerɛ sɛ negative
nea ɛkyerɛ a nono?
aseɛ kyerɛ sɛ ghost nso.•[5]

1 • Tobias Wendl and Nancy du Plessis, *Future Remembrance - Photography and Image Arts in Ghana*, 1988.
2 • Tierno Bokar cited in Amadou Hampâté Bâ, “The living tradition” in *General history of Africa, I: Methodology and African prehistory*, ed. Joseph Ki-Zerbo, (London: Heinemann Educational Publishers) 1980, 166.
3 • “Toni Morrison's ‘Good’ Ghosts,” NPR, September 2004: https://www.npr.org/2004/09/20/3912464/toni-morrisons-good-ghosts?t=1655648623388.
4 • This destruction of negatives, often through burning, was done for several reasons. These included the loss of dedicated studios due to the decline of studio photography and negatives quickly degrading due to the climate and not being properly fixed. The negatives were burnt to prevent them being accessed by strangers in order to protect the integrity of the photographer as someone to be trusted with private material or to protect those represented from having their image fall into the wrong hands.
5 • This exchange between myself and a photographer in Accra reads as follows:
I have some *saman* for you.
What does *saman* mean?
It means negative.
Is that the only meaning?
It means ghost too.

With that, the project with no real plan had a name, Saman Archive, and the photographic negatives I'd been gathering took on a different kind of agency; objects becoming figures in the research that could offer social, ethical and temporal guidance. In being able to name my desired relationship with the photographic negative as an interest in gathering (with) ghosts, the scope of the work became more capacious. While, initially, my encounter with these photographs gave me some insight into a life that *could-have-been*, had I grown up in Ghana, my interest in the photographs grew beyond a personal desire to reconnect with my homeland and eventually morphed into something that encompassed a broader community.

MORE THAN GHOSTS: SAMAN, ŊƆLI AND SISA

The relationship between ghosts, haunting, photography, and film is extensively theorised, as is evident elsewhere in this volume. However, the language(s) and environmental conditions acting on the photo-objects constituting this archive led me to grapple with its ghosts in specific, localised ways. In addition to the *saman* of the Akan were the *sisa* of the Ga and *ŋɔli*, sometimes *luhor,* of the Ewe. Each term is slightly different in meaning and usage, but is translatable as "ghost" in English, and sometimes is used to describe the photographic negative. Shifting my focus to the object of the negative drew in additional useful associations as I considered the social functions of the photo-gathering I had embarked on. One photographer described the negative not so much as a ghost, but instead as a "sketch"•6 of the photograph, its *prototype*, holding the potential of all that the photographic image/object could be. Not the thing itself, but the thing that makes the thing possible, "a figure of possibility and suspension where relationships and objects can be at once more than many, less than one."•7

More than a dead or absent person/presence, the ghost emerged as a social figure, one whose investigation could lead to dense sites where "history and subjectivity make social life."•8 As I moved through the Ghanaian landscape, gathering (with) and encountering ghosts, I was also navigating the polysemous nature of photography. In a country with over 70 ethnic groups – many closely related but each with its own specific and well-rehearsed narratives of migration, settlement, and relation to land – navigating the nature of photography required grappling with the particularities of each location I collected from. These particularities had to be understood in relation to how my Fante and Akan ethnic identity informed my reception and understanding of the sites I came across. Given that ghosts operate as continuations rather than as endings of relation, and possess an uncanny ability to extend our spatio-temporal vision, once I started to gather (with) ghosts around shrines and slave forts, these haunted sites began to re-orient my historical imagination, directing me towards multiple *befores.*•9 Before European contact, before Christianisation, before racial capitalism. These hauntings also directed me across the Atlantic Ocean and the African continent, as I contended with migration stories beginning as far away as what is now Mali, Sudan, Ethiopia, and Egypt.

This is the context in which I began to build an archival and organisational logic around Saman Archive. The worlds that gathering (with) spectres opened up became the driving force in my approach to expanding Saman Archive from an informal assembly of photographic negatives into a research space. These spectres continuously guided me towards questions about the distance between us – people of African descent – as told from Ghana and its coastal regions in particular. I developed a

6 • Asante 'Obra Photo' Joseph, interview with Adjoa Armah, 2017, Accra.
7 • Alberto Corsín Jiménez, "Introduction, The prototype: more than many and less than one," *Journal of Cultural Economy,* Vol. 7, No. 4, 2014, 383.
8 • Avery F. Gordon, *Ghostly Matters: Haunting and the Sociological Imagination*, (Minneapolis and London: University of Minnesota), 1997, 8.
9 • Robert Maniura and Rupert Shepherd, eds., *Presence: The inheritance of the Prototype within Images and Other Objects*, (Aldershot: Ashgate), 2006, 20.

place-based relationship with the *saman*, as photographic negative, and took note of the ways its relationships with the material conditions of its locale were inscribed upon it – I am speaking here of the images' scratched surfaces, dust particles, and distorted colours. I additionally opened up the domain of my archival practice to multiple descriptive sciences and modes of writing, in other words, various "-graphies," which this archive and its associated hauntings had shown me to be within the scope of my work. There is, of course, the -graphy of photography, but also the following:

> Ethnography - the primary method of the anthropological discipline, aiming to collect scientifically important cultural information, primarily from Euro-America's racialized *others*.
>
> Historiography - the descriptive science of a discipline that had claimed the African continent had no meaningful history.
>
> Cartography - the method by which the continent was carved up for colonising forces, as though the land had no people or histories that a map had to contend with.

Each of these -graphies are implicated in histories of colonialism and imperialism, as well as slavery. I began to attend to the domain of cartography in navigating the length and breadth of Ghana, organising land and water bodies, and building relations with them through gathering *saman*. I attended to the concerns of historiography in speaking with and listening to elders. And finally, I attended to ethnography by living in and with various communities. Through formal and informal conversations with community members, I was able to incorporate their knowledges into how I understood the photographic negatives gathered in each location. I list these elements of my experience separately for clarity here, but in fact they were never treated or understood as separate. They are living parts of an entangled culture and sociality in the way of oral traditions.•[10] The role of photography, of collecting *saman* and documenting my journeys, was also inseparable from this larger whole. As Saman Archive grew into a research and publishing space, the function of *saman* became one of multiple ways to relate to Afro-diasporic epistemologies situated in what is now Ghana. Even as I worked with photography, I aimed to get closer to knowledge and how that may be transmitted *beyond* the description of knowledge. I wanted to go where description could not go.

KNOWLEDGE BEYOND DESCRIPTION: WHAT DO OUR EPISTEMOLOGIES OPEN UP?

Oral epistemologies call for a relationship with knowledge that does not seek to split the world into slices. For knowledge to be shared, strong "chains of transmission" are required.•[11] With my gathering *saman* and my regular visits to particular communities, I began to enter various chains and hear particular stories being repeated. I was most drawn to oral narratives that rehearsed stories of intracontinental migration. These stories often contained allegorical flourishes and offered formal reminders of that which animated the land and guided the future.

To tell a story is always to "invoke ghosts, to open a space through which something other returns ... [as such] all stories are, more or less, ghost stories."•[12] In considering these stories, we are left with the understanding that if Black theorising is often delivered in "narrative form" across the African

10 • See Amadou Hampâté Bâ, "The living tradition" in *General history of Africa, I: Methodology and African prehistory*, ed. Joseph Ki-Zerbo, (London: Heinemann Educational Publishers), 1980.
11 • Amadou Hampâté Bâ, "The living tradition," 167-177.
12 • Julien Wolfreys, *Victorian Hauntings: Spectrality, Gothic, the Uncanny and Literature*, (London: Palgrave Macmillan) 2001, 3.

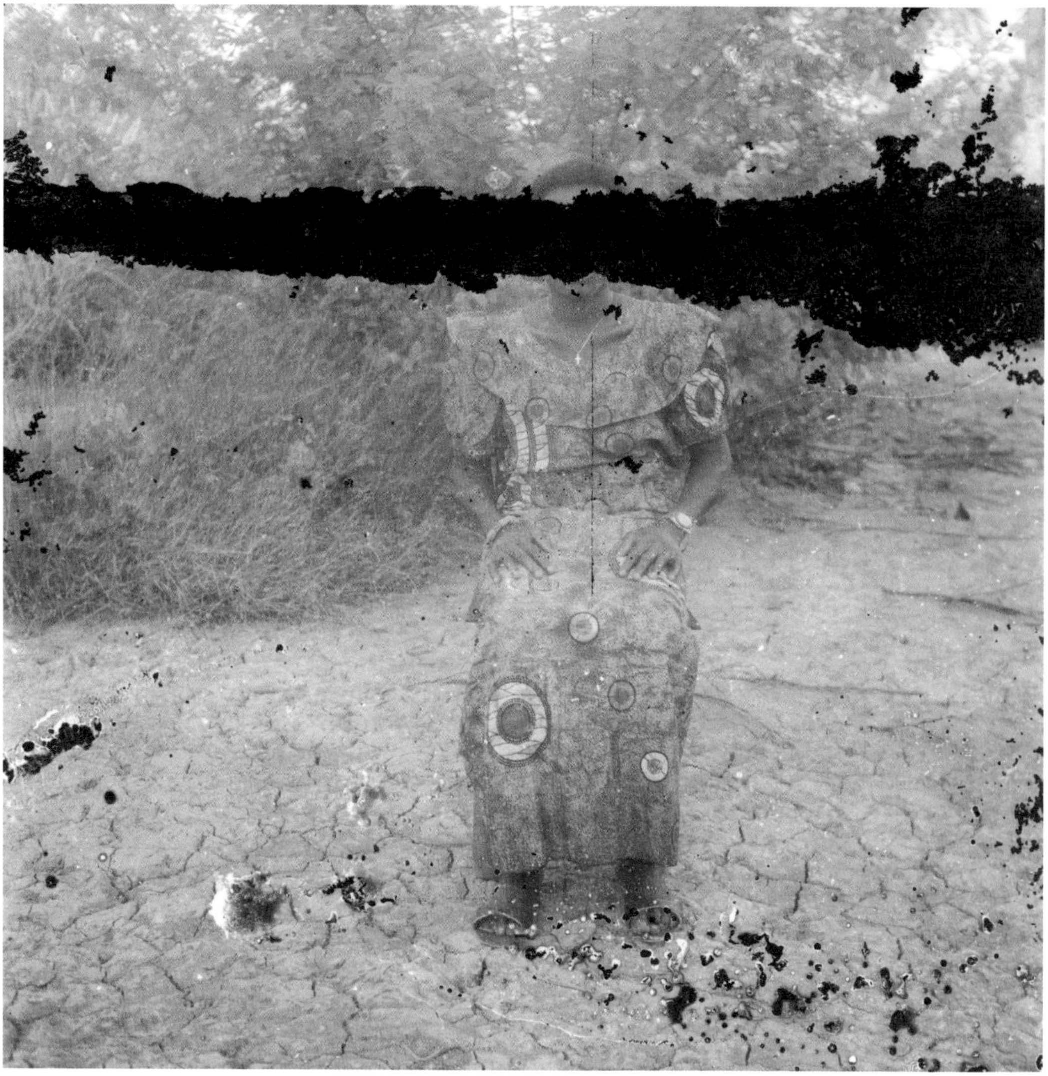

Portrait of female sitter from damaged negative.
Courtesy of Saman Archive, date unknown, Agbozume.
Photographer: Patrick Doe Gakpetor.

diaspora, then that is in part due to our memory of the narrative heart of the oral cultures of the African continent.•[13] Storytelling is a necessarily multifarious, relational, and interdisciplinary practice that makes representative demands outside of itself.•[14] The telling and retelling I was encountering became an extension of my relationship with ghosts. In addition to gathering *saman*, once my interest in the language of ghosts became apparent, ghost stories would be shared with me by elders, photographers, and new friends. For Avery F. Gordon, ghost stories "not only repair representational mistakes, but also strive to understand the conditions under which a memory was produced in the first place, toward a countermemory, for the future."•[15]

By remaining open to being haunted, in space and through stories, I was drawn into an experience of transformative recognition that was always "magical."•[16] These "magical" registers of haunting pulled me into the logics of animist technology, a convergence of objects, techniques, substances and subjects that enable communing across spatio-temporal distances and recognise the interdependent relatedness of the physical and spirit realms. If modernist epistemology understands the world as composed of "separated essences, approached ideally from a separated viewpoint," animist knowledge understands relatedness "from a related point of view within the shifting horizon of the related viewer."•[17] Like the chains of transmission required to ensure the viability of oral cultures, animism's relational nature engenders affective presences that extend relations in ways ghosts make us receptive to. Given the importance of animist pedagogies within much of traditional African spiritual - which is to say life - practices, re-orienting oneself towards an animist worldview is an important part of seeking out the continent's *befores* and *elsewheres*.

Below, I would like to briefly offer an example of how haunting, animism, and storytelling connect with peoples, lands, and bodies across multiple temporalities and towards relation. I will focus on a single geographic area encountered as part of an ongoing research project being conducted under Saman Archive titled, *In our language, the word for the sea means "the spirit that returns."*•[18] This project is an attempt to *map* the Ghanaian coast beyond the realm of the material world, making it understood in such a way as to account for multiple layers of time. My Saman Archive collaborators and I are also working towards creating portraits of the various communities and land surrounding dozens of identified slave fort locations between the borders of Ivory Coast and Togo. What this project is particularly interested in is how one may speak to, and from, the consciousness of The Door of No Return in such a way as to account for both those that passed through and those that did not.•[19] I am interested in the implications of this mapping beyond description, of these portraits of place beyond form, in how we, people of African descent, consider the space between us, our multiple geographies, our shared histories, and imagined futures.

I HAVE COILED OVER

Within the popular Ghanaian imagination, Anloland evokes sandy beaches. In a part of the country well-known for the relationship its people have with their land, key towns are named after these beaches: For example, there is the town of Kedzi, meaning the top of the sand, and Keta, meaning the head of the sand.

13 • I refer here to Barbara Christian's writing: "And I am inclined to say that our theorizing (and I intentionally use the verb rather than the noun) is often in narrative forms, in the stories we create, in riddles and proverbs, in play with language, because dynamic rather than fixed ideas seem more to our liking." Barbara Christian, "The Race For Theory," *Feminist Studies*, Vol. 14, No. 1, 1988, 68.

14• Katherine McKittrick, *Dear Science and Other Stories*, (Durham: Duke University Press), 2021, 7.

15 • Avery F. Gordon, *Ghostly Matters: Haunting and the Sociological Imagination*, (Minneapolis and London: University of Minnesota), 1997, 22.

16 • According to Avery F. Gordon, "Being haunted draws us affectively, sometimes against our will and always a bit magically, into the structure of feeling of a reality we come to experience, not as cold knowledge, but as a transformative recognition." Ibid. 8.

17 • Nurit-Bird David, "'Animism' Revisited: Personhood, Environment, and Relational Epistemology," *Current Anthropology*, Vol. 40, February 1999, 77.

18 • This research is being conducted collaboratively with input from Hamza Moshood, Henneh Kyereh Kwaku, Yaw Asare Mankatah, and Anakwa Dwamena. See "In our language the word for the sea means "the spirit that returns," Graham Foundation, June 2021: http://www.grahamfoundation.org/grantees/6182-in-our-language-the-word-for-the-sea-means-the-spirit-that-returns.

19 • See Dionne Brand, *A Map to the Door of No Return: Notes to Belonging*, (Toronto: Vintage Canada), 2001.

Anloland is also a place known for peoples of spiritual acumen and for a migration story that narrates escape from tyranny. Located on the Bight of Benin, Anloland is on what was known as the slave coast. One of its key towns, Keta, is located near a Danish-built slave fort, Fort Prinzenstein, built in 1784. On this land, particularly in and around Keta, is the convergence of multiple hauntings, absences, and stories of people seeking out otherwise futures. Having suffered coastal erosion over the past century, these absences refer to multiple waves of (forced) emigration and to the scarred land itself. A conversation with an elder in Keta made palpable the feeling of loss that has overcome the town, especially in more recent years:

> Look, the sea is mild in the day. Very mild, but before the day breaks five, six, ten buildings they've been taken. Before the day breaks. Beautiful storey buildings. Wonderful buildings. The Keta you are seeing today is no more Keta. Before, the trading markets were some of the best in the country. The schools too, some of the best. But the people lost their trust to stay here. Now, the people of Keta, many of them build in places like Accra and Kumasi because the sea doesn't disturb them there. Those people who normally struggle for the goodness of the town, they've moved their families. Even though they have their homes over here, scarcely they visit. Some of the children don't even know their houses because of the broken heart their parents and their grandparents got here.[20]

Keta is a place of multiple ghostly timescapes. The market where traders would leave captured slaves on their way to approach the governor of Keta is known as *Ŋɔlivishime*, meaning market of the ghosts. These ghosts are still believed to reside in the location as proper rites had not been performed to enable their departure.[21] Sites such as the nearby Atorkor Slave Market are also memorialised for their relationship to the transatlantic slave trade.

Fort Prinzenstein is amongst the structures partially lost to the sea. In conversation with learned people in the area, what remains of the fort is told through the efficacy of mercury's supposed magical properties and its interactions with European presences.[22] The Danish were not here for long, abolishing the slave trade in 1792, eight years after building the fort. In this time there were numerous instances of people with well-trained spiritual capabilities being captured and finding themselves in the fort's dungeons. These newly captured folk would link arms with others in the dungeons, forming chains of touch through which they could all escape, by "magic," back home. To prevent such escapes, mercury – a substance with long-established spiritual uses to either extend/block spiritual powers, bring luck, or open/close paths – was taken up by the Danish and placed within the thick walls of the fort. The story goes that when the sea came to take its portion of the fort, the remains of those that had tried to escape, but whose fugitive magical powers were unfortunately neutralised, were rendered visible in the mercury-clad walls.

The theme of escape appears elsewhere in the Anlo Ewe imaginary. For instance, the telling and retelling of the Anlo Ewe migration story, particularly in the thin strip of land between the Atlantic Ocean and Keta Lagoon, rehearses another story of flight. The Anlo Ewe are as rooted in this land and on its beaches as in its peoples' bodies, tongues, and the postures they take in the telling of its history. Particular attention here should be paid to how words, or sounds, animate and are animated. The "Anlo" of Anloga has its root in the body posture known in Euro-American contexts as the foetal position. As the migrating party moved

20 • Paul Badu, interview with Adjoa Armah, September 2021, Keta.
21 • Midawo Dzilah and Victor Wornu cited in Christina M. Dietrich, "Spirit Messengers, Divine Encounters: Practitioner Inhabitants of the Anlo-Ewe Spirit World," PhD diss., (University of California, Santa Barbara, 2012), 122.
22 • Magic here is understood as one of the earliest forms of human technology, as efficacious action on objects and subjects, See Jean-Pierre Warnier, "Technology as Efficacious Action on Objects...and Subjects," *Journal of Material Culture*, Vol. 14, No. 4, 2009.

along this thin strip of land, following their departure 300 years ago from tyranny, their leader Torgbui Atsu Wenya, upon arrival at his final destination, proclaimed "*Nyeamea meŋlɔ afiaɖekeyiyi megale nunye o.*" Translated as, "I am rolled or coiled [or folded] up from exhaustion and I cannot travel further."•[23] With that his followers stopped, the community becoming Anloga, meaning Big Anlo, derived from the *ŋlɔ* of rolling, coiling, folding.•[24]

Ŋlo on this land is a foundational aspect of one's Anlotowo (people), Anlogbe (language), and Anloga (ancestral homeland). It symbolises "freedom from enslavement and exhaustion from the flight, joy for the arrival at a new homeland and sorrow for those who died along the way."•[25] It places the Anlo Ewe simultaneously in the space-time of escape from tyranny and in the space-time of contemporary Anloland, the eventual resting home of an initially displaced population. Like the many seeds of ancestral knowledge and experience contained in the stories told along the Ghanaian coast, *ŋlɔ* animates the land surrounding the slave fort, making it, for me, a valuable point from which to stand at The Door of No Return and speak to both those that passed through it and those that did not. This word, and its capacities, can serve as a bridge of sorts.

The utterance of *ŋlɔ* contorts the body, requiring the mouth to roll or curl up in a manner that resonates with Torgbui Atsu Wenya's coil. The word's aural dimension itself prompts "feelings of a kind of texture and timbre of roundness."•[26] It stores recursive time in the body. *Ŋlɔ* can be considered as technically onomatopoeic, creating a feeling of "roundness or an inward-spiraling kinesthetic return to the center."•[27] *Ŋlɔ* is an animated word. If we understand well-being within an animistic worldview – as being a matter of interconnected flows of energy, matter, substance, and information – the utterance of this word is a ritualisation of this relation.

Torgbui Atsu Wenya's rolled-up position, in its repetition by the body and the tongue, invites those that utter *ŋlɔ* to enter into an indeterminate repetition of flight and, thus, an endless movement towards freedom. This is a logic of repetition able to respond to the conditions of the present moment of each successive repetition. In other words, the escape is still possible; we can still move, find an elsewhere and an otherwise. Perhaps our bodies will not live to see what happens there but the *ŋlɔ* reverberates. One could conclude that – akin to the recursive potentialities of the prototype, the ghost's capacity to dislodge temporality via haunting, and animisms's capacity to reroute us ontologically – *ŋlɔ* and the various other seeds planted within our myriad stories allow us to remember and relive where we have been as well as rehearse where we may go. Beyond the limitations of mere description (though objects and methods for description have their place), taking heed of these oral stories and the ghosts they contain cements our relationships with all that our ancestors have known.

Ŋlɔ's ancestors are not restricted to Anloland. They are part of a story that passes through Notsie, in present day Togo, and Ilé-Ifé, the Yoruba homeland, meaning *place of dispersion*. It is in the latter location that earlier generations of the migrating party, who eventually found their resting home in Anloga, learnt the art of divination. With these intraregional waves of influence and relation, the knowledge and possibilities that *ŋlɔ* opens up offers an expansive *us* - peoples of African descent, past, present, and future – a connection to the ancestors, their imaginaries and their futurities. There is something in all of our stories for all of us.

23 • Kathryn Geurts, "On embodied consciousness in Anlo - Ewe worlds: A cultural phenomenology of the fetal position," *Ethnography*, Vol. 4, No. 3, 2003, 368-369.
24 • Ibid.
25 • Kathryn Geurts, "Toward an Understanding of Anlo Forms of Being-in-the-World," in *Culture and the Senses: Bodily Ways of Knowing in an African Community*, (Berkeley: University of California Press), 2003, 119.
26 • Kathryn Geurts, "Toward an Understanding of Anlo Forms of Being-in-the-World," 2003, 117.
27 • Ibid.

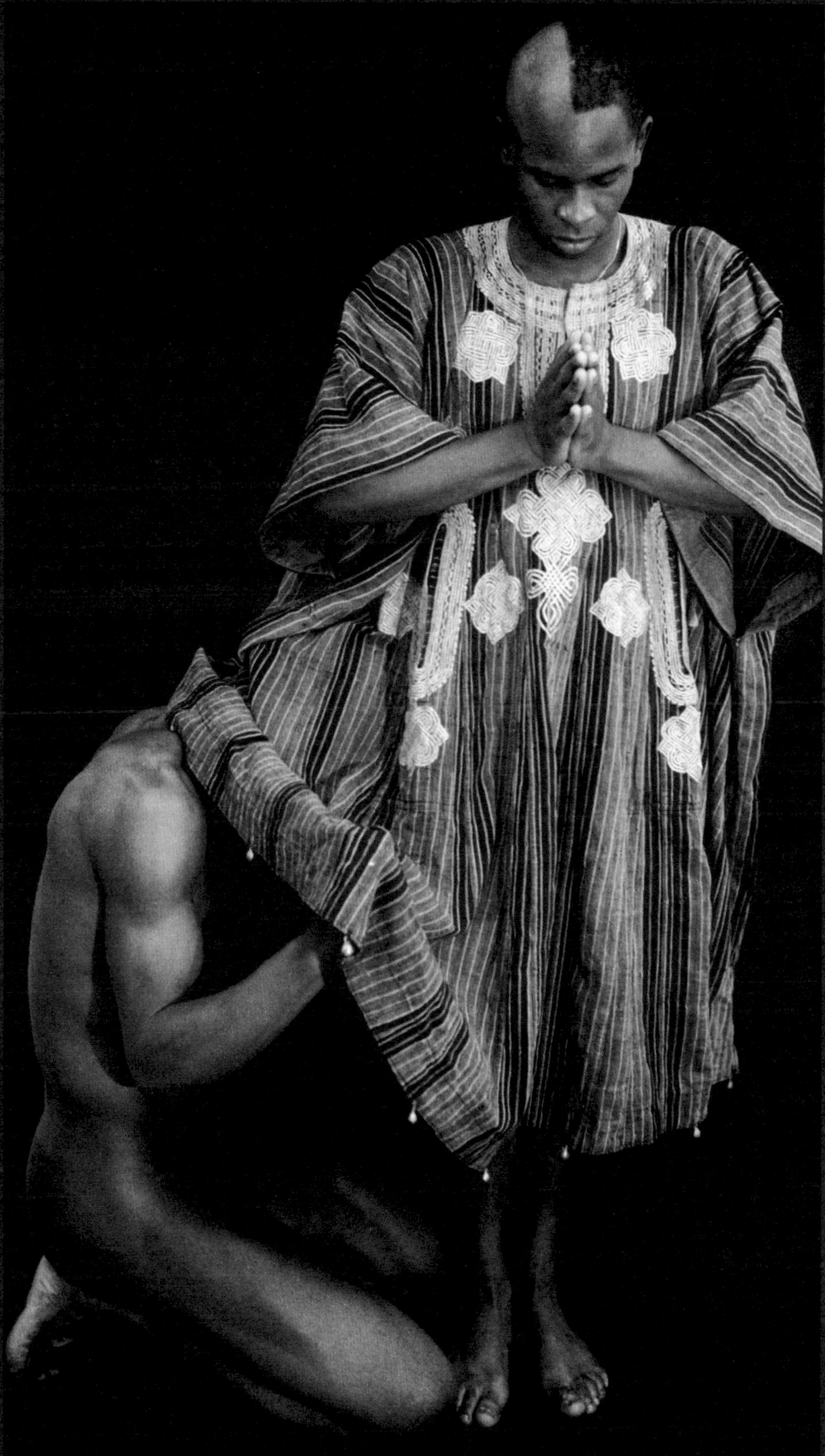

Rotimi Fani-Kayode, *Sonponnoi*, 1987. Hand printed gelatin-silver print, 61 cm × 50.8 cm

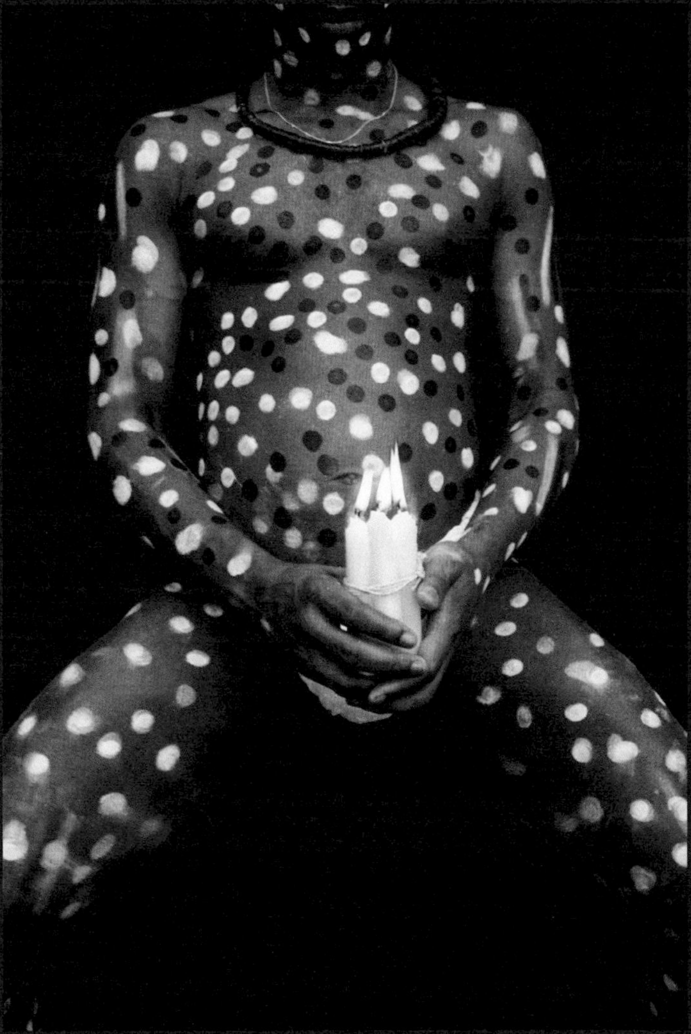

Rotimi Fani-Kayode, *Under the Surplice*, 1989. Hand printed gelatin-silver print, 60 cm × 50.8 cm

For The Time Being: Verve & Vertigo In the Nowhere of Modernity

by JOSHUA SEGUN-LEAN

"beyond their bodies' dark delirium they find clear flight."
– Kamau Brathwaite

"All facts are not created equal: some leave physical markers, others do not...What happened leaves traces, some of which are quite concrete – buildings, dead bodies, monuments, political boundaries that limit the range and significance of any historical narrative."
– Michel-Rolph Trouillot

"Radically, then, one works not for a future present, but imagining the blank certitude of a future anterior. And the audience is the unimaginable."
– Gayatri Chakravorty Spivak

"The starting point of critical elaboration," Gramsci writes, "is the consciousness of what one really is, and is 'knowing thyself' as a product of the historical process to date which has deposited in you an infinity of traces, without leaving an inventory".•[1] For the Black person, we know that the work of knowing oneself is one which, within the world-as-is, exceeds the full provisions of cartesian materialism. Furthermore, that the conditions which are believed to produce both knowledge and selfhood, and the process by which that self may come to be understood by its own mind have been defined according to a dubious metre which sees Europe as the locus of all rationalism, and indeed of all thought. It is for this reason that consciousness for Black people begins as a set of "epistemic practices from the positionality of the unthought," which "puts blackness as a challenge to the world that denies the existence of blackness."•[2] It is from this positionality that the stakes of Black life become apparent and we recognize "dehumanization, not only as an ontological possibility but as an historical reality."•[3] A historical reality whose disjunctive and violent character is abstracted within a naturalized so-called modernity.

The nature of the contemporary African experience is that it is made to bear the anxious weight of multiple interruptions, that of the pre-colonial world disrupted by European imperialism, the racialized colonial state brought into global circuits of production, and the postcolonial state which marked not a break from but an extension of the previous. Thus, the infinity of traces does not simply reveal itself in a broken yet chronological sequence. Rather, it flares up and wanes, spreads or contracts in response to material developments, (re)articulations, and (re)distributions of power. As Stoler writes, "Colonial pasts, the narratives recounted about them, the unspoken distinctions they continue to "cue," the affective charges they reactivate, and the implicit 'lessons' they are mobilized to impart are sometimes so ineffably threaded through the fabric of contemporary life forms they seem indiscernible as distinct effects, as if everywhere and nowhere at all."•[4]

It is the ambition of the postcolonial African state to flatten these fractures within founding myths of a self-existing, independent structure capable of engendering a progressive national consciousness. A framework through which it elides its own contradictions. Against social change

1 • Antonio Gramsci, Quintin Hoare, and Geoffrey Nowell-Smith, *Selections from Prison Notebooks*, (New York: International Publishers, 1972), 687-88.
2 • Tendayi Sithole, *The Black Register* (Cambridge: Polity Press, 2020), 21.
3 • Paulo Freire, *Pedagogy of the Oppressed*, trans. Myra Bergman Ramos, (New York: Continuum, 2000), 59
4 • Ann Laura Stoler, *Duress: Imperial Durabilities in Our Times* (Durham: Duke University Press, 2016), 5.

it considers disruptive, it mobilises the absent presence of precolonial tradition whose inner lining reveals Victorian era puritanism and colonial logics of disciplining difference. In pursuit of "economic progress", it deploys neoliberal policies which intensify rather than limit exposure to debt and exploitation. The result of this is a biopolitics which, entangled with colonial hierarchies of being, forestall, intercept, and delimit social practices through which people resist alienation, create strategies of survival, and build alternative forms of power. As Fanon writes, "Instead of being the coordinated crystallization of the people's innermost aspirations," national consciousness becomes nothing more than "a crude, fragile shell" facilitated by a ruling class unwilling to "betray the vocation to which it is destined."•[5]

What marks the transition from subject to citizen in the face of state capture before and after the fact of the "rule of law"? What marks the transition from subject to citizen in the face of borders and the violence by which they are both maintained and contested? Attempts to situate African being-in-time through reclamations of archives or projections into this or that afrofuture remain insufficient against conditions that render the present unliveable. And if, as Prakash argues, "at stake is not simply the issue as to whether or not former colonies have become free from domination, but also the question as to how the history of colonialism and colonialism's disciplining of history can be shaken loose from the domination of categories and ideas it produced", how can we produce a reading of our moment that is not only a naming of this entanglement but through which we might reorient ourselves in new relations?•[6] By seizing upon a sense of ourselves as fragmented might we develop modes of errancy and slippage? In other words, by learning to sit "in a room with history" can we resist the overdetermining status of the event?•[7] Can we from within or under or at the edge of modernity, resist the closed horizon of the state through which modernity is historicised?

As #EndSARS protesters gathered at the Lekki Toll Gate in Lagos in October 2020, waiting for the government to respond to their demands, a nimbleness came into their movements. It was more than the looseness in mood and pose that naturally comes into a group as they become more familiar with their surroundings and with each other. It was the attunement of a shared gaze, of faces looking in the same direction. They sensed themselves on the verge of something, the force of a possibility for which there was not yet a name. They brought music and food and dance. And under the constant threat of imprisonment, made legal aid available. A direct engagement with the carceral system which challenged not only its terms of operation but its foundational use as a solution to the problem of unsociable bodies. Such acts of refusal and sustenance became constitutive of a discursive mode for which there was no preparation or theoretical basis. It arose in direct response to the situation. That is, as Mignolo writes, its meaning derived "from the action itself."•[8] The occupation became a third space where the symbolic and material of the toll gate as a source of government revenue and a critical point in the urban flow of goods and people were disrupted and replaced with an invitation and insistence to refuse "the call to order."•[9] Similarly, in #RhodesMustFall, we recognize an awareness that "every political order depends on a relationship to inhabitable space," and a form of resistance to that order through desecration was critical. •[10] It is an engagement with colonial history which lays it open to subversive interrogations, to ulterior motives. Against the rampant, unabated deterritorialisation which offers indigenous lands as commodity and forces Black South Africans into increasingly precarious living conditions.

We foreground space here not simply to take note of the situated strategies of these struggles but

5 • Frantz Fanon, *The Wretched of the Earth*, trans. Richard Philcox, (New York: Grove Press, 2004), 18, 233.
6 • Gary Prakash, "After Colonialism," in *After Colonialism: Imperials Histories and Postcolonial Displacements*, ed. Gary Prakash (Princeton: Princeton University Press, 1995), 5.
7 • Dionne Brand, *A Map to the Door of No Return* (Canada: Vintage Canada, 2001).
8 • Walter D. Mignolo and Catherine E. Walsh, *On Decoloniality: Concepts, Analysis, Praxis*, (Durham: Duke University Press, 2018), 37.
9 • Fred Moten and Stefano Harney, *The Undercommons: Fugitive Planning & Black Study*, (Wivenhoe: Minor Compositions, 2013).
10 • Kelly McBride and Margaret Kohn, *Political Theories of Decolonization: Postcolonialism and the Problem of Foundations*, (Oxford: Oxford University Press, 2011), 99.

to observe the centrality of "property relationships" to colonial matrices of power and consequently to the deployment of decolonial visions. In the monumentalised landscape, we encounter traces of the past that are not past. This is evident across various former African colonies. On Ghana, Victoria Ogoegbunam Okoye writes:

> "When the British colonize the settlement and surrounding territories (formally, from 1874–1957), they produce the 'Gold Coast' through subjugating and joining together diverse peoples and their territories into a single colony. They position Accra as colonial capital, drawing it into the global landscape of British empire. Accra's land emerges as a principle asset to the colonial administration, which stakes its dominance through multiple violences. The spatial violence of colonialism lies in its practices of unseating Indigenous uses and relations, through the epistemic, physical and material violences of devaluing and dismissing Indigenous land claims, spatial relations and ways of living: the principles of *terra nullius* and *tabula rasa*; the demolition of and claim to territory; then the work of colonial architects and planners to produce spatial and urban transformations, grounded in modernist visions and projecting westernised concepts, designs and control onto these peoples and their lands. The colonial administration transforms land through the expropriative forces of seizure, design and planning, along with, as Amarteifio points out, infrastructure: the roads, streets, corridors, ports and railways necessary for colonial extraction and globalisation. These are predicated on and entangled with land ordinances and regulations – laws created by the colonial authority to control the use of land and space in everyday life, formalising the dispossession and curtailment of Indigenous custodianship and spatiality, in order to transplant a western concept of property, with enduring ramifications."•[11]

I must admit to being less interested in the supposed success or failure of contemporary resistance movements than I am in how they help us understand the ways in which public space and indeed the larger public sphere remain arenas of "contested meanings" in which "different and opposing publics manoeuvred for space."•[12] If at all any such evaluations are necessary, it is only by viewing them as modalities of rehearsal whose measure is neither in the perfection of method nor the realisation of an event but in the insistence on the will to live. A practice whose point, in Motenian terms, is *practice*. In which we accustom ourselves to dispersal and fragmentation, to the rhythm of "non-static registers; conditions and ways of relating to one another that remain subterranean to the cartographic gaze."•[13] It is always fundamentally generative, contingent, and emergent. An accumulation of experiments in living which are not "necessarily converging toward a single point, trend or cycle" but "harbour the possibility of a variety of trajectories."•[14] Implicit in rehearsal is the awareness that life is happening, and from this awareness it invites strangeness and incoherence and noise; a drawing further into the minor gesture on which Erin Manning contemplates:

> "And yet the minor gesture is everywhere, all the time. Despite its precarity, it resurfaces punctually, claiming not space as such, but space-of-variation. The minor invents new forms of existence, and with them, in them, we come to be. These temporary forms of life travel across the everyday, making untimely existing political structures, activating new modes of perception, inventing languages that speak in the interstices of major tongues."•[15]

11 • Victoria Ogoegbunam Okoye, "The Colonial Afterlives of Encroachment," *L'Internationale Online*, 11 December 2021. https://www.internationaleonline.org/research/decolonising_practices/207_the_colonial_afterlife_of_encroachment/
12 • Geoff Eley, "Chapter Ten, Nations, Publics, and Political Cultures: Placing Habermas in the Nineteenth Century" In *Culture/Power/History: A Reader in Contemporary Social Theory*, eds. Nicholas B. Dirks, Geoff Eley, and Sherry B. Ortner, (Princeton: Princeton University Press, 2021), 297-335.
13 • Emmanuel Admassu and Jen Wood, "Architecture Without Measure: Notes on Legibility," e-flux, 30 July 2021. https://www.e-flux.com/architecture/survivance/404210/architecture-without-measure-notes-on-legibility/
14 • Achille Mbembe, *On the Postcolony* (Berkeley: University of California Press, 2001), 16.
15 • Erin Manning, *The Minor Gesture*, (Durham: Duke University Press, 2016), 2.

In the minor gesture we grow sceptical of cohesive narratives, of the three-act structure, of a reading of time realised in fixed temporalities. This discipline, rather, remains attentive to aggregated potentialities, to forced eruptions, afterlives, ripples, spillages; in short, those movements of matter and force that are not immediately recognizable as History or Change, those data which resist dominant methods of analysis, which require attention to the micro and rhizomatic, to histories that seem to lie in wait, that seem to travel incognito, histories that may show up in the blood, in songs, stories, in dreams of a commons beyond all economies of dispossession. Dreams, Fanon reminds us, are not simply the stuff of fantasy but the means through which the colonised subject nurtures an "aggressive vitality."

Though we may make our way, haltingly and by dim lights, from a "past order that is rejected" to an "absurd present,"[16] bearing strange burdens and even stranger gifts, the shelters in which we gather are necessarily makeshift, imagined, felt, made piece by piece, composed of seemingly disparate pedagogies, paradigms, and perspectives. Along these haunted grounds, we may join the students at Cape Town who stand now, in the absence of that shadow, in the shadow of that absence, singing Yinde Le Ndlela Esiy'hambayo.

For the road, indeed, is long.

16 • Édouard Glissant, *Caribbean Discourse: Selected Essays*, (Charlottesville: University Press of Virginia, 1989), 131.

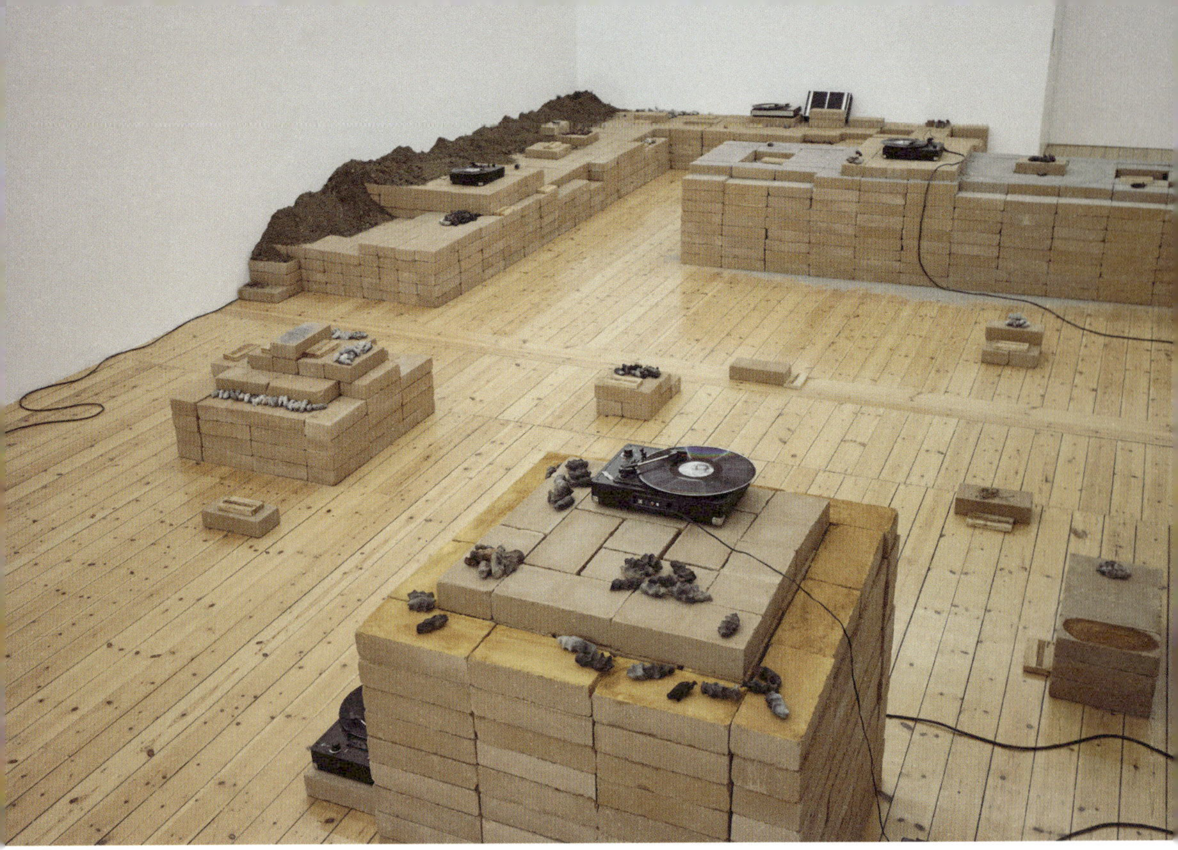

Dineo Seshee Bopape, *Lerole: footnotes (The struggle of memory against forgetting)*, 2018, Exhibition view, Sfeir-Semler Gallery Hamburg, 2018

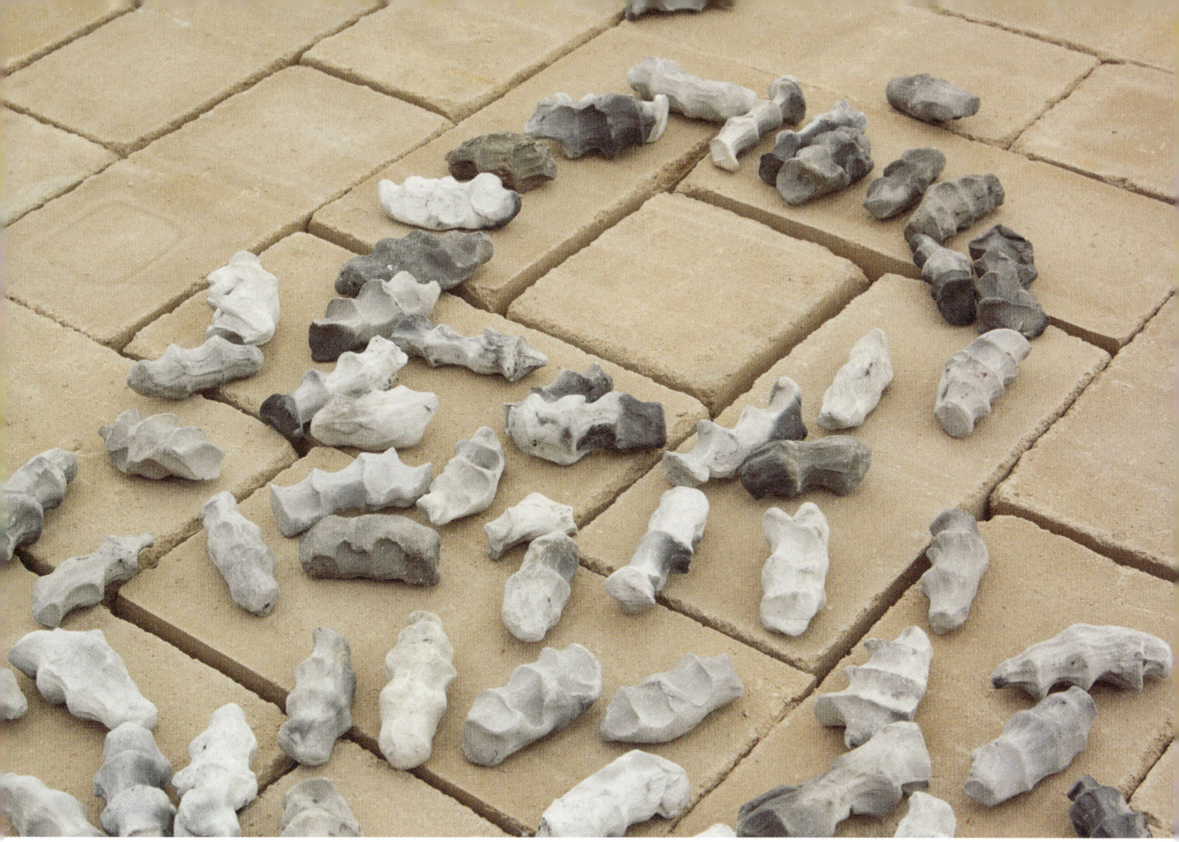

Further reading

Abraham, Nicolas. "Notes on the Phantom: A Complement to Freud's Metapsychology." *Critical Inquiry*, Vol. 13, No.2, Winter 1987, 287-292

Baucum, Ian. *Specters of the Atlantic: Finance Capital, Slavery, and the Philosophy of History.* Durham and London: Duke University Press, 2005

Behrend, Heike. "Spaces of Refusal: Photophobic Spirits and the Technical Medium of Photography" in *Trance Mediums and New Media: Spirit Possession in the Age of Technical Reproduction*. ed. Heike Behrend, Anja Dreschke, and Martin Zillinger, *Fordham Scholarship Online*, 2015, 202-220

Blanco, María Del Pilar and Peeren, Esther (eds.). *The Spectralities Reader: Ghosts and Haunting in Contemporary Cultural Theory*. London and New York: Bloomsbury, 2013

de Bacque, Antoine and Jousse, Thierry, "Cinema and Its Ghosts: An Interview With Jacques Derrida." trans. Peggy Kamuf. *Discourse*, Volume 37, No. 1-2, Winter/Spring 2015, 22-39

Césaire, Aimé. *Discourse on Colonialism*. trans. Joan Pinkham. New York: Monthly Review Press, 2000

Cole, Teju. "When the Camera Was a Weapon of Imperialism. (And When It Still Is.)," *New York Times*, February 6, 2019: https://www.nytimes.com/2019/02/06/magazine/when-the-camera-was-a-weapon-of-imperialism-and-when-it-still-is.html

Demos, T.J. *Return to the Postcolony: Specters of Colonialism in Contemporary Art.* Berlin: Sternberg Press, 2013

Derrida, Jacques. *Specters of Marx: The State of the Debt, the Work of Mourning and the New International.* trans. Peggy Kamuf. New York and London: Routledge, 1994

Eng, David L. and Kazanjan, David. *Loss: The Politics of Mourning*. Berkeley, Los Angeles, London: University of California Press, 2003

Enwezor, Okwui. "Modernity and Postcolonial Ambivalence." *South Atlantic Quarterly*, Vol. 109, Issue 3, Summer 2010, 595-620

Fanon, Frantz. *The Wretched Of The Earth*. trans. Richard Philcox. New York: Grove Press, 1963

Freud, Sigmund. "Mourning and Melancholia" in *On Freud's "Mourning and Melancholia."* eds. Leticia Glocer Fiorini, Thierry Bokanowski, Sergio Lewkowicz. London: Karnac Books, 2009

Gordon, Avery. F. *Ghostly Matters: Haunting and the Sociological Imagination*. Minneapolis and London: University of Minnesota, 1997

Hartman, Saidiya. *Lose Your Mother: A Journey Along the Atlantic Slave* Route. New York: Farrar, Strauss, and Giroux, 2006.

Hofmeyr, Murray. "From Hauntology to a New Animism? Nature and Culture in Heinz Kimmerle's Intercultural Philosophy." *TD: The Journal for Transdisciplinary Research in Southern Africa*, Vol. 3, No.1, July 2007, 1-38

Ingawanji, May Adadol. "Cinematic Animism and Contemporary Southeast Asian Artists' Moving-Image Practices." *Screen*, Vol. 62, Issue 4, Winter 2021, 549-558

James, C.L.R. *A History of Pan-African Revolt*. Oakland: PM Press, 1969

Kelley, Robin D.G. *Freedom Dreams: The Black Radical Imagination*. Boston: Beacon Press, 2002

Khanna, Ranjana. *Dark Continents: Psychoanalysis and Colonialism*. Durham, NC: Duke University Press, 2003

Lugones, Maria. "Heterosexualism and the Colonial/Modern Gender System." *Hypatia*, Winter, 2007, Vol. 22, No. 1, Winter, 2007, 186-209

Marks, Laura U. *The Skin of the Film: Intercultural Cinema, Embodiment and The Senses.* Durham and London: Duke University Press, 2000

Mbembe, Achille. *Necropolitics.* Durham: Duke University Press, 2019

Mbembe, Achille. *On the Postcolony*. Berkeley, Los Angeles, and London: University of California Press, 2001

Mbembe, Achille. *The Critique of Black Reason.* Durham: Duke University Press, 2017

Mignolo, Walter D. "Delinking: The Rhetoric of Modernity, The Logic of Coloniality and the Grammar of Decoloniality." *Cultural Studies,* Vol 21, Issue 2-3, 449-514

Mignolo, Walter D. and Walsh, Catherine E. *On Decoloniality: Concepts, Analytics, and Praxis.* Durham, NC; London: Duke University Press, 2018

Mudimbe, V.Y. *The Invention of Africa: Gnosis, Philosophy and the Order of Knowledge*. Bloomington and Indianapolis: Indiana University Press, 1988

Ndlovu-Gatsheni, Sabelo J. *Coloniality of Power in Postcolonial Africa: Myths of Decolonisation.* Dakar: CODESRIA, 2013

Ndlovu-Gatsheni, Sabelo J. *Epistemic Freedom in Africa: Deprovincialization and Decolonization.* New York: Routledge, 2018

Ndlovu-Gatsheni, Sabelo J. and Ndlovu, Morgan (ed.). *Marxism and Decolonization in the 21st century: Living Theories and True Ideas*. Abingdon and New York: Routledge, 2021

Neocosmos, Michael. *Thinking Freedom in Africa: Toward a Theory of Emancipatory Practice.* Johannesburg: Wits University Press, 2016

Nkrumah, Kwame. *Neocolonialism: The Last Stage of Imperialism*. London: Thomas Nelson & Sons, Ltd., 1965

Nora, Pierre. *Realms of Memory: The Construction of the French Past, Volume I – Conflicts and Divisions,* trans. Arthur Goldhammer. New York: Columbia University Press, 1996

Oyěwùmí, Oyèrónkẹ́. *The Invention of Women: Making an African Sense of Western Gender Discourses.* Minneapolis and London: University of Minnesota Press, 1997

Quijano, Aníbal. "Coloniality and Modernity/ Rationality." *Cultural Studies*, Vol. 21, No. 2, 168-178

Robinson, Cedric J. *Black Marxism: The Making of the Black Radical Tradition*. Chapel Hill and London: The University of North Carolina Press, 1983

Santos, Boaventura de Sousa. *Epistemologies of the South: Justice Against Epistemicide.* London and New York: Routledge, 2014

Scotini, Marco and Galasso, Elisabetta (ed.). *Politics of Memory: Documentary and Archive.* Berlin: Archive Books, 2017

Scott, David. "The Re-Enchantment of Humanism: An Interview with Sylvia Wynter." *Small Axe* 8, 2000, 119-207

Sharpe, Christina. *In the Wake: On Blackness and Being.* Durham: Duke University Press, 2016

Sithole, Tendayi. *The Black Register.* Cambridge and Medford: Polity Press, 2020

Stewart, Tyson. *Cinema Derrida: The Law of Inspection in the Age of Global Spectral Media.* New York: Peter Lang, 2020

Stoler, Anne Laura. "Colonial Archives and the Arts of Governance." *Archival Science 2*, 2002, 87-109

Trouillot, Michel-Rolph. *Silencing the Past: Power and the Production of History*. Boston: Beacon Press, 1995

Vergès, Françoise, *A Decolonial Feminism*. trans. Ashley J. Bohrer. London: Pluto Press, 2021

Wong, Annie. "How to Burn Paper for the Dead." *MICE Magazine*, 2017: https://micemagazine.ca/issue-three/how-burn-paper-dead

Wynter, Sylvia. *Black Metamorphosis: New Natives in a New World*

Wynter, Sylvia. "Unsettling The Coloniality of Being/Power/Truth/Freedom: Towards The Human, After Man, Its Overrepresentation - An Argument." *The New Centennial Review*, Vol. 3, No. 3, Fall 2003, 257-337

List of works

Mathieu Kleyebe Abonnenc
Foreword to Guns for Banta, 2011
Mixed Media: Synchronised slide show transferred to HD, 25 minutes, 40 seconds; Poster, 120 × 160 cm
Courtesy of the artist

Dineo Seshee Bopape
Lerole: footnotes (the struggle of memory against forgetting), 2018
Mixed media
Variable dimensions
Courtesy of the artist and Sfeir-Semler Gallery

Nolan Oswald Dennis
biko.cabral (time/place), 2020
Receipt Printer, microcontroller
Variable dimensions
Courtesy of the artist and Goodman Gallery

Torkwase Dyson
Black World Building (Hypershape), 2022
Wood, graphite, acrylic
111.8 × 112.4 × 3.8 cm
Courtesy of the artist and Pace Gallery

Torkwase Dyson
Enclosure/Encounter – Studies #4 (Hypershape), 2022
graphite and pen on paper
29.7 × 42 cm
Courtesy of the artist and Pace Gallery

Torkwase Dyson
Enclosure/Encounter – Studies #5 (Hypershape), 2022
graphite and pen on paper
29.7 × 41.9 cm
Courtesy of the artist and Pace Gallery

Torkwase Dyson
Symbolic Geography #1 (Hypershape), 2022
wood, graphite, acrylic and glass
49.5 × 58.4 × 8.9 cm
Courtesy of the artist and Pace Gallery

Rotimi Fani-Kayode
Sonponnoi, 1987
Hand printed gelatin-silver print from the original negative
61 × 50.8 cm
Courtesy of The Walther Collection and Autograph ABP, London

Rotimi Fani-Kayode
Under the Surplice, 1989
Hand printed gelatin-silver print from the original negative
60 × 50.8 cm
Courtesy of The Walther Collection and Autograph ABP, London

Rotimi Fani-Kayode
Nothing to Lose VII (Bodies of Experience), 1989/2021
C-type archival print
121.9 × 121.9 cm
Courtesy of Hales Gallery, London and New York; and Autograph, London

Rotimi Fani-Kayode
Nothing to Lose IX (Bodies of Experience), 1989/2021
C-type archival print
121.9 × 121.9 cm

Courtesy of Hales Gallery, London and New York; and Autograph, London

Bouchra Khalili
Foreign Office, 2015
Mixed media: single-channel digital film, 22 minutes, 6 seconds; 15 digital prints on paper; silkscreen print on paper
Courtesy of the artist and Mor Charpentier, Paris

Abraham Oghobase
Constructed Realities, 2022
Wood, inkjet on fibre paper, inkjet on silk organza
130.6 × 373.5 × 226 cm (depth variable)
Courtesy of the artist

Tako Taal
I fa mo ketta (It's been a long time), 2017
HD Video, no sound
9 minutes, 27 seconds
Courtesy of the artist

Tako Taal
Absence/Baduja (the state of being away, the condition of being related), 2021
Watercolour on paper, imitation leather, gold chain, seashell
34.4 × 85 × 3.2 cm overall installed dimensions
34.4 × 34.4 × 3.2 cm individual frame
Courtesy of the artist

Cameron Rowland
Mooring, 2020
AB-001-013

William Rathbone and Sons was a timber merchant company founded in Liverpool in 1746. "[T]he foundation of the Rathbone fortune and business was built on the Africa slave trade."[1] During the 18th century, they imported timber felled and milled by slaves in the West Indies and operated a number of trading ships that sailed to West Indian colonies as well as the Southern States of America.[2] Rathbone and Sons' yard occupied a large portion of the Liverpool South Docks.[3] Rathbone and Sons supplied timber for slave ship builders in Liverpool until at least 1783.[4] These ships carried enslaved black people who were sold in the West Indies and in British North America. Ships built in Liverpool also carried the slaves who were sold on Negro Row at the Liverpool South Docks.[5]

Liverpool built the world's first wet dock in 1716, allowing cargo ships to dock directly at the port. By 1796, Liverpool had built 28 acres of docks.

> Liverpool's proximity to Ireland also not only facilitated a profitable trade, but provided a relatively safer route that allowed Liverpool ships less chance to be captured by French privateers. Additionally, the copper and brass manufactures in Lancashire and Ireland allowed for local companies that manufactured African trade goods such as manillas to carry on a prosperous export trade, further giving Liverpool a competitive edge. The relationships forged with nearby merchants not only helped secure trade goods, but also valuable credit terms.[6]

In 1784, Rathbone and Sons imported the first consignment of raw cotton to England from the United States.[7] From this point, they became stated abolitionists and free trade advocates.[8] The abolition of the "West Indian monopoly" on the import of goods to the British Isles would allow for the expansion of U.S. cotton trading. Liverpool became the primary port of 19th-century cotton importation to England. Rathbone and Sons imported American cotton to Liverpool through the American Civil War.[9] The company continues to operate as the investment and wealth management firm Rathbone Brothers Plc.

The mooring at the Albert Dock: AB-001-013 is on the former location of the Rathbone warehouse. This mooring has been rented for the purpose of not being used. It continues to be rented for this purpose indefinitely.

Courtesy of the artist and Maxwell Graham/Essex Street, New York

1 • Jehanne Wake, *Kleinwort Benson: The History of Two Families in Banking* (New York: Oxford University Press, 1997), 15.
2 • Wake, 16.
3 • Adam Bowett, "The Jamaica Trade: Gillow and the Use of Mahogany in the Eighteenth Century," *Regional Furniture* 12 (1998): 22.
4 • Wake, 16.
5 • Eric Williams, *Capitalism and Slavery*, 2nd ed. (1944; repr. Chapel Hill: The University of North Carolina Press, 1994), 52.
6 • Katie McDade, "Liverpool Slave Merchant Entrepreneurial Networks, 1725–1807," *Business History* 53, no. 7 (2011): 1094.
7 • Eleanor F. Rathbone, *William Rathbone: A Memoir* (London: Macmillan and Co. Limited, 1905), 11.
8 • Wake, 15, 31.
9 • Sheila Marriner, "Rathbones' Trading Activities in the Middle of the Nineteenth Century," *Transactions of the Historic Society of Lancashire & Cheshire* 108 (1956): 118.

Contributors for *Living with Ghosts: A Reader*

KJ Abudu is a critic and curator based in London, Lagos, and New York. Informed by anti/post/de-colonial theory, queer theory, African philosophy, and Black radical thought, his writings and exhibitions focus on critical art and aesthetic practices from the Global South (particularly Africa and its diasporas) that respond to the world-historical conditions produced by colonial modernity. KJ holds an MA in Modern & Contemporary Art: Critical and Curatorial Studies from Columbia University, and a BA from Duke University, where he studied philosophy and political science. The first iteration of his ongoing curatorial project, *Living With Ghosts*, opened at the Wallach Art Gallery, New York, in March 2022. KJ is a 2022-23 Helena Rubinstein Curatorial Fellow at the Whitney Independent Study Program and will be curating a pavilion-bound exhibition, *Traces of Ecstasy*, for the fourth edition of the Lagos Biennial in 2023.

Adjoa Armah is an artist, educator, writer, and editor with a background in design and design anthropology. Her practice is concerned with the entanglement between narrative, the archive, pedagogy, black ontology, infrapolitics, design methods, and spatial consciousness. She is the founder of Saman Archive, a gathering of photographic negatives encountered across Ghana, through which she explores models of institution-building grounded in Akan temporalities and West African technologies of social and historical mediation. She is also a managing editor and research fellow at Afterall. Armah holds a Masters in Material Anthropology Design from University College London and is a practice-led DPhil researcher in Fine Art at Ruskin School of Art at the University of Oxford.

Emmanuel Iduma was born and raised in Nigeria, where he trained as a lawyer. He is the author of the travelogue *A Stranger's Pose* (Cassava Republic Press, 2018), which was longlisted for 2019 Ondaatje Prize. He has contributed nonfiction and criticism to *Granta*, the *New York Review of Books*, *Aperture*, *n+1*, *Artforum*, *Best American Travel Writing 2020*, and *Art in America*, among other places. His art writing has been honored with the Andy Warhol Foundation Arts Writers grant, the inaugural Irving Sandler Award for New Voices in Art Criticism from AICA-USA, and the C/O Berlin Talent Prize for Theory. In 2020, he was listed in *Apollo International Art Magazine*'s 40 under 40 Africa for the broad social impact of his work *I Am Still With You*, a memoir on the aftermath of the Nigerian civil war, which was awarded a Silvers Grant for Work in Progress, and is forthcoming from Algonquin (US) and William Collins (UK) in March 2023. He received a Windham-Campbell Prize for Literature in 2022.

Bouchra Khalili is a French Moroccan artist based in Berlin. Encompassing film, video, installation, photography, printmaking, and publishing, Khalili's practice explores imperial and colonial continuums as epitomised by contemporary forced illegal migrations and the politics of memory of anti-colonial struggles and international solidarity. Deeply informed by the legacy of post-independence avant-gardes and the vernacular traditions of her native Morocco, Khalili's approach develops strategies of storytelling at the intersection of history and micro-narratives. Combining documentary and conceptual practices, she investigates questions of self-representation, autonomous agency, and forms of resistance of communities rendered invisible by the nation-state model. Khalili's work has been the subject of many international solo exhibitions, including at the Museum of Fine Arts, Boston (2019), Museum Folkwang, Essen (2018), Jeu de Paume, Paris (2018), Secession, Vienna (2018), The Museum of Modern Art, New York (2016), and Palais de Tokyo, Paris (2015).

Avery F. Gordon is a writer, educator, and radio producer living in London. Currrently Visiting Professor at Birkbeck School of Law University of London, she is the author of *The Hawthorn Archive: Letters from the Utopian Margins, The Workhouse: The Breitenau Room, Ghostly Matters: Haunting and the Sociological Imagination, Keeping Good Time: Reflections on Knowledge, Power and People,* and *Mapping Multiculturalism,* among other books and articles.

Achille Mbembe, born in Cameroon, obtained his PhD in History at the Sorbonne in Paris in 1989 and a D.E.A. in Political Science at the Institut d'Etudes Politiques (Paris). He was Assistant Professor of History at Columbia University, New York (1988-1991), a Senior Research Fellow at the Brookings Institute in Washington, D.C. (1991-1992), Associate Professor of History at the University of Pennsylvania (1992-1996), and Executive Secretary of the Council for the Development of Social Science Research in Africa (CODESRIA) in Dakar, Senegal (1996-2000). He was also a Visiting Professor at the University of California, Berkeley (2001), Yale University (2003), University of California at Irvine (2004-2005), Duke University (2006-2011) and Harvard University (2012).

Walter D. Mignolo is Distinguished William H. Wannamaker Professor of Romance Studies and Professor of Literature; he is also the Director of the Center for Global Studies and the Humanities at Duke University. He was Associated Researcher at Universidad Andina Simón Bolívar, Quito, (2002-2018) and an Honorary Research Associate for CISA (Center for Indian Studies in South Africa), Wits University at Johannesburg (2015-2019). He was Senior Advisor of DOC (Dialogue of Civilizations) Research Institute, based in Berlin (2016-2020).

Sabelo J. Ndlovu-Gatsheni is Professor and Chair of Epistemologies of the Global South with Emphasis on Africa at the University of Bayreuth in Germany. He is a leading decolonial theorist with over one hundred publications in the fields of African history, African politics, African development, and decolonial theory. He previously worked as the Acting Executive Director of Change Management Unit (CMU) in the Vice Chancellor's Office at the University of South Africa (UNISA), Director of Scholarship at CMC, and founding Head of Archie Mafeje Research Institute for Applied Social Policy (AMRI). He is a member of the South African Academy of Science (ASSAf). His research interest is predominantly in African history, particularly Zimbabwean and South African history as well as contemporary African politics; hence, his research focus is mostly cultural and colonial encounters, and colonial and post-colonial forms of governance.

Joshua Segun-Lean is a writer and researcher. His writing engages contemporary issues across visual and literary culture, Black studies, gender, spatiality, and politics. With a background in International Business, Joshua tries to understand how social practices interdict, respond to, and intersect flows of capital in the 'globalized' world. His writing has appeared in *The Republic Magazine*, *TSA Art Magazine*, *A Long House*, and elsewhere. His current research is informed by the relationship between protest and performance, protest as performance, and divergent modernisms in music, architecture, and literature. He is also interested in fiction.

Jacques Derrida (1930 - 2004) was an Algerian-born French philosopher known for his major contribution to the study of semiotics and phenomenology. In 1949, he relocated to France to study at the elite École Normale Supérieure (ENS) before teaching philosophy at the Sorbonne (1960–64), the ENS (1964–84), and the École des Hautes Études en Sciences Sociales (1984–99). He published numerous seminal books and essays including *L'Écriture et la différence* (1967), *De la grammatologie* (1967), and *La Voix et le phénomène* (1967), and *Spectres of Marx* (1993). Derrida also lectured at prestigious institutions in the US including the University of California, Yale University, and Johns Hopkins University. His theory of 'deconstruction' had a significant and far-reaching influence on psychology, literary theory, cultural studies, linguistics, feminism, sociology, and anthropology.

C.L.R. James (b. Cyril Lionel Robert James, 1901 - 1989) was a Trinidadian historian, journalist, and political activist who served as a leading figure in the Pan-African movement throughout his lifetime. In 1932 James moved to England, where he published *The Life of Captain Cipriani* (1932; revised as *The Case for West-Indian Self-Government,* 1933). Known for his autodidactism, his book *Minty Alley* (1936) was the first novel by a Black West Indian to be published in the UK. During the 1930s James was a cricket correspondent for the Manchester Guardian and became increasingly involved in Marxist politics and the African and West Indian independence movements. His most notable work was *The Black Jacobins* (1938), a Marxist study of the Haitian Revolution of the late 18th century, which won him widespread acclaim.

Artist Biographies

Abraham Oghobase (b. 1979, Lagos, Nigeria) is an artist based in Toronto, Canada. In his photography-based practice, he interrogates human existence and uncovers interior worlds by deconstructing traditional modes of making and experimenting with the narrative and multisensory potential of images and objects, including archival materials.

Bouchra Khalili (b. 1975, Casablanca) see previous page.

Cameron Rowland (b. 1988, Philadelphia) lives and works in New York. Their work has been exhibited in solo exhibitions at the Institute of Contemporary Arts, London; Museum of Contemporary Art, Los Angeles; Galerie Buchholz, Cologne, Germany; Établissement d'en face, Brussels; Kunsthalle Freiburg, Switzerland; Artists Space, New York, and Maxwell Graham / Essex Street, New York. They have participated in group exhibitions at the Museum fur Moderne Kunst, Frankfurt, Germany; 33rd Bienal de São Paulo, Brazil; Secession, Vienna; The Museum of Modern Art, New York, and elsewhere.

Dineo Seshee Bopape (b. 1981, Polokwane, South Africa) lives and works in Johannesburg, South Africa. Bopape spent her youth in Limpopo. At 12 years of age she began to follow a hunger for an elsewhere, beginning with Durban, South Africa, where she studied painting and sculpture. She is a 2007 graduate of De Ateliers in Amsterdam and in 2010 completed an MFA at Columbia University, New York. She was the main prize winner of the Future Generation Art Prize 2017 by PinchukArtCentre, the recipient of a 2010 Columbia University Toby Fund Award, and the winner of 2008 MTN New Contemporaries Award. She has shown her work in national and international exhibitions and was the recipient of the Artes Mundi 9 Prize by National Museum Cardiff, Wales.

Mathieu Kleyebe Abonnenc (b. 1977, Paris/French Guiana) is an artist, curator, and researcher interested in exploring the history of the colonial encounter and its effects on memory and identity. In his work as an artist, he uses video, drawings, installations, and photographs, as well as interviews and archives, to counter collective amnesia and erasure of experiences and traumas. He was a resident at the French Academy in Rome - Villa Medici in 2016-2017, and a guest artist at the DAAD, Berlin for 2019. Selected solo exhibitions include *Gods Moving in Places – The Day Reader*, Ifa Gallery, Berlin (2022), *The Music of Living Landscapes*, Kestner Gesellschaft, Hanover (2022), *Le palais du Paon* at the Musée départemental d'art contemporain de Rochechouart (2018); and *Concerning Solitude* at the Jumex Foundation, Mexico City (2018).

Nolan Oswald Dennis (b. 1988, Zambia) is an interdisciplinary artist from Johannesburg, South Africa. His practice explores what they call 'a black consciousness of space': the material and metaphysical conditions of decolonisation. Their work questions the politics of space and time through a system-specific, rather than site-specific, approach. They are concerned with the hidden structures that condition our social and political imagination, which transverse multiple realms (technical, spiritual, economic, psychological, etc), and works to produce counter-diagrams of these sometimes opposed, sometimes complimentary systems. Dennis has exhibited in various solo and group shows, including the 9th Berlin Biennale (2016), the Young Congo Biennale (2019), and the CAN Centre d'art Neuchâtel, Switzerland (2022). Dennis will be in residence at The Mirror Institution in Sweden in July 2022.

Torkwase Dyson (b. 1973, Chicago, Illinois) describes herself as a painter working across multiple mediums to explore the continuity between ecology, infrastructure, and architecture. Examining environmental racism as well as the history and future of black spatial liberation strategies, Dyson's abstract works grapple with the ways in which space is perceived and negotiated, particularly by black and brown bodies. In 2019, Dyson's solo exhibition *I Can Drink the Distance* was on view at The Cooper Union, New York, and her work was also presented at the Sharjah Biennial. In addition to participating in group exhibitions at the Smithsonian National Museum of

African Art, Washington, D.C.; Whitney Museum of American Art, New York; The Museum of Modern Art, New York; and California African American Museum, Los Angeles, Dyson has had solo exhibitions and installations at Colby College Museum of Art, Waterville, Maine; Graham Foundation for Advanced Studies in the Fine Arts, Chicago; Schuylkill Center for Environmental Education, Philadelphia; and Suzanne Lemberg Usdan Gallery, Bennington College, Vermont.

Tako Taal (b. 1989, Wales) is an artist, filmmaker, and programmer based in Glasgow. At stake in her artistic practice are the psychic structures of colonial relations, and the question of how vivid they remain in the present. In 2021 Taal presented her first institutional solo exhibition, *At the shore, everything touches,* at Dundee Contemporary Arts and her work was included in *Survey II*, Jerwood Arts (Touring UK); NADA House, Governors Island, New York; *Meet me at the Threshold*, Talbot Rice Gallery, University of Edinburgh, and *Mis(sing) Information*, Perth Museum and Art Gallery. She was a 2019 RAW Academy fellow at RAW Material Company, Dakar, and a Committee Member at Market Gallery, Glasgow (2016-18).

Rotimi Fani-Kayode was born in 1955, in Lagos, Nigeria, to a prominent Yoruba family before moving to England following the outbreak of civil war. He later studied at Georgetown University and the Pratt Institute in the US, before settling permanently in London in 1983, where he lived and worked until his untimely death in 1989. Fani-Kayode is a highly influential figure in the history of art who, despite a tragically brief career, produced a complex body of photographic work that explores themes of race, sexuality, spirituality, and the self. At the core of Fani-Kayode's art is an emphasis on difference and otherness. The status of 'outsider' was one with which he identified on multiple fronts — from his 'geographic dislocation' to the exclusion he experienced as a result of his sexuality and artistic career — and which motivated him throughout his life. Fani-Kayode's powerful legacy continues to speak to urgent issues concerning identity politics, belonging, and desire, and has deeply impacted subsequent generations of contemporary artists and photographers.

Published on the occasion of
Living With Ghosts
July 8 – August 5, 2022

Pace Gallery
5 Hanover Square
London

Front cover, clockwise from top:
Rotimi Fani-Kayode, *Under the Surplice*, 1989;
Torkwase Dyson, *Enclosure/Encounter – Studies #4 (Hypershape)*, 2022; Abraham Oghobase, *Constructed Realities*, 2022; Dineo Seshee Bopape, *Lerole: footnotes (The struggle of memory against forgetting)*, 2018; Nolan Oswald Dennis, *biko.cabral (time/place)*, 2020.

Back cover, clockwise from top:
Nolan Oswald Dennis, *biko.cabral (time/place)*, 2020; Tako Taal, *I fa mo ketta* (It's been a long time), 2017; Bouchra Khalili, *Foreign Office*, 2015; Mathieu Kleyebe Abonnenc, Set photographs of the shooting of the film *Guns for Banta* by Sarah Maldoror, 1979; Tako Taal, *I fa mo ketta* (It's been a long time), 2017; Bouchra Khalili, *Foreign Office*, 2015.

Spine, top to bottom:
Nolan Oswald Dennis, *biko.cabral (time/place)*, 2020;
Tako Taal, *I fa mo ketta* (It's been a long time), 2017.

Photography:
Damian Griffiths: pp. 1, 4, 7.
Suzanne Lipinska: p. 45.
Damian Griffiths: pp. 102, 104.
Nicholas Moss: pp. 103, 105-109.
Richard Gary: pp. 126-127.
Photocity Archives: p. 134.
Patrick Doe Gakpetor: p. 138.

Design: Johanne Lian Olsen
Editor: KJ Abudu
Copyediting: Saskia Flower
Rights & Reproductions: Vincent Wilcke
Production: KJ Abudu

Typeset in Nocturne and Suisse Int'l
Printing: Studio Elphick, London

ISBN: 978-1-948701-59-4
Library of Congress Control Number: 2022946610